The Assessment of College Performance

*A Handbook of Techniques
and Measures for
Institutional Self-Evaluation*

Richard I. Miller

The Assessment of College Performance

Jossey-Bass Publishers

San Francisco • Washington • London • 1979

THE ASSESSMENT OF COLLEGE PERFORMANCE
A Handbook of Techniques and Measures for Institutional Self-Evaluation
by Richard I. Miller

Copyright © 1979 by: Jossey-Bass, Inc., Publishers
433 California Street
San Francisco, California 94104
&
Jossey-Bass Limited
28 Banner Street
London EC1Y 8QE

Library of Congress Catalogue Card Number LC 79–83575

International Standard Book Number ISBN 0-87589-406-2

Manufactured in the United States of America

JACKET DESIGN BY WILLI BAUM

FIRST EDITION

Code 7911

The Jossey-Bass Series
in Higher Education

Preface

E valuation is a valuable means to the end of improving the performance of individuals and institutions. It facilitates progress toward goals and objectives, and it is essential for determining both efficiency and effectiveness. As society demands better-run and higher-quality institutions, including colleges and universities, effective institutional administrators need to conduct repeated and continuing assessments and appraisals as part of decision making.

The evaluation of colleges and universities as a whole is both old and new. The 1910 Flexner Report is well known, although it focused on medical education rather than on institution-wide evaluation, and the North Central Accrediting Association's six volumes on appraising member institutions were completed in the 1930s. Institutional self-studies, as required by regional accrediting associations, have been with us since the turn of the century. These studies have sometimes served as institutional evaluations, but most are not designed to help administrators make and act on difficult decisions about program quality, internal priorities, and management. These kinds of rigorous evaluations are increasingly needed today.

The current heightened interest in collegiate evaluation started with faculty evaluation in the mid sixties, spurred by student protests on some campuses. In the 1970s administrative evaluation came on the scene, and it too has developed rapidly. One should not be surprised, therefore, to find new interest in assessing programs and departments, as well as institutions. In other words, all aspects of colleges and universities are being increasingly evaluated.

The Assessment of College Performance will serve its purpose if readers are aided in developing better criteria and procedures for institutional appraisal. This book reviews the elements that combine to form a college or university; it identifies measures, policies, and procedures that can help ascertain the extent to which an institution is going where it wants to go; and it advocates a manageable and flexible approach to appraising the overall quality of an institution. It is an effort to assist chief administrative officers, faculty leaders, trustees, state educational officials, and others to analyze and better understand their institutions and thereby make more effective educational decisions about the present and future.

Chapter One focuses on some basic assumptions, considers the validity of any kind of institutional evaluation, and introduces forty-five criteria for making assessments. Chapters Two through Eleven, covering ten areas of institutional life, further explore these criteria. The material on each standard is designed to explain, to highlight its important characteristics, and to provide specific methods and approaches, including a series of questions that consultants, administrators, or members of a self-evaluation team might find helpful. Chapter Twelve suggests several ways to conduct institutional evaluation and describes some operational principles for self-study. Appendices A and B review a variety of institutional studies, and an annotated bibliography points to other useful works.

My purpose in this book is to strike a balance between two different views of institutional assessment: those of some humanists, who believe the most significant facts about education and about its institutions cannot be measured numerically, and those of the systems analysts and cost-effectiveness experts, who are reluctant to concern themselves with "soft" evidence because it is messy and unquantified. I believe we must push for better, more specific data while not neglecting the evidence of observation, experience, and common sense. I do not believe the current paucity of "valid and reliable" appraisal measures should deter assessment efforts. It is better to develop one's own procedures where none currently exist and to adapt established methods to individual situations than to forgo any evaluation at all. I advocate a simple model composed of goals and objectives, the human and material resources needed to achieve these aims, and evaluation to determine progress toward the desired ends. Qualitative judgments are important, and they will be made by one means or another. I seek in this book to assist their being made better.

Many individuals have been most helpful, and I am grateful to them—to each one. The great assistance of others in every aspect of the book is sincerely appreciated, but of course I take full responsibility for what is said, somewhat in the spirit of Sir Thomas More, who said to his executioner: "Help me up. On the way down I will shift for myself."

The financial support of the Association of Governing Boards through its small-grant research program was instrumental in allowing this project to get under way.

The moral support and assistance of my wife, Peggy, has been significant in the evenings, mornings, weekends, and leave-time that have constituted this marathon effort. And our three daughters—Joan, Diane, and Janine—were helpful in showing interest in what was sometimes a bit beyond them (and sometimes beyond me also), but their interest was a source of satisfaction and encouragement.

Brockport, New York RICHARD I. MILLER
February 1979

Contents

The Author

RICHARD I. MILLER is vice president for educational services (one of two academic vice presidents) at the State University of New York at Brockport. He has served as associate director with the Illinois Board of Higher Education; vice president for academic affairs at Baldwin-Wallace College; professor and department head at the University of Kentucky, where he also was director of the program on educational change and executive secretary for the President's Commission on Supplementary Plans and Centers; and associate director of the National Project on Instruction for the National Education Association.

Miller completed his undergraduate degree at the University of Nebraska in biology and education and his doctoral degree from Teachers College, Columbia University. He has taught at Adelphi University, Pennsylvania State University, the University of Kentucky, and the University of Illinois at Urbana.

His professional activities include service on several national task forces, boards, and special studies as well as numerous consultations here and abroad. Beginning with undergraduate academic and athletic distinctions, he has received several professional awards and honors.

Among Miller's publications are several dozen articles, chapters in books, booklets, and six books where he served as editor and chapter author. He is the author of *Dag Hammarskjold and Crisis Diplomacy, Teaching About Communism, Education in a Changing Society, Evaluating Faculty Performance* (Jossey-Bass, 1972), and *Developing Programs for Faculty Evaluation* (Jossey-Bass, 1974).

He resides in Brockport, New York, with his wife, Peggy, and their three daughters.

To Peggy Miller

The Assessment
of College
Performance

A Handbook of Techniques
and Measures for
Institutional Self-Evaluation

1

Planning Effective Institutional Self-Study

If the past is prologue, then accountability, evaluation, financial constraints, curricular review, and government concern about higher education will be prominent challenges for colleges and universities in the decade that is almost upon us. Departmental and institutional evaluators should begin by developing some basic assumptions about evaluation and about what will be assessed. I suggest the following ones as a beginning.

- *Institutional evaluation will be an increasing part of higher education in the 1980s.*

    All phases of national life will be subjected to greater examination in the eighties, leading to what might be called "the great reappraisal." The speed of change, the complex nature of alterna-

1

tives, continuing inflation, the "taxpayer's revolt," greater consumer consciousness, and more careful study of the impact of consequences will shift more attention to evaluation. And a healthy skepticism (not to be confused with cynicism) also will raise evaluative types of questions. Thus higher education will find itself in this not altogether hospitable setting in the next decade.

Several factors are bringing about increasing interest in institutional appraisal as an integral aspect of accountability. National enrollment projections for postsecondary education indicate a leveling off of the number of entering freshmen by the early eighties, then a decline until about 1990, at which time enrollment in postsecondary institutions is expected to return to the 1972 level. Where state educational authorities use enrollment-driven funding formulas for colleges and universities, this impending decline alone can have a major impact on the available human and material resources.

Even those institutions that are not troubled by enrollment decreases may face more or less continuous internal reappraisal because limited state and federal funding will allow only modest new program development and very little bricks-and-mortar expansion. Most state governments have reduced significantly the *percentage* of public money appropriated to postsecondary education, and a significant reversal of this current situation is unlikely in the near future. The disenchantment with colleges and universities among state and federal legislators that took place in the middle and late 1960s remains more deep-seated than many educators realize. A related factor is the increasing competition for public money from other public-service agencies, such as those for public welfare, elementary and secondary education, transportation, and safety. These agencies have learned the lessons of lobbying well, and usually their "act" is more together than is that of people developing the case for higher education.

Private colleges and universities will also find formidable foes in the shrinking pool of high school graduates and in rising costs, as well as in the more intense and effective student recruiting campaigns by public institutions.

• *Institutional evaluation is already being done by someone, somehow.*

Appraisals of institutional quality take place more often than we realize. When a trustee votes on priority matters, when parents and their youth in secondary school select an institution of higher education, when federal and foundation grants are awarded, when the media report on a college, when state agencies allocate resources: at these and many other times, colleges and universities are evaluated. The problem is, How?

Old school ties, academic prestige, athletics, vitality, costs, size, propinquity, the quality of the faculty, the number of graduates, the president's personality, the success of the alumni, and the attractiveness of the physical plant are among the rational and not so rational criteria that are used to judge "the whole thing," but are these eclectic bases adequate for the future? How institutional evaluation is perceived and performed depends on who is doing it. Some types of assessment such as those conducted by state higher education officials minimize the measurement of student learning, because the data from such measurements cannot be plugged into the formulas that are increasingly being advocated by government personnel who are not involved in education. Students, who vote with their feet, are not concerned with state-level formulas but with the vitality of the environment, the quality and concern of the faculty, and the relevance of the program. Legislators evaluate because they are interested in receiving "more for less." Trustees are concerned with appraising the whole institution because they are mandated to do so by the governing statutes of the institution. And chief administrative officers must fulfill administrative responsibilities. It seems that although everyone has a piece of the action along with some fleeting and impressionistic views of the Gestalt, only trustees and chief executives have a legal obligation to consider the institution as a whole. Thus they must develop a rational and comprehensive approach to their charge. This book and other efforts that will follow attest to the belief that assistance is needed in coping with this very difficult but necessary institution-wide perspective.

- *If public postsecondary institutions do not undertake vigorous evaluation, likely it will be done for them.*

The new forces of direct, significant influence on higher education from outside the immediate campus environment have come to bear within the past fifteen to twenty-five years. The members of these influential groups tend to treat colleges and universities more as other state agencies than as unique societal institutions, and therefore we should not be surprised to find that these groups, often staffed by younger persons with accounting and statistical skills, expect more rigorous internal analyses from educational institutions, as well as expect subsequent internal reallocations based on established priorities. Some postsecondary institutions already have found that failure to put their own house in economic order means more state controls and quite possibly fewer human and material resources. Even private colleges and universities are under increasing pressures from their governing boards and their key constituents to undertake vigorous evaluations, and these pressures can be expected to build in the 1980s.

- *The overall purpose of institutional appraisal should be to improve the academic enterprise.*

      Just as faculty and administrative evaluations should have better performance as their central purpose, so institutional appraisal should have overall academic improvement as its ultimate objective. Ultimate does not mean exclusive, however. Improving academic quality may require difficult decisions about reallocating resources, decisions based on prior analyses of such factors as departmental or college quality, the need or demand for particular resources, and their centrality of programs and activities to the institution's goals and objectives. Just as data for faculty evaluation can and should be used also for personnel decisions, so information for institutional evaluation can be used in making internal reallocations.

      The emphasis on academic improvement is important to the success of the overall institutional appraisal, but some individuals may feel this approach has tinges of a con game if evaluative data are used to make decisions about releasing individuals or decreasing the size of departments. Those directly affected by such actions need extraordinary statesmanship not to feel the human hurt and anger that normally are triggered by these decisions. Yet any organized enterprise—business, military, nonprofit—survives and flourishes because it is able to keep general purposes and objectives at the heart of its decision-making processes.

- *Institutional evaluation can be done objectively and perceptively.*

      The following statement by Allan Cartter (1966, p. 3) argues the case for systematic evaluation: "Diversity can be a costly luxury if it is accompanied by ignorance. Our system works fairly well because most students, parents, and prospective employers *know* that a bachelor's degree from Harvard, Stanford, Swarthmore, or Reed is ordinarily a better indication of quality and accomplishment than a bachelor's degree from Melrose A&M or Siwash College. Even if no formal studies were ever undertaken, there is always a grapevine at work to supply impressionistic evaluations. However, evaluation by rumor and word of mouth is far from satisfactory, particularly in advanced training for scholarship and professions."

Some people contend that a college or university is too complex and changing to be evaluated by anything other than guesswork and subjectivism. There is some truth in this position, and all institutional evaluators need to recognize the serious problems and potential shortcomings of their endeavors. Yet because evaluations are taking place with increasing frequency, we must face the choices: relegating this responsibility to others outside education, continuing with mysticism and subjectivism, or expecting educators to assume the challenge themselves.

We have enough examples of objectively and perceptively conducted institutional evaluations to believe that educationally sound outcomes can result from such efforts. And as sincere and thoughtful programs are undertaken, the process will become more effective.

• *Institutional quality can be defined.*

This and the preceding assumption are undoubtedly the most difficult to "prove," but if we do not accept them, there is little point in going further. In attempting to define quality, we can easily be distracted by the great diversity among postsecondary institutions, forgetting all they have in common. For instance, all obviously have students, faculty members, administrators, alumni. They share certain curricular features: freshman English in some form, American history, and so on. All are guided by some policies and procedures; all have some politics to cope with; all have some type of evaluation; and all are influenced (in varying degrees) by the social milieu and the regional and national economy. And of course they share one primary goal—educating students.

Although the details of these goals, policies, programs, and so on are arranged uniquely in each institution, high-quality colleges and universities also have some more specific characteristics in common: Their members have reached general agreement on where they want to go, how their limited resources can be employed in making progress toward these goals, and whether they are moving toward where they want to go. Their academic programs contribute to the students' ability to think clearly, communicate effectively, act wisely, discriminate among values, and progress toward career aspirations (these aims are adapted from the Report of the Harvard Committee, 1945). Their faculty members are on the growing edge of their academic fields, seeking new ideas, materials, and approaches to improvement; they work closely with students in formal and informal teaching and learning circumstances; and they participate meaningfully in institutional governance. Their administrators exercise dynamic, and sometimes courageous, leadership in helping to make crucial decisions about the institution's future, and they use human and material resources prudently and in accordance with established goals and objectives. And finally, the trustees of high-quality colleges and universities support their institutions while serving as friendly critics, provide policy direction, differentiate between policy development and operational procedures, and evaluate institutional effectiveness.

• *Institutional quality is a composite of inter-dependent elements.*

Whether or not one agrees that a high-quality institution would have all the characteristics cited above, it is clear that an assessment of its quality cannot be based on a single indicator or even on a cluster of similar indices. "Prestige," for example, is commonly considered an indicator of quality, yet it should never be used alone, and in some cases it shouldn't be used at all, because it can be inaccurate or misleading. A prestigious reputation derives from a variety of institutional characteristics, some of which may have little to do with educational quality, such as size, age, and a distinguished football record. Land-grant universities, for instance, by virtue of their land-grant status and their long existence, have prestige that may be quite deserved or otherwise. Once an institution acquires such a reputation, it is unlikely to lose it, because public opinion tends to perpetuate that status regardless of current merit. National ratings of prestigious universities have varied little over the past forty years. So regional state universities, community colleges, and other relatively new institutions have difficulty cracking the top ranks. And therefore the fact that they have little or no national prestige tells us almost nothing about the caliber of the education they provide.

Another indicator that may be misused is financial efficiency. Certainly good money management is an important part of institutional quality, especially where limited resources do not allow colleges to smother their problems and inefficiencies with more money, but this element must be seen for what it is, a means to the larger end: learning. This perspective must be zealously guarded, lest efficiency for the sake of survival become an end in itself.

Some will argue that institutional quality should be judged largely on the basis of how much students learn. Yet even if we accept this as the most important indicator—as my comment above about means and ends implies that we should—we still cannot use this as the only criterion. After all, if the institution is managed so badly that it dies, it cannot teach anybody anything. If the faculty is poor or overworked, students are likely to learn little. If the physical plant is limited and out of date, this too affects the outcomes of college attendance. And so on. All these factors, as well as the caliber of the goals and objectives, the design of the curriculum, the behavior of the governing board, the nature of external influences, are parts of the whole called institutional quality, and therefore all must be evaluated.

To assist in conducting whatever kind of assessment the institutional evaluators decide upon, this book suggests that they examine ten aspects of the academic enterprise and consider the following forty-five evaluative criteria related to those ten areas.

Goals and Objectives

1. The goals statement serves as an effective guide for the present and future.
2. Objectives reinforce goals.
3. The institution has adequate planning capabilities.
4. Institutional admissions policies and procedures are consistent with institutional goals and objectives.
5. The institution's goals and objectives help it maintain a reasonable identity within a statewide system of institutions.

Students' Learning

6. Students give a good rating to their advising and counseling system.
7. Retention rates are reasonable.
8. An array of individualized and compensatory learning resources is available.
9. The student affairs administration is effective.
10. Satisfactory progress is evident toward learning goals.

Faculty Performance

11. Current policies and procedures for evaluating individual faculty members are satisfactory.
12. Current instructional improvement/faculty development programs serve their purposes.
13. Faculty personnel policies and procedures are considered satisfactory.
14. Faculty salary scales and fringe benefits are competitive.
15. The overall quality of the faculty's performance is optimal.

Academic Programs

16. The institution has effective policies and procedures for developing new programs.
17. The institution has effective policies and procedures for the review and evaluation of existing programs.
18. The general education component is an intellectually stimulating and integral part of the curriculum.
19. The quality and size of the graduate program are consistent with institutional goals and objectives.
20. The library or learning resources center provides good service to the academic community.

Institutional Support: Services

21. The physical plant and facilities are adequate for the size of the student body and for the nature of the academic program.
22. The institution has a relevant and current long-range plan for developing and maintaining its physical plant.
23. Salaries and other benefits for support personnel are sufficient to attract and retain competent individuals.

24. Systematic procedures are used for evaluating the performance of support personnel.

Administrative Leadership

25. The administration gives adequate attention to planning.
26. The chief campus administrator and his team have effective working relationships with other campus administrators.
27. Institutional governance policies and procedures allow for effective institutional management.
28. The policies and procedures established for administrative evaluation and for professional development are satisfactory.
29. The institution has an effective affirmative action program.

Financial Management

30. The tuition and fee structure is compatible with the institution's needs and with the students' capacity to pay.
31. The institution has an efficient management system for accounting and financial reporting.
32. Costs and expenditures are comparable with benchmark institutions.
33. The investment portfolio is well managed.
34. The institution has an effective system for demonstrating its accountability.

Governing Board

35. The policies and procedures for conducting board affairs are satisfactory.
36. Trustees understand the differences between policy formulation and policy implementation and apply this knowledge.
37. The governing board works effectively with external constituencies.
38. The board contributes positively to improving the institution.

External Relations

39. The institution's activities contribute to the quality of life in its primary service area.
40. The institution has effective relationships with the state higher education (coordinating or governing) office.

41. The institution has an effective relationship with the federal government.
42. The institution is able to secure acceptable levels of funding from private sources and foundations.

Institutional Self-Improvement

43. The institution seeks improvement through innovation and experimentation.
44. Campus groups have positive attitudes toward self-improvement.
45. The institution has established procedures for evaluating its own effectiveness.

With these criteria as guidelines, as well as the assumptions presented in this chapter and the operational principles described in Chapter Twelve, the institutional evaluator should be able to develop an approach suited to his or her particular institution and its unique circumstances.

One might question the validity of these ten subjects and forty-five criteria, just as one should question criteria of quality from any source. Are they figments of the imagination drawn from a midsummer night's dream, or do they have some basis in research, common practice, or expert opinion? As far as my suggested ten areas and forty-five criteria, I have derived them from studying the criteria used successfully in many circumstances by institutions and associations and from discussing with numerous educators and trustees the standards that should be used for institutional evaluation. Thus, there is virtually complete agreement in the literature and research about the importance of evaluating students, faculty members, and academic programs and services, and attention has been increasing in recent efforts at institutional evaluation to assess the governing board, administrative leadership, financial management, and goals and objectives. Only the areas of institutional self-improvement, external relations, and institutional support seem to be considered the least necessary or valid subjects of appraisal, although even they are beginning to increase in prominence. And of the forty-five criteria, probably well over half would already be used in most institutions' self-appraisals. Their wording might be somewhat different, but the data sought would be essentially the same.

Nonetheless, in the final analysis, the validity of any criteria of institutional quality is a matter of judgment. "Quality is an elusive attribute, not easily subjected to measurement," Allan Cartter (1966, p. 4) wrote. "In the operational sense, quality *is* someone's subjective judgment, for there is no way of objectively measuring what is in essence an attribute of value." Any one person or any single institution will weigh the importance of these criteria differently in terms of the value they attribute to them within their own definition of educational quality. The specific evaluation efforts described in this book—of Oklahoma State University, Princeton University, the State University of New York at Buffalo, the University of Rhode Island, and others—may not be valid for other institutions, because the stimuli for the evaluation and what it seeks to accomplish may be different in each case. In fact, the worst thing an evaluator could do regarding any criterion or procedure advocated in this book would be to *adopt* it rather than *adapt* it to local circumstances. These criteria and practices have a built-in flexibility that can facilitate their adaptation, and they will be of greatest value if they stimulate thought and sharpen approaches among those who seek to use them.

Institutional evaluation is a complex, large-scale, and in many ways still a subjective enterprise. It has a long history and an extensive literature, as evidenced by the review in the annotated bibliography. It is a far more complex and ambiguous endeavor than the evaluation of particular departments, programs, or personnel (the literature of such evaluation is reviewed in Appendix A). But much more is known about institutional evaluation than is usually applied. Because crucial decisions affecting institutional quality must be made every day, greater application of this knowledge about institutional evaluation should result in improved decisions.

2

Assessing
the Relevancy
of Institutional
Objectives

The distinctive feature of organizations that sets them apart from other kinds of social systems is the primacy of goal attainment relative to all other problems. Therefore every postsecondary institution should know where it is going, what human and material resources are needed to get there, and how well it is progressing toward where it wants to go. And since these are basic components in any simple systems model, every college and university should be guided by such a model.

Despite the desirability of these components, however, several types of colleges and universities have particular difficulty in developing realistic, agreed upon goals and objectives statements —and for different reasons. Many private liberal arts institutions, for instance, especially those with enrollment problems, have conflicting goals. The reason is that many current students (as much as 75 to 80 percent), as well as an increasing number in the future, are in professional curriculums, such as business and economics and education. At the same time, the presidents and board members continue to describe their schools as liberal arts institutions, and their catalogues continue to speak primarily of liberal arts traditions. Although these institutions still require their students to take more liberal arts classes than do public institutions—it is possible, for example, for engineering students at some large land-grant universities to complete their four years with only fifteen to twenty-one credit hours in courses outside those related to engineering—and thus although liberal arts institutions come closer to developing the "well-rounded person" than do the more specialized programs at some large public universities, the necessities of economic sufficiency are pressing them to extol the virtues of a liberal arts education while expanding their professional school programs and developments. These pressures complicate developing mission and scope statements.

Regional state universities have another kind of goals conflict. Established initially as teachers' colleges and universities they experienced very substantial growths in the 1960s. Some aspired beyond their capabilities, some promised more than they could deliver, and others were caught in changes in state plans. Their academic programs and personnel policies were modeled on those of state land-grant universities, and this approach worked reasonably well as long as higher education was expanding rapidly. In the seventies, however, their rising expectations have been met with fiscal austerity and declining enrollments. As a result, many regional state universities have established much tighter personnel policies and severely curtailed academic program expansion. The light course load, graduate assistantships, research assistance, travel, secretarial assistance, and amenable office space in many cases have been adversely affected by such austerity measures. Hence academic personnel are caught in a reality that differs markedly from that which they experienced when recruited, and the forecasts do not engender optimism about an upturn in the 1980s. Professors and administrators who viewed regional state colleges and universities as moving significantly toward the prestige afforded to state land-grant universities can no longer realistically harbor such aspirations. And young professors who perceived academic conditions at these institutions as conducive to meeting the research and publication requirements that would allow upward mobility are frustrated. But these hopes and aspirations die hard, and thus realistic adjustments of the institutions' mission and scope to current conditions and future expectations are difficult.

A third type of conflict over goals is found in the large state land-grant universities, which have developed along the lines of the Germanic research institutions, where the emphasis on research was evident in the rewards system. Faculty committees that make the crucial recommendations on promotion and tenure have been dominated by comparatively conservative senior faculty members, who hold on to a research bias even if they themselves have not been particularly good examples of its practice. Promotions and tenure committees, therefore, tend to give considerable weight to this orientation. Two factors may be changing this pattern somewhat. The decreasing mobility resulting from fiscal austerity has given younger professors a greater voice in personnel decisions, and the student demonstrations of the late sixties, as well as the declining student pool, have given greater importance to teaching. But academic decisions on promotion and tenure are still largely controlled by senior faculty members, and thus continue to emphasize research and publication.

The presidents and board members of large land-grant universities have a different orientation. Their successful competition for state funds rests to an increasing extent on evidence of effective public service and teaching. Chief administrative officers, recognizing the strong agricultural and other public service dimensions of their institutions, realize that a continued and even greater stress on teaching and public service is necessary to receive favorable treatment from funding sources. (In many a state legislature, half its members rise with a rendition of the fight song of the state's major football power!) Thus, large land-grant universities have a built-in contradiction between those who manage or manipulate the internal rewards system and those who mold the institution's image for its external constituents.

Colleges and universities that have these difficulties in arriving at honest, useful goals should therefore give particular attention to the first of the forty-five evaluative criteria.

1. **Does the goals statement serve as an effective guide for the present and future?**

I am assuming here that no institution of higher education is without some kind of goals statement. The problem, therefore, is to assess the accuracy and utility of the current one and then to revise it as needed. In making this appraisal, the evaluator will probably want to review the literature not only to see what statements other colleges have used that might be adapted to his or her institution but also to analyze the results of several studies of goals and objectives and to find applicable guides to evaluation. (Incidentally, in this section the usual distinction is made between "goals"—the large purposes that the college hopes, or strives, to achieve—and "objectives," the more limited, specific targets.)

An almost countless number of goals statements can be found in the literature. Particularly useful are the chapters on goal systems in Richman and Farmer (1974); the catalogue of goals in Bowen (1977, pp. 55–59); Part I in Dressel (1976); and the Institutional Goals Inventory published by the Educational Testing Service. This Inventory, which presents most of the important kinds of goals established by a broad spectrum of colleges and universities, consists of ninety goal statements arranged in twenty categories called "goal areas," plus ten miscellaneous goal statements. The twenty goal areas are in turn broken down into outcome goals (relating to academic development, intellectual orientation, individual personal development, humanism/altruism, cultural/aesthetic awareness, traditional religiousness, vocational preparation, advanced training, research, meeting local needs, public service, social egalitarianism, and social criticism/activism) and process goals (pertaining to freedom, democratic governance, community, intellectual/aesthetic environment, innovation, off-campus learning, and accountability/efficiency). Up to twenty more goal statements that are relevant specifically to an individual campus or system can be added.

Another source worth reviewing because of its influence over the years is *General Education in a Free Society,* perhaps better known as "the Harvard Report," produced in 1945. The Harvard committee concluded that above all others general education should develop the abilities "to think effectively, to communicate thought, to make relevant judgments, to discriminate among values" (Report . . . , 1962, p. 65).

Knowledge of the national picture can provide useful yardsticks for comparing goals and objectives for one's own institution. Several studies have surveyed various groups about what goals they prefer. One by Gross and Grambsch (1968) probed how several clienteles viewed goal definition and achievement. (Data for the 1968 study were gathered in 1964, so they were not much influenced by student unrest.) Sixty-eight public and private universities, all with graduate schools, were included in the study; not surveyed were church-controlled institutions, liberal arts colleges, teachers' colleges, and technical institutions. About 7,200 usable returns were received from a sample including presidents and other administrators and 10 percent of the faculty at each institution. Forty-seven goals were presented to the respondents, who were to rank both the goals they "perceived"the university to have and those they themselves "preferred." Table 1 presents the top seven and bottom four perceived and preferred goals.

Concern for the instruction and welfare of students is conspicuously absent from top seven, and one notes that improving undergraduate instruction is ranked forty-fourth in importance; yet eighteen of the forty-seven goals in the questionnaire focused on students. On administrator and faculty member congruence, the study indicated "clearly that administrators and faculty tend to see eye to eye to a much greater extent than is commonly supposed and therefore the greater power of administrators should not be regarded as necessarily inimical to the faculty or inconsistent with the fundamental role and purposes of the university" (p. 115).

Gross and Grambsch replicated their 1964 study in 1971, and a comparison revealed little overall change in the rankings of the forty-seven goals (Gross and Grambsch, 1974). Faculty matters and career interests remain at the top of the list. Two noticeable

Table 1. Perceived and Preferred Goals

Seven Perceived Top Goals	Seven Preferred Top Goals
1. Protect academic freedom	1. Protect academic freedom
2. Increase/maintain prestige	2. Train students for scholarship/research.
3. Maintain top quality in important programs	3. Cultivate students' intellect
4. Ensure confidence of contributors	4. Maintain top quality in all programs
5. Keep up to date	5. Disseminate new ideas
6. Train students for scholarship/research	6. Keep up to date
7. Carry on pure research	7. Maintain top quality in important programs

Bottom Four Goals	Bottom Four Goals
44. Emphasize undergraduate instruction	44. Emphasize undergraduate instruction
45. Involve students in university governance	45. Cultivate students' taste
46. Preserve institutional character	46. Involve students in university governance
47. Cultivate students' taste	47. Preserve institutional character

Source: Gross and Grambsch (1968).

changes, however, are evident: involvement of the faculty and students in university governance moved in faculty ratings from twenty-fifth to ninth as a perceived goal and from nineteenth to twelfth as a preferred goal. Graduate study dropped from eighteenth to twenty-fifth as a perceived goal and from twenty-seventh to forty-second as a preferred goal.

Gross and Grambsch concluded that in 1971 as compared with 1964 the internal constituencies (faculty members, students, administrators) had more similar goal orientations than did the external constituencies (regents, governments, citizens). (The views of administrators and faculty members reflect their conclusions about students, which is one source of information—the one that generally prevails.) By 1971 the authors found not only that noticeable cleavages had developed between external power holders and the internal constituencies, cleavages which could significantly affect the goals of the university, but that power was shifting toward external groups. Richman and Farmer (1974, p. 100) reached a similar conclusion in their analysis of the 1964 and 1971 data.

In a comprehensive study of community colleges, D. S. Bushnell obtained goal ratings from 2,500 faculty members, 10,000 students, and 90 presidents. This study found "a high degree of consensus among community junior college administrators, faculty, and students on the major goals to be served by their colleges. Differences do occur, however. Presidents emphasize responding to community needs; faculty place greater stress on the student's personal development; and students press for more egalitarian goals, like the concept of the 'open door' and expanded financial aid. Community junior college presidents place significantly greater weight on output goals (that is, changes in student performance) than do university administrators. Only one of seven top-ranked goals of university administrators focused on serving the needs of students . . . while five of the top third (five out of nine) of the community junior college presidents' goals are student-oriented" (1973, p. 63).

The literature also contains a number of lists of criteria for appraising the quality of mission statements. One general example is offered by the Commission on Higher Education of the Middle States Association of Colleges and Schools in its "Characteristics of Excellence in Higher Education and Standards for Middle States Accreditation," which can be used as a checklist for appraising the quality of the goals. This report states that well-defined aims are "(a) clear, appropriate to higher education, intellectual in emphasis, and broad in scope; (b) identifiable with the particular institution; (c) stated in terms of results sought, not merely the means by which they are to be attained; (d) susceptible of attainment in reasonable degree; (e) honest in describing what the institution plans and constructs its programs to accomplish; (f) expressed in simple terms; (g) understood and accepted within the institution as guides for thought and action" (1977, pp. 2–3).

2. Do objectives reinforce goals?

Having a general goals statement is necessary for the next, more concrete, step—formulating objectives. Each goal should have subordinate objectives that lead to outcomes that are reasonably measurable. "Reasonably measurable" is a realistic guide based on the premise that it is better to be generally right than precisely wrong in these matters. Colleges and universities have a tendency to err either on the side of vague generalities or toward the other extreme of unattainable and time-consuming specificity.

Management by objectives (MBO) is one effort to bring objectives, programs, and evaluation together as parts of a whole that is greater than the sum of the parts. The major purpose of MBO is to translate the statement of organizational purpose into more specific operational objectives, plans, and budgets so as to influence the members of the institution to support the goals. Drucker has written (1954, pp. 135–136) that MBO is a principle of management that "will give full scope to individual strength and responsibility, and at the same time give common direction of vision and effort, establish teamwork and harmonize the goals of the individual with the common weal. . . . It makes the common weal the aim of every manager. It substitutes for control from the outside the stricter, more exacting and more effective control from the inside. It motivates the manager to act not because somebody tells him to do something or talks him into doing it, but because the objective needs of his task demand it." Numerous higher education articles have adapted this concept of business management to higher education; Lahti (1973) approaches the matter in some depth.

Linking programs to measurable objectives that are consistent with larger goals is difficult but worth pursuing. In one sense almost every college and university makes this effort, in that its administrators do ask fairly regularly, "Where are we going?" Yet the discipline required to take the next steps is often lacking. These steps are guided by questions such as these: Is where we are going where we want to be in three or five years? If not, how do we modify current directions, and what checkpoints can be established to help us know how effectively we are moving toward objectives that are consistent with agreed-upon general directions?

The budget-making and allocating processes should be closely related to goals and objectives. An institution's real priorities can be ascertained by looking at where it puts its money; therefore, a continuous self-questioning should take place about the relation between goals and objectives and allocating and reallocating resources.

Stating objectives in measurable terms has facilitated developing clear-cut targets that can be used by professors to plan instruction and by students to guide their study. Opponents of the behavioral-objectives approach contend that the method focuses principally on detail at the expense of large, more interrelated, dimensions. Anderson, Ball, Murphy, and Associates (1975, pp. 182–183) have offered these compromises that would probably be accepted by both advocates and opponents:

> (1) Objectives expressed in measurable, behavioral terms are appropriate for basic skills and for other areas where there is agreement about the components of an instructional program. (2) For most purposes, behavioral objectives need not be reduced to trivial detail. The degree of specificity may vary and should relate to the purpose of instruction and the understanding of students and instructors. (3) The use of behaviorally stated objectives should be contained in an instructional model which recognizes and provides for individual differences. (4) Complex and long-range objectives should be included in a set of objectives, even though they cannot be described in precise terms or measured with a high degree of accuracy. (5) Educational objectives must be appropriate to the social milieu at a given time, and students should participate with their instructors in finding objectives that make sense to them. (6) In times like the present, when technological and social changes are rapid and the future is uncertain, the desired behaviors should be adaptable to situations other than the existing one. The ultimate usefulness of behavioral objectives will depend upon how effectively they may be adapted to quite different learning needs and situations.

These six generalizations can serve as guidelines for assessing the quality of behavioral objectives.

Another, older set of criteria, the result of an extensive study undertaken by Zook and Haggerty (1936) for the North Central Association in the mid 1930s, can be used to judge the effectiveness of both goals and objectives statements. In this case, points are awarded (one, five, or ten points) according to the assessed quality of the statements in each of four categories: clearness of conception, scope, acceptance by the faculty, and relation between stated purpose and contributory activities. Each of these categories is in turn divided into nonoccupational and occupational aims.

Thus, in appraising the *clearness of conception* of nonoccupational aims, the evaluator gives ten points to statements in which each announced purpose of the institution is unequivocally presented, which is clear to the students, the faculty, and the public, and in which there is complete harmony among the stated aims. Five points go to a partial statement, or to one containing some confused or vague aims, or to one that shows evidence of conflict among aims. Only one point is awarded to a statement demonstrating "conspicuous conflict and confusion." With respect to occupational aims, ten points go to a statement that clearly sets forth the purpose of each occupational and preoccupational curriculum, specifies the conditions of entrance and length in years, and presents a well-organized outline of content. When the purposes are not stated but each occupational and preoccupational curriculum carries specifications and a careful outline, or when the purposes are stated but some curricula lack specifications, or an outline, or both, five points are awarded. If the purposes are either not stated or stated vaguely and the curriculum descriptions are inadequate, one point is given.

In evaluating the *scope* of nonoccupational goals, the assessor gives ten points to a statement that includes the aims of the institution, of each division, and of each curriculum or department and that has aims covering all activities but nothing beyond those. If the statement presents the aims of the institution but of only part of its divisions, or if it describes some activities outside the stated aims or some aims that overreach the program, it gets five points. If it presents the institutional aims only, or a portion of the divisional aims only, and it also describes activities outside the aims or aims beyond the activities, it receives one point. With respect to the scope of occupational aims, a ten-point goal statement describes the purpose of each occupational program, refers to institutional goals, and offers a well-organized, adequate curriculum for each occupational or preoccupational aim stated. If the purposes are omitted but a well-organized, acceptable curriculum is presented for each occupation for which occupational or preparatory training is offered by the college, five points are awarded. When purposes are stated that have no attached curriculum, or when the curricula described are loosely organized and inadequate, one point is given.

In the category of *faculty acceptance*, the award system is more or less the same for nonoccupational and occupational aims. The evaluator gives the institution ten points if there is unmistakable evidence that the faculty understands and accepts the goals and that the institution has a plan to acquaint (and does acquaint) incoming members of the faculty with its essential purposes before their appointment. The evaluator awards five points if he sees evidence that the aims of the institution have been considered and in the main accepted by the faculty and if there is no apparent opposition to essential aims. If he finds no evidence of understanding and acceptance of the aims (general or occupational), and if in fact there is some discord and opposition with respect to some goals, he gives the college only one point.

The last category, the *relation between purposes and activities* (or goals and objectives), partly overlaps the earlier ones but is nevertheless scored separately. In this case, if the goals and objectives statement (of nonoccupational aims) provides specific activities intended to accomplish each stated purpose and avoids presenting activities for which no purpose is given, it receives ten points. When most of the stated aims are accompanied by contributory activities, or when a few of the activities described are not directed toward some purpose, five points are awarded. But if there are no apparent relations between purposes and activities, or there is conflicting evidence, the statement gets the lowest score. The scoring for occupational goals is similar: an aim is stated for each occupational or preoccupational curriculum, and a well-organized, adequate curriculum is provided for each stated aim (ten points); aims are not stated but fairly apparent in well-organized curricula (five points); aims are stated but not sustained by adequate curricula, or inadequate curricula also lack stated aims (one point). These points, criteria, and guidelines should provide useful ideas for evaluators while they develop approaches to determining the extent to which objectives reinforce goals.

3. Does the institution have adequate planning capabilities?

The goals and objectives statements and planning are closely related. It is not possible to do long-range planning without such statements; nor is it possible to have effective goals and objectives statements without considerable planning. Therefore one might ask: Is there also a relationship between long-range planning and institutional success? Research on this question has been rather extensive in the business world. For example, studies by Thune and House (1970), Karger and Malik (1975) and Herold (1972) reach similar conclusions (see the Annotated Bibliography for descriptions of all three). The Karger study measured the effects of formal integrated long-range planning (FILRAP) on commonly accepted financial performance measures in industrial companies. Ninety U.S. companies took part in the survey representing five generic groups—clothing, chemicals, drugs and cosmetics, electronics, and food and machinery. In most cases companies that did long-range planning significantly outperformed the nonplanners. The planners were more aggressive and better sellers of goods, controlled margins to show greater profits, and earned higher returns on capital. The Thune and House study found that formal planning firms in the drug, chemical, and machinery industries consistently out-performed informal planners; no clear associations were established in the food, oil, and steel industries. Positive economic performance and formal planning were most strongly related in the medium-size companies that have rapidly changing markets. Whether similar results would be produced by a study of planning and success in academic organizations is not known, although one suspects they would be. In other words, in those colleges and universities that plan well, plans are more likely to serve as guides to the future than would be the case for what industry calls the nonplanners.

What sort of procedures does the institution have for making plans? One commonly used arrangement is an office of institutional research which does both short- and long-range planning. This is a relatively recent development, however. Rourke and Brooks (1964) point out that most colleges and universities established their offices or bureaus of institutional research (IR) only a few years before 1963. Indeed, the 1957 American Council on Education conference on institutional self-study had difficulty locating individuals to whom invitations could be extended. But only five years later sixty people attended a national conference of institutional research officials held at Northern Illinois University, and in the following year more than two hundred attended a similar meeting at Wayne University in Detroit. Institutional research has continued its rapid growth and development.

However, probably less than half of all colleges and universities have separate IR offices, although almost every college or university does some kind of institutional research. Hodgkinson and his associates at the Center for Research and Development in Higher Education (1975, p. 233) surveyed 342 institutions which they had identified "as doing something different and perhaps 'innovative' in higher education at the undergraduate level." The survey asked whether the institutions had an institutional research office with a full-time director. The results indicated that about 51 percent had such an office, and an additional 2 percent had one with a part-time director. Thus only about 53 percent of the institutions, even though they were selected for their innovative characteristics (one can assume that more of these institutions would have institutional research offices than would a random sample of institutions), had an office devoted to planning, evaluation, and related tasks. The status of these offices may be indicated by the fact that only 30 percent of the respondents were IR directors. The authors concluded: "The questionnaire (sent to the president's office) apparently was routed to some individuals who felt that they should respond rather than the director of institutional research. What this tells one about the political role of the directors of institutional research offices on campus can only be speculated about, but one wonders if some of them are perhaps seen as clerical functionaries rather than line administrators" (p. 234).

In addition to being low, at least in some institutions apparently, the status of IR may also be vague. The Carnegie Commission survey on institutional research (Bogard, 1972, p. 20) found that institutional research "was difficult to locate within the organization; it was hard to identify specifically; and its exact role or function in the administration was not easily determined. The typical administrator in the sample survey perceived himself as competent and as possessing highly adequate information for the decisions he made. He attributed the same characteristics to his colleagues. He was aware of only one constraint—insufficient time to make decisions. It is interesting to note that there was no evidence reported of a correlation in the minds of the administrators between this time constraint and the usefulness of a centralized IR office."

The following criteria for evaluating an institutions' goals and its plans for realizing them were developed by the Young Presidents' Organization in cooperation with the Association of Governing Boards, the Association of American Colleges, and the National Association of College and University Business Officers (Armacost and others, 1976, pp. 3–6). With respect to the *college mission*, the following questions can be asked: For whom does the college exist? To whom, besides the faculty and staff, would it make a difference if the college ceased to exist? Is the stated mission desired by the majority within each of the constituent groups on campus? How widely shared and deeply held is the statement of mission within and among these groups?

Related particularly to *long-range planning*, these questions are pertinent: Is there a clearly articulated set of long-range goals? How does fulfilling each of these aims help in attaining the mission of the college? Is the plan based on clear and realistic assumptions? Are the methods for achieving each of the goals clearly stated? Have alternative means to reaching the objectives been carefully considered? Are the methods consistent with available resources? Are there contingency plans in case of "down-side risks," such as enrollment decline? Are the relative priorities among the objectives clearly stated and understood?

The following questions may be asked about the *planning process*. How does the board ensure that the long-range plan is up to date? How is the advice and knowledge of the various constituencies incorporated in the planning process? Is the term of the plan long enough to accommodate changes in society and institutional changes needed in order to adjust to social movement?

And what about *annual objectives and the budget*? Are there clearly articulated annual management objectives? Does achieving the annual objectives result in reasonable progress toward fulfilling long-range goals? Does the budget allocate resources in support of the objectives and in the order of their priority?

With respect to communicating the plan, are the long- and short-range objectives clearly understood throughout the administration and faculty? What devices are being used to positively disseminate the plan?

Finally, a number of questions should be asked about the annual performance appraisal. What progress has been made during the year in accomplishing each objective? By what means and with what criteria does the board annually assess the performance of the president? Of the other administrative officers? Does the institution have a board-approved regular and systematic program to measure the effectiveness of its faculty and its other employees? Is there adequate and timely follow-up to deal with substandard performance? Do salary and promotion decisions adequately reflect superior performance? And are there enough opportunities for professional development related to institutional needs and the professional goals of the employees?

4. **Are institutional admissions' policies and procedures consistent with institutional goals and objectives?**

The admissions process is intimately involved not only with the entire educational endeavor and the institution's goals and objectives but also with the values and aspirations of the surrounding society. Clearly, then, it is more than just an administrative detail. Thresher (1970, pp. 3–4) has pointed out, "The admissions function constitutes a major conduit or tap-root between the college and the society that generates and sustains it. Properly to perform this function imposes the obligation to hold out and make known the institution's offer of educational opportunities in ways which speak to the needs and aspirations of youth which constitute its natural clientele."

Armacost and others (1976, pp. 4–6) have developed the following criteria to assist colleges and universities to better define and evaluate the key elements of admissions:

A. *Defining the Market*

1. *Geographically.* What is our geographical market? Which states and which cities are most important to us? Why does this pattern exist? What trends are occurring within our geographical markets? What is driving these trends?
2. *Academically.* Which areas of study, general interest, and career interest represent those market segments in which we are

strongest? What are the forecasted trends or changes in trends within these market segments?

3. *Philosophically.* Which distinct religious or philosophical constituencies represent major markets for us? Is our relationship with them, and the results growing from it, expected to be strengthened or weakened in the future?

4. What other significant characteristics of the college further define our served market (such as its single-sex or coed status, or its size)?

5. What other variables need to be analyzed in order to clarify further our marketing opportunities?

B. *Identifying the "Target Student"*

1. Exactly what kind of person does the college seek to attract?

2. What quantitative measures exist which ensure that we are admitting students who reflect our target criteria?

3. What is the desirable "mix" of students in order to have sufficient diversity to be educationally productive and yet enough commonality to support the general college purposes?

C. *Clarifying the College Selection Process*

1. What are the determining factors about each college that influence students to choose one institution over another?

2. Who are the key people involved with the student during the decision-making process, and what role does each play?

3. What is the most effective way to influence these key people in favor of our college?

D. *Assessing the Competition*

1. Does the marketing plan reflect accurate knowledge of the nature of the competition for students and the strengths and weaknesses of our primary competitors?

2. What is the source of such information, and does it adequately reflect the views of prospective students?

E. *Defining the College in Terms of Market Needs*

1. What are the distinguishing characteristics of our college which set it apart from other colleges and which can be effectively promoted to prospective students?

2. Do our promotional materials present a clear, appealing, and memorable picture of the college that emphasizes points which complement one another and distinguish the college from others?

3. Are prospective students of the type defined as our "target" likely to be interested in the kind of college depicted in the materials?

4. Do the promotional materials accurately reflect our knowledge of the market for the college?

F. *Developing a Recruitment Strategy*

1. Is there a central and carefully planned strategy for recruitment which capitalizes on the strengths of our college and which takes advantage of the comparative weaknesses of our competitors?

2. Is the strategy such that it can be implemented well with present resources?

G. *Developing a Recruitment Objective for the Year*

1. Does the recruitment plan accurately reflect the long-range planning goals and the budget needs of the college?

2. Does the plan include realistic goals for the number of prospects, candidates, applications, and acceptances in light of our previous experience, on the one hand, and our needs, on the other hand?

H. *Spelling Out the Tactics*

1. Does the college have a realistic, thoughtful, and imaginative plan for the specific allocation of staff time, financial resources, and the use of volunteers (alumni, parents, faculty members, students) which reflects the goals, strategic considerations, market definition, "target student" and the nature of the competition?

2. Are the timetables clear and reasonable?

I. *Managing for Results*

1. Is there an adequate system of reporting which indicates periodically the results obtained, how much they cost, and how they compare with what was planned?

2. Is the information reported in such a way as to facilitate timely corrective action?

In struggling colleges and universities now and in additional ones joining this group in the 1980s, admissions policies and procedures will be driven significantly by a noticeable decrease in the available pool of full-time, residential students. Talking to a struggling institution about more selective admissions criteria is like telling a man near starvation to mind his manners during his first meal. Fewer four-year colleges and universities will have the luxury of numbers in the 1980s, but *survival with purpose and quality* likely will rest significantly upon redefining goals and objectives, meshing admissions policies and procedures with chosen institutional directions, and fastening down the hatches and trimming the sails for the rough seas ahead.

5. **Have the institution's goals and objectives helped it maintain a reasonable identity within a statewide system of institutions?**

Since public postsecondary institutions are related to some larger governing or coordinating system, they compete directly or indirectly with affiliated institutions for funds. And in states with systems within a state system (such as Illinois and Massachusetts), each system competes with other systems for funds and, to a lesser extent, for programs. State-level coordinating/governing boards can complicate the goals picture.

Statewide master plans usually show the stress and strain of political accommodation with individual institutions' aspirations. A couple of years ago I was visiting a fine regional university in a state that had a nationally and internationally known land-grant university. I happened to call this land-grant university the titular institution in the state, and a couple of the deans were not at all happy that any particular institution could be so designated. Perhaps "titular" is not the best term, but some recognition of the vertical as well as the horizontal roles of the various state institutions may be a necessary beginning for developing missions and scope objectives that reflect a statewide perspective.

Differences between goal statements developed by institutions and by statewide boards are almost inevitable. Inasmuch as expansionism has been a way of life in higher education since the mid 1950s, chief administrators understandably seek to include as much as possible in their goals and objectives statements to keep their options open, with the result that such statements tend to be expansive, optimistic, noble—and quite alike. Administrators can defend some nebulousness because colleges and universities are complex and developmental institutions where "bottom line" results are very difficult to ascertain, and because of some optimism on the basis of a belief in a better tomorrow, and because of some similarities, owing to the common elements found in all four-year institutions of higher education. Yet they should be aware that educational officers with state boards/systems see things differently. Increasing competition for all public funds and undesirable academic program duplication cause state-level officials to expect institutions to limit and to more carefully define their aims. Such requests inevitably arise during any statewide master planning process and may bring about an "us" and "them" situation if institutional and system perspectives and sensitivities are not understood.

Returning to the criterion question: The answer concerning the "reasonable self-identity" will depend largely on the soundness, dynamism, and priorities developed in the goals and objectives statement; on evidence of interinstitutional understanding; on the statement's length; on budgetary realities; and on the artistry of institution/system relations.

The first point is self-evident. The second one, about interinstitutional understanding, sometimes is not so discernible—some institutions develop their goals and objectives as though other public institutions, the private sector, community colleges, and proprietary institutions did not exist. But elimination of unnecessary program duplication and curtailment of graduate programs, particularly at the doctoral level, will occur in most states for some time to come; therefore, goals and objectives statements that do not discourage low-priority programs or those in obvious duplication with offerings by other institutions can expect serious trouble at the state level. Negative decisions by the state only frustrate the faculty and administration and add to the natural tensions that exist between an institution and its governing board(s).

The length of the goals and objectives may seem an insignificant detail, and it is if the campus develops two statements: one that flows on to its natural length of several pages and a shorter one for the governing or state agency. State-level master-planning efforts usually require brief statements of similar length from all institutions. Since problems inevitably arise when institutions stand on their multipage documents and let state officials do the cutting, campus designates should make these adjustments themselves.

And, finally, goals and objectives statements should be developed in coordination with system and state officials. Antagonistic relationships serve nobody's basic interests and should be avoided if possible. State educational officials are paid to be concerned and to perform something ·of a watchdog function with respect to statewide directions and priorities, new and existing programs, unnecessary duplication, fiscal effectiveness, interinstitutional coordination and cooperation, and evaluation. The effective institutional officer will therefore develop and maintain amicable and effective working relations with appropriate state officials, and they will have some preliminary discussions on goals and objectives in order to establish the general parameters.

The following questions can serve as guidelines for appraising institution-state relationships with respect to goals and objectives statements: (1) Does the chief administrative officer maintain good working relations with state education officials? (2) Do those who are developing the campus goals and objectives statement have full knowledge of state requirements? (3) Will the statements be forward-looking for the campus yet compatible with basic state requirements and directions? (4) Will the statement be drafted sufficiently in advance of its required submission date to allow ample formal and informal interaction between campus and state officials?

Strategies for Institutional Planning

The common approach to curricular change, the one assumed in the earlier parts of this chapter, is to begin with objectives and move through programs, resources, and evaluation. As originally propounded by Tyler (1949), it has proven constructive in many cases. Yet there is another approach that can be more effective in some circumstances. There are times when developing or redefining the goals and objectives statement may be the last step. This strategy begins with the most pressing problems of the institution. In most instances such concerns are no secret to experienced and perceptive faculty members and administrators. They include attrition, retention, faculty evaluation, budget processes, the academic calendar, and curricular and instructional changes. Task forces, or "study and action committees," if you are tired of the term *task forces*, can develop recommendations on these matters.

This approach has the advantage of tackling pressing concerns directly and immediately, and the possibility of achieving some concrete results is greater when individuals sense the necessity for some action to improve a situation that everyone agrees is undesirable. This strategy also has a greater chance of succeeding than the more complicated and sensitive process of developing or refining goals and objectives statements for the whole institution. By making headway with "smaller" problems, people gain confidence for other ventures. (Nothing succeeds like success.) A faculty that has tackled successfully its immediate difficulties may then be in a better position to address the larger issue of institutional goals and objectives.

Another strategy outlined by Pace (1972), begins with the central question "What are the consequences?" rather than with what he considers to be a more limiting one, "What are the objectives?" The style of inquiry is more aptly characterized by the word *exploration* than by the words *control* and *forms*. In this case the evaluator acts as a social scientist instead of a teacher, missionary, reformer, or staff officer to the practitioners. The purpose of this approach is to provide more complex bases for informed judgment. Pace contends that "decision making" is too narrow for describing the purpose and role of evaluation, and "explanation" is too abstract and impersonal; "judgment," as he sees it, should be the central aim of evaluation studies (p. 3).

Planning in Perspective

Planning in perspective refers to the right balance among planning, operations, and evaluation. Planners and evaluators can be expected to see the institution through their eyes, and these views can call for inordinate amounts of time and paperwork; from the administrators' standpoint, keeping daily operations running smoothly and efficiently is the primary responsibility, and they therefore gravitate toward ad hoc planning or meeting immediate needs, sometimes to the detriment of planning. Obviously some balance is required between these two groups.

A philosophical difference exists between planners who believe in orderly progress toward known goals and objectives and those who believe the planning mentality reduces creativity, enthusiasm, and ultimately the quality of the end product. In sum, planning should be taken more seriously, but planners should not take themselves too seriously. They need to recognize that for the student many aspects or unexpected concomitants of the collegiate experience—marriage, part-time employment, academic learning, extracurricular social and governance activities, and so on—can have much more import than a statement of students' goals and objectives. And colleges, in the final analysis, are for students.

Regardless of whether one begins or ends with statements of intended outcomes, or how seriously one plans, however, the fundamental consideration in evaluating an institution is its *actual* effects, not the adequacy of any published statements of purpose. The next chapters consider these real effects or results.

3

Appraising
the Extent of
Student Learning

Learning is the *raison d'être* of the collegiate experience. This many-splendored thing may be defined as acquiring, through classroom teaching or independent effort, affective, cognitive, and psychomotor knowledge, values, and skills. A lifelong process, it includes perpetuating, discovering, applying, and changing. At the bottom of a mimeographed newspaper published in an Eskimo village seven hundred miles north of the Arctic Circle, this one-liner captured the essence of learning: "When you're through learning, you're through."

In treating this very broad subject, one might start with major aspects of adolescent and young-adult development, which have been termed "growth trends" and "developmental tasks."

Chickering (1969, pp. 8–19) uses the terms "vectors of development" and identifies these seven: *Achieving competence*—this vector has three elements: intellectual ability, physical and manual skills, and social and interpersonal competence. The last "is the one of greatest concern to the young adult and one where significant development frequently occurs without explicit support from family, employer, or college." *Managing emotions*—the two major impulses to manage are aggression and sex. *Becoming autonomous*—"to be emotionally independent is to be free of continual and pressing needs for reassurance, affection, or approval." *Establishing identity*—this one depends on, but is more than, other vectors already mentioned: competence, emotion, management, and autonomy. *Freeing interpersonal relationships*—a sense of identity liberates relations with others. *Clarifying purposes*—it requires "formulating plans and priorities that integrate avocational and recreational interests, vocational plans, and life-style considerations." *Developing integrity*—it involves "three overlapping stages: the humanizing of values, the personalizing of values, and the development of congruence."

In the college environment, what elements are necessary or at least highly desirable for students' development? Grant (1974, pp. 71–75) identifies stimulation, security, order, freedom, and territoriality. The milieu must be interesting and challenging, yet students should feel secure against undesirable stimuli and circumstances. Order is necessary to support security and intellectual activities. Freedom allows students to create and respond to the environment in their own way. And territoriality means the ability of a student to stake out a piece of the environment over which he or she can have optimum control, and in which there are acceptable levels of security, stimulation, order, and freedom. In the ideal environment for learning, according to Miller and Prince (1977, pp. 111–113), the various elements serve common institutional goals; there is a purposeful relationship between formal learning and the student's growth outside the classroom; a reasonable degree of compatibility exists between an individual and the institution; there is an understandable relationship between what occurs on campus and what happens in the "real world"; and the milieu responds to the developmental needs of its students.

It is clear from the foregoing general discussion of the complex nature of students' learning and the proper environment for fostering it that the evaluator's task is formidable. He or she must analyze and try to measure a great many slippery variables. This task is strongly influenced by the current emphasis on accountability and on numerical measures of educational results. Spurred by such factors as the colleges' increasing competition with several powerful public agencies for public support, the increased use of computers and technology to provide data on social and educational problems, a sluggish economy, and student unrest in the 1960s are stimulating more questions like "Are taxpayers receiving fair value for their significant investment in higher education?" Educators need to address this question carefully because budget experts in state houses and governors' offices are beginning to do so. Their criteria—degree production, cost per full-time-equivalent (FTE) student, cost per credit hour of instruction, and so forth—are almost wholly quantitative. Such experts tend to ignore benefits from higher education that are difficult to measure, and as Trow (1974, p. 16) cautions, "To infer from the difficulty of measurement that these effects don't occur . . . is to make the most serious error . . . , the error of believing that if a phenomenon can't be measured, it doesn't exist." Because of these trends, one can easily conclude, with Astin (1977, p. x), education is now being shaped more by economic considerations than by concern for enhancing student progress."

What general outcomes of college going can be identified? Hundreds of studies have examined various aspects of students' learning. Two decades ago Jacob (1957) found that college does not make a fundamental difference for most students, although "there is more homogeneity and greater consistency of values among students at the end of their four years than when they begin. . . . The impact of the college experience is rather to *socialize* the individual, to refine, polish, or 'shape up' his values so that he can fit comfortably into the ranks of American college alumni" (p. 4).

The work of Jacob set researchers in motion. As a result, several major studies and syntheses of the literature have been published in the past ten years. (In addition to those discussed here, Solomon and Taubman, 1973, is an excellent summary.)

Feldman and Newcomb (1969, p. 4) in their comprehensive study of the impact of college said: "In a sense, our conclusions are more optimistic than Jacob's. There are conditions under which colleges have had (and, we assume, will continue to have) impacts upon their students, and not least upon student's values. Moreover, the consequences of these impacts often persist after the college years."These researchers found that freshman-to-senior changes in several characteristics have been occurring with considerable uniformity in most colleges and universities in recent decades. More specifically:

> Declining "authoritarianism," dogmatism, and prejudice, together with decreasingly conservative attitudes toward public issues and growing sensitivity to aesthetic experiences, are particularly prominent forms of change—as inferred from freshman-senior differences. These add up to something like increasing openness to multiple aspects of the contemporary world, paralleling wider ranges of contact and experience. Somewhat less consistently, but nevertheless evident, are increasing intellectual interests and capacities, and declining commitment to religion, especially in its more orthodox forms. Certain kinds of personal changes—particularly toward greater independence, self-confidence, and readiness to express impulses—are the rule rather than the exception [p. 326].

Two more recent books (Astin, 1977; Bowen, 1977) also speak authoritatively on this subject. Astin's longitudinal data, derived from studies that collectively involved some two hundred thousand students:

> Show clearly that students change in many ways after they enter college. They develop a more positive self-image as reflected in greater interpersonal and intellectual competence, and they develop more liberal political views and attitudes toward social issues. At the same time, they show less religiousness and altruism and show reduced interest in athletics, business, music, and status. Some of these attitudinal and personality changes are accompanied by parallel changes in behavior. Most dramatic is the decline in religious behavior and the accompanying increase in hedonistic behavior. Freshmen appear to be less studious

and to interact less with instructors than they did in high school, but studiousness and interaction with faculty increase with time in college [p. 212].

Bowen based the following conclusion on a comprehensive analysis of the individual and societal value of education:

> The sum of the benefits [of education] exceeds the total cost by a factor of three or more. The monetary returns alone, in the form of enhanced earnings of workers and improved technology, are probably sufficient to offset all the costs. But over and above the monetary returns are the personal development and life enrichment of millions of people, the preservation of the cultural heritage, the advancement of knowledge and the arts, a major contribution to national prestige and power, and the direct satisfactions derived from college attendance and from living in a society where knowledge and the arts flourish. These nonmonetary benefits surely are far greater than the monetary benefits—so much greater, in fact, that individual and social decisions about the future of higher education should be made primarily on the basis of nonmonetary considerations and only secondarily on the basis of monetary factors [1977, p. 447].

In sum, at least four benefits are derived from the collegiate experience. First of all, most students make an initial career choice in college, or at least serious career inclinations are developed at this time. And required credentials for the professions are gained only by the collegiate route.

The collegiate experience also acquaints students with man's past, with present issues, and with future opportunities, needs, and problems. Students begin to see the world outside themselves and to take some steps toward analyzing and understanding it.

Further, the four-year experience is a symbolic loosening of the ties between parents and children. More mothers than care to admit it have cried most of the way home after dropping off their daughter at the college dormitory to begin that first fall term, and more "cool" teenagers than care to admit it have felt quite miserable when Mom and Dad were not at their elbow. But both parents

and offspring survive, and both become stronger in their own resources as new friends and challenges face students away from
home and parents away from students.

A fourth positive influence of the collegiate experience is
personal adjustment. The influence of peer groups, more powerful
than parental influences in many instances, is a dominant factor in
the teen years, and it continues to be persuasive in college. In the
collegiate environment, where new faces and circumstances are the
rule, students must adjust to their new peers. In this caldron of
swirling forces and counterforces, different ways of coping and
succeeding are developed. Sometimes the secondary school and the
home have made these adjustments relatively easy, but other environments may not have prepared young adults, and they experience severe trials and problems before learning to handle the situation (and of course not all do learn). College, then, can provide a
vast environmental laboratory where one can fail without the
stigma or consequences that may be at stake later. To fail an
examination or receive a poor grade in a course is one thing; to lose
a sales account or one's job is another.

The four-year residential instution provides a certain kind
of experience; the two-year community college, the four-year
commuting institution, and nontraditional programs offer
others—and to a rapidly growing number of students. Part-time
students now constitute approximately half of all postsecondary
students, and this proportion will increase somewhat in the future.
Though colleges and universities are ready and eager to reap the
monetary benefits of enrolling these students, the programs and
policies to accommodate their particular interests and needs have
developed slowly. Finally, however, lifelong learning is becoming a
major educational theme as more individuals retire early and develop new interests and careers, as more people seek to escape the
routine of a highly structured environment, as job obsolescence
requires more or less continuous education, and as fiscal austerity
and severe competition for public funds foster more delivery systems that are not placebound. The four-year residential learning
experience will continue to be important, but significant institutional adjustments are necessary to capitalize on the opportunities
presented by the trend toward lifelong learning.

The following five criteria are designed to assist in evaluating the institution's ability to bring about both intellectual and other learning.

6. **How do students rate their advising and counseling system?**

Three new kinds of students place additional burdens on college advising. The adult part-time student requires as much advising time as the full-time residential student, and sometimes more; and to help part-timers the adviser must have a broader knowledge of the institution, the ability to plan and work out individualized programs that often are of greater complexity, and the capacity to creatively adapt schedules and programs to adult learners. The second kind of student is described by various terms, such as "disadvantaged," "culturally deprived," "underprepared," and "high-risk." Cross (1972) describes them in this manner: "The majority of them are the white sons and daughters of blue-collar workers, although a significant number are from ethnic minorities. . . . These New Students have been unlikely to find rewards for good performance within the school system. . . . They don't seek intellectual stimulation from their classes, nor do they anticipate discovering the joy of learning; they just hope to survive and to protect themselves against too obvious failure. . . . They learn job-related material well because it is usually concrete and its usefulness is apparent."

Chickering (1973, pp. 70–71) identifies a third new group of students "from the pool of middle- and upper-class high school graduates between the ages of sixteen and twenty-five who have traditionally been the primary constituents of colleges and universities. These students are 'new' in the general maturity of their orientation toward college, toward work, toward marriage and family life, and toward the place of education in their total existence."

The problem of adequate advising is most evident at large public universities, where few, if any, "brownie points" are given to professors for taking the time necessary for constructive, informed advising. Commenting on this issue, Dressel (n.d.) has written that "academic advising suffers at the undergraduate level because few of our faculty in the present day have any conception of what undergraduate education is all about. The horizon of each professor is limited by the barriers thrust up around the disciplines, and the large number of courses piled helter skelter inside these barriers impedes discussion and understanding of the curriculum offerings even within the discipline. . . . If faculty members are to accept academic advising as a really important function, they are going to have to spend time on it, and administrative officials are going to have to recognize that time is necessary."

Effective advising calls for a good comprehension of general education, a knowledge of institutional policies and procedures in addition to those of the department and college, and a knowledge of career patterns. And advisers need to recognize the human tendency to favor their own subject area. As Solomon, Bisconti, and Ochsner (1977, p. 165) point out: "The danger for a professor of classical literature if he recommends that his students sample psychology or business is that the students might decide that psychology or business is either more interesting or more marketable than classics. The classics professor could lose a student rather than gain a student who knows classics but has broader skills."

Helping students analyze their *career* interests is an important dimension of the advising/counseling function, as I suggested above, yet how many advisers keep abreast with occupational trends and directions? Gilford (1975) sought information on the postsecondary plans of sixteen thousand high school seniors in the spring of 1972. He found that 45 percent wanted to go into professional work, 17 percent planned on vocational/technical education or apprenticeship, and 14 percent wanted to be craftsmen, to go into technical work, or to get some type of clerical, service, managerial, or sales job that would require vocational education. These aspirations do not match the actual distribution of employment in 1970 or the projected distribution for 1980. In 1970 only 14 percent of the labor force was in the professional and technical occupations, yet 45 percent aspired to these types of occupations, and the 1980 projection is 16 percent. And whereas only 25 percent aspired to careers as sales workers, craftsmen, semiskilled workers, service workers, laborers, and farm workers, these categories comprised 58 percent of the 1970 labor force and will probably include 55 percent in 1980.

These discrepancies can create problems for students and counselors in high school and college. The excessive amount of floundering that accompanies choosing a career field suggests that current counseling facilities and procedures need improvement.

No one best way exists for determining advisee load or for assigning advisees to faculty members. Each institution might examine its commitment to the advising and counseling program as a starting point; then organizational and advising procedures should follow from basic philosophical and policy commitments. These commitments are measurable, and the student appraisal form (see p. 45 in the *Evaluating Faculty Performance,* 1972) can assist in this process. Whether academic advising or personal counseling or both are provided depends on a number of factors that should be decided by each institution or unit.

Another, more general, type of evaluation may be undertaken through seeking answers to a series of questions such as these: (1) To what extent are advisers informed and up to date about programs, procedures, and requirements? How can deficiencies be remedied? This point has two aspects: How can new advisers be educated about institutional programs, procedures, and requirements; and how can veteran advisers be updated effectively? Does the institution have an updated handbook for advisers? (2) Are advisers accessible? What procedures for arranging appointments are most effective? (3) How does an institution identify those who are most interested in advising and who are most effective at it? (4) How does an institution work toward providing every student with at least one faculty member with whom he or she can discuss problems and concerns? (5) What recognition is given to the time and expertise required for effective advising? Should everyone have an advising load even if the person has little interest or competence in this area?

7. Are retention rates reasonable?

"Reasonableness" is a judgment that depends on the particular campus. Some attrition is inevitable and desirable. When there are too many incompatibilities between the institution and the student, a parting of the ways may be in the best interests of both parties; or a change in a student's interests may point toward a different institution; or the maintenance of academic standards may cause some attrition.

Although some student attrition should be expected, I agree with the contention of Bowen and Minter (1976, p. 7) that "perhaps the most conspicuous mark of a healthy college or university is its capacity to attract and hold students. And among the most important indicators signaling impending or actual distress are declining numbers and qualifications of applicants, increasing student attrition, and declining enrollments." Viewing the retention problem in monetary terms, Binning (1971, p. 117) found that "a student with the ability to pay represents $2914 annually to the average private college when tuition, fees, room, board, and the cost of student recruiting are totaled. The average private college dismissed or suspended for academic reasons forty students during academic year 1969–70. Looked at another way, the average private college flunked out nearly $120,000—about the size of the average private college deficit." Thus, it behooves every institution to do all it can to retain students.

In evaluating his institution's retention rate, the assessor will want to compare it with that of benchmark colleges. In four-year residential colleges, the degree-completion rate has remained relatively constant since the first national study in the 1930s indicated that approximately 60 percent of the entering freshmen did not earn a baccalaureate degree in four years (McNeely, 1938). A similar study conducted by Iffert (1957) concluded that 40 percent of entering freshmen nationwide did not graduate. More recent reviews of the literature, according to Maxey (1975), confirmed earlier findings: About 40 percent of entering freshmen nationwide never earn a baccalaureate degree. In community colleges the dropout rate is higher than the rate for four-year colleges: about 50 percent of the entrants do not return for a second year. Of those remaining, about half complete the requirements for an associate degree (p. 2).

College-graduation rates are related directly to selectivity. Less selective institutions have the highest rates of attrition, sometimes as high as 80 percent. Attrition rates are also generally higher in city- and state-supported institutions than at private ones. Attrition rates among private and public institutions vary considerably,

**Table 2. Estimated Eventual Bachelor's Degree-Completion Rates
by Type of Institution**

Type of Institution	Percentage of Students Earning Degrees
Prestigious private universities	90–95
Better public universities	80–85
Typical state universities	60–70
State colleges	40–50
Junior and community colleges[a]	20–30
Proprietary schools	Unknown

[a]Earning B.A. degree after transferring.
Source: Maxey, 1975, p. 2.

ranging from 10 percent at some highly selective private liberal arts colleges to 80 percent at less selective state colleges. Table 2 estimates the graduation rates for various types of institutions (Maxey, 1975).

What factors are most commonly associated with academic failure in college? On the basis of the experience of the Educational Development Center, which conducted a number of ten-week educational rehabilitation programs for several hundred college failures who wanted to continue their collegiate experience, Pitcher and Blaushild (1970, pp. 25–40) identified these ten most common *causes* for academic failure in college:

- Lack of potential
- Inadequate concept of the meaning of work
- Other activities being viewed as more important than the academic program
- Interference from psychological problems
- Failure to assume responsibility
- Inhibition of language functions
- Lack of internalized standards of quality
- Inappropriate choice of major
- Vagueness about long-range goals
- Selection of the wrong college

The *reasons* students give for dropping out are somewhat different. Astin (1975) reported on the results of a national survey

Table 3. Students' Reasons for Dropping Out

	Percentage of Men	Percentage of Women	Percentage of All Students
Boredom with courses	36	25	32
Financial difficulties	29	27	28
Some other reason	31	24	28
Marriage, pregnancy or other family responsibilities	11	39	23
Poor grades	38	14	22
Dissatisfaction with requirements or regulations	24	20	22
Change in career goals	19	20	19
Inability to take desired courses or programs	12	9	11
Good job offer	10	6	9
Illness or accident	7	7	7
Difficulty commuting to college	3	3	3
Disciplinary troubles	2	2	2

Source: Astin, 1975, pp. 14–15.

of forty-one thousand graduates at 358 representative two- and four-year institutions and also of a follow-up questionnaire administered four years later. Table 3, which is based on the 1972 questionnaire, indicates the reasons students gave for leaving college. The substantial percentage in the "some other reason" category probably reflect personal problems.

What are the best predictors of collegiate success? The Astin study (1975, pp. 174–175) reached these conclusions:

> The most important entering characteristics are the student's high school grades, degree aspirations, and religious background: students with good grades, plans for postgraduate degrees, Jewish parents, and Jewish religious preferences have the best chance of finishing college; those with poor grades, plans for only a bachelor's or "other" degree, Protestant parents, and no religious preference have the poorest chance. (For black students, being a cigarette smoker is also among the strongest predictors of dropping out.) The entering characteristics next in importance for staying in college are having good study habits, having high expectations about academic performance in

college, having highly educated parents, being married (for men), and being single (for women). Other entering characteristics that add significantly but less powerfully to college persistence are high scores on college admissions tests, being Oriental, being a nonsmoker, and growing up in a moderate-size city or town.

Once students are enrolled, certain experiential factors enhance their chances of finishing college. The key is involvement, which manifests itself in many ways. Again turning to the Astin (1975) research, we find that "the most important of these [esperiential factors] is getting good grades in college. Next in importance are staying single (for women) and not having children (both sexes), living in a college dormitory rather than at home, and having a part-time job (full-time jobs are to be avoided). Persistence is also enhanced by participation in ROTC or in extracurricular activities such as sports and fraternities or sororities. Being supported by one's parents also helps, as does having a scholarship or grant, but loans add little, and, for men, they reduce chances of finishing college. Students who transfer from one four-year college to another also have somewhat reduced persistence chances." (p. 175)

Several environmental elements are also important in increasing retention. A major one is faculty concern—concern about the student as an individual learner and as a person, about good programs, about special learning opportunities for those who need them, and about early warning systems for those students who are heading for academic trouble. Residence-hall control is another element. Students who are reasonably serious about their academic work, and certainly serious students, are turned off by loud stereo sets and by excessively boisterous behavior. And administrators who place students first in their planning constitute a key element. This attitude manifests itself in the importance administrators give to advising in the reward system and in how they allocate human and material resources.

In making an overall assessment of this aspect of institutional activity, the evaluator might consider the following questions: (1) Are up-to-date attrition data available? Does the study make distinctions between academic and personal reasons for leaving college, and are personal reasons asked in such a way as to elicit specific answers? Does the study also differentiate between students who withdrew in good standing and those who were dismissed for academic reasons? (2) Have institutional retention policies and procedures been examined for their relevance, timeliness, effectiveness, and costs? (3) What current policies and practices, as well as academic programs, have been analyzed with a view toward improvements that would increase retention? (4) Have new methods for increasing retention been considered in conjunction with admissions, advising and counseling, new programs, and the overall campus environment, including residential living arrangements where they exist?

8. **Is an array of individualized and compensatory learning resources available?**

Colleges and universities in the United States, with their essentially open admissions policies as compared with those in other countries, have developed a variety of learning modes for individuals and groups. The need for "learner-centered" programs became quite evident when the surge of Second World War veterans hit the campuses; then the unrest of students in the 1960s and the new clienteles mentioned at the beginning of this chapter amplified the need for individualized programs for average and talented students as well as programs to assist those who are underprepared or have particular learning problems.

The learner-centered movement places the individual student at the center of the educational process and uses a greater array of individualized learning approaches, as well as more traditional ones, to assist in learning. Flexibility in programs characterizes the movement. It also includes many kinds of individualized or self-paced learning materials for regular academic work and for enrichment or supplemental interests. For example, the impact of the "Keller Plan" since it was introduced in 1968 has been dramatic, with around one thousand PSI courses in psychology alone in operation in 1976. Individually Prescribed Instruction (IPI) has been expanding at a rapid rate also. And the PLATO computerized self-paced learning program developed at the University of Illinois at Urbana-Champaign is developing a nationwide clientele for its learning modules. As a whole, the trend toward individualized learning is probably the most significant instructional development of this decade, although it is really an acceleration of what has been under way for some years.

The learner-centered movement does have its critics, however, and several of them wrote articles in a double issue of *Daedalus* that served as a final report for the Assembly on University Goals and Governance. For example, Frankel (1974, p. 25) wrote: "Consider the following phenomena: grade inflation; the progressive elimination of foreign-language requirements from the curricula; the steady dilution even of mild distribution requirements; the regularity with which curricular reforms turn out to involve simply less reading and writing; the living conditions in dormitories, from which universities have almost entirely withdrawn their supervisory authority although they continue to pay the bills."

O'Neil (1975, p. 7) pointed out, in discussing the critics of learner-centered reform, that "if one seeks a scapegoat for what is wrong with higher education, reform appears to be a vulnerable candidate." And London (1976, p. 94) concluded with respect to the learner-centered movement and its critics, that "while the rhetoric has become more vituperative in each camp, in practice the lines are converging. The old guard has liberalized its curriculum so significantly that the once easily defined liberal arts courses are a gallimaufry of everything from Greek philosophy to modern dance. And the reformers, in an effort to establish legitimacy for their programs, have had to develop evaluation techniques that may differ in kind but in many instances are as sophisticated as tests in traditional classrooms."

Whatever the outcome of this controversy, however, individualization is a significant aspect of students' learning and also of programs. And each institution should therefore compile, analyze, and evaluate what is currently available in the way of individualized learning opportunities, as well as what should be available. A number of special provisions should be made especially for poorly prepared students, such as summer courses, reduced course loads, counseling services, tutorial help, and programs for improving their skills. The Learning Skills Center at the State University of

New York at Brockport, for example, offers these services: (1) *Writing*—grammar and writing mechanics; paragraph development; essay organization; term papers and reports; spelling; résumé/application writing; thesaurus usage; vocabulary development; and preparation for graduate school tests. (2) *Study skills*—marking the textbook (underlining and marginal notes); previewing and study reading; preparing an outline; taking notes from lectures or textbooks; preparing for exams; taking various types of exams; and preparation for professional tests, such as the Graduate Record Examination, Law School Admissions Test, and Miller's Analogy Test. (3) *Reading*—reading comprehension skills, such as evaluation, interpretation, recall, and association; recognition of main ideas; rate of reading comprehension; identification of organizational patterns; critical reading skills; skimming/scanning; vocabulary development; reading flexibility; word analysis (attacking unfamiliar words); content area reading (history, science, psychology, and so on); and speed reading and versatility. (4) *Research*—knowledge and utilization of various indices; facility in using the card catalogue; and knowledge and utilization of various divisions of the library. (5) *Mathematics*—metric measurement and conversions; basic arithmetic skills; statistics and test interpretation; trigonometry; Euclidean geometry; beginning, intermediate, and advanced algebra skills; functions, analytic geometry, and calculus; preparation for the quantitative Graduate Record Examinations; individual programs to best fulfill a student's needs; and help on a drop-in basis with specific math problems. (6) *Tutoring service*—tutors are qualified, certified, and ready to help; and service is free to students needing help.

Many, if not most, two- and four-year colleges have not made the effort necessary to handle students who are poorly prepared or who have special learning problems. Bushnell and Zagaris (1972, p. 120), speaking about faculty participation in this effort, concluded: "Those selected for the job frequently enjoy low seniority and no tenure. Such assignments reflect the fact that teaching a remedial course is still a low-prestige assignment. The inexperienced faculty member, often fresh out of graduate school, has had little in the way of orientation or training in coping with the special needs of this group of students. . . . The absence of alternative ways of linking students and tutors, faculty and students, and students with students fuels the fires of frustration."

How successful are compensatory education programs? One recent study (Dudley, 1977) looked into the effectiveness of the remedial courses offered to underprepared freshmen by the Learning Skills Center of the State University of New York at Brockport. The study revealed statistically significant differences in the retention of those who took special courses and those who did not. This finding corroborates that of Roueche and Kirk (1973, pp. 58–59) in their study of *successful* compensatory education programs at five community colleges:

> Students in remedial programs earned significantly higher grades than did high-risk students in non-remedial programs. (2) High-Risk students of like race-ethnic groups earned higher grades in remedial programs than did those in non-remedial programs. (3) In each college, grades earned by successive year-groups enrolled solely or predominantly in courses in developmental studies improved each year. (4) Academic performance of students in remedial programs dropped significantly after they entered regular college programs. . . . (5) Students in remedial programs persisted in college to a greater extent than did high-risk students in non-remedial programs. (6) At each college, students in remedial programs expressed greater satisfaction with the instructor/instructional component of the remedial program than they did with the counselor/counseling component.

Regarding the general results of compensatory education in four-year colleges (in contrast with the outcomes of reputedly successful programs in two-year colleges), Tinto and Sherman (1974, p. *vi*) found "limited consequences as compared with [compensatory courses] at the secondary level." And on the basis of a general literature review, Roueche and Kirk (1973, p. 6) stated that "little hard data exists to support the contention that these programs do indeed help the student remove or remedy his deficiencies."

New and more carefully designed research studies are needed, because earlier ones may not reflect recent advances on many campuses. The results of compensatory programs may need to be analyzed by means of case studies as well as experimental procedures. And even if the studies continue to demonstrate limited overall benefits, the political realities favor continuation. With the scramble for students institutions will need to provide special assistance for inadequately prepared students in order to attract and retain them. And most important, this approach is educationally sound.

These questions can serve as guidelines for evaluating the effectiveness of compensatory programs:

1. Does the college or university work toward the goal of serving all its students?
2. Are instructors who teach compensatory courses volunteers, or have they been chosen at random or forced to participate?
3. Is the developmental program a separately organized unit with its own staff and administrative head? (The unit should report directly to one of the vice presidents.)
4. Do regular courses and programs also give adequate individual attention to some learning problems? (Do professors grade papers for grammar, spelling, and mechanics and assist those who have poor study habits, for instance?)
5. Does the developmental program work closely with related campus units, such as academic advising and personal counseling?
6. Does the program undertake fairly continuous research studies of itself and its effectiveness in order to answer questions such as the following (taken from Roueche and Kirk, 1973, p. 10)?
   A. To what extent do students in selected programs persist in college?
   B. How well do students in remedial programs perform or achieve academically in college?
   C. Is the academic performance of students in remedial programs, as measured by gradepoint average, superior to that of comparable students enrolled in nonremedial programs?
   D. Are students in remedial programs more persistent, as measured by enrollment in and completion of subsequent semesters, than comparable students enrolled in nonremedial programs?

   E. Are there significant relationships among the variables of
      student attitude, persistence, and academic performance
      when low-ability students are statistically categorized in the
      major racial and ethnic groups?
   F. Are there significant differences in persistence, academic
      performance, and attitude among students in remedial
      programs at different colleges?

9. **How effective is the student affairs administration?**

   Alumni often claim that the most significant gains from the
college experience were not obtained in the classroom. The total
college environment, then, needs to be evaluated in terms of its
impact on learning.

   The nonacademic aspects of this environment are often considered the general responsibility of the student affairs office, one
of whose tasks is to oversee the residence halls. Much research has
shown that living on campus (whether in dorms or fraternities and
sororities) has a significant impact in students' development and
adjustment. Astin (1977) reaches these conclusions about the place
of residence: "Residents show slightly greater increases than commuters in artistic interests, liberalism, and interpersonal self-
esteem and show slightly larger declines in musical interest. Effects
are substantially larger, however, on behavior: Residents show
much larger declines in religiousness and much larger increases in
hedonism. Residents are also more likely to interact with faculty, to
become involved in student government, and to join social fraternities and sororities. . . . Living on campus substantially increases
the students' chances of persisting in college and of aspiring to
graduate or professional degrees. . . . Residents express much
more satisfaction than commuters with their undergraduate experience, particularly in the areas of student friendships, faculty-
student relations, institutional reputation, and social life" (pp.
220–221). And in his book-length discussion of the matter, Chickering (1974, pp. 84–85) makes the point still more emphatically:
"Whatever the institution, whatever the group, whatever the data,
whatever the methods of analyses, the findings are the same. Students who live at home with their parents fall short of the kinds of
learning and personal development typically desired by the institu-

tions they attend and which might reasonably be expected when their special backgrounds are taken into account."

The student affairs administration also has charge of such other influential factors as health services and counseling, student government, social and athletic activities, and dining halls and cafeterias. Hence the effectiveness of the student personnel staff must be assessed too. The Student Life Survey (shown in part in Table 4), developed by the State University of New York at Cortland, provides a method for evaluating the student affairs administration.

The student affairs staff also can be evaluated in terms of their professional skills. Five criteria, based on those presented in Miller and Prince (1977, pp. 42–43) are suggested. The staff member (1) is familiar with the various "values clarification" approaches and able to assist students in identifying what they prize, cherish, and believe; (2) knows what general and specific outcomes can normally be expected from completing the various developmental tasks; (3) is skilled at using the goal-setting process and at teaching others how to apply it; (4) is able to motivate students and get them to take responsibility for setting goals and making decisions; and (5) has consultation skills in order to help students locate the settings in which their particular goals and objectives may best be mastered (pp.42–43).

10. **Is satisfactory progress evident toward learning goals?**

What students learn from the collegiate experience can be considered a "value added," in which case the knowledge, values, and skills developed during the two or four years are measured at the outset and at the finish; or it can be determined by judgments made at the end of two or four years, irrespective of the starting point.

The value-added approach takes into account what students bring to college with them, and several studies have shown that this suitcase, so to speak, is significant. For example, Astin (1968b, p. 667) found that "differences in student achievement during the senior year were much more highly dependent upon variations in student characteristics that existed before entrance into college than upon the characteristics of the undergraduate college at-

Table. 4. Student Life Survey

In the column below marked A, check each agency or office that you could describe (that is, do you know where it is located, its main purpose, and what services it provides?).

In the column below marked B, check the appropriate box to indicate how many times you have dealt in person or by telephone with each agency or office.

	A	B			
	You Could	No		Frequency	
Agency or Office	Describe	Contact	1–2	3–7	8 or more
Academic Advisement Office (Twin Towers)					
Business Office (Student Accounts)					
Campus Security					
Career Resource Library (Twin Towers)					
College Court					
Counseling Office					
Financial Aid Office					
FSA Business Office					
Health Services (Infirmary)					
Housing Office					
Orientation					
Placement					
Reading and Study Skills Office					
Registrar's Office					
Union and Activities Offices					
Veterans Affairs Office					

This section of the survey is designed to find out your overall impression of the services (that is, offices and agencies) listed below. Please indicate your satisfaction with those offices and agencies with which you have had personal contact by checking the appropriate column.

Agency or Office	1 Extremely Dissatisfied	2 Dissatisfied	3 Mixed	4 Satisfied	5 Highly Satisfied
Academic Advisement Office (Twin Towers)					
Business Office (Student Accounts)					
Campus Security					
Career Resources Library (Twin Towers)					
College Court					
College Store (Bookstore)					
Counseling Office					
Custodial and Cleaning Service					
Financial Aid Office					
Food Service (Dining Halls, Snack Bar)					
FSA Business Office					
Health Services (Infirmary)					
Housing and Residence Life Offices					
Orientation					
Placement					
Reading and Study Skills Office					
Registrar's Office					
Union and Activities Offices					
Veterans Affairs Office					

Table 4. Student Life Survey (Continued)

Please respond to the statements below by checking a YES or NO to indicate your agreement or disagreement with each of the statements in items 2 through 7, but only for those offices or agencies with which you've had contact. In items 1, 5, and 6, the term Professional Staff (PS) refers to such persons as the directors of placement, financial aid, and housing; physicians; and coordinators of various functions. The term Classified Staff (CS) refers to such persons as stenographers, typists, clericals, nurses, accountants, and receptionists. The terms Not Helpful (NH), Sufficiently Helpful (SH), and Very Helpful (VH) are used in item 8. If you've not had contact with an agency or office, leave blank.

Your Present Residence Hall Director
Housing & Residence Life Offices
Academic Advisement Office
Union & Activities Offices
Career Resource Library
Veterans Affairs Office
Financial Aid Office
Counseling Office
Registrar's Office
Placement Office

1. My principal contact was with   PS   CS
2. The staff seemed to know their job   NO   YES
3. The staff were pleasant and courteous   NO   YES
4. The staff were readily available   NO   YES

5. I generally have
good feelings
about the PS

NO
YES

6. I generally have
good feelings
about the CS

NO
YES

7. I have enough
confidence to
go to the office
or agency for
assistance

NO
YES

8. This office,
agency, or
person was

NH
SH
VH

Please answer the following questions about the offices and agencies with which you are familiar.

Academic Advisement
Career Planning & Placement
Career Resource Library
Health Service (Infirmary)
Financial Aid
Counseling
Housing

1. Do you feel that
the hours of this
office are
adequate?

NO
YES

2. Do you feel that
the location of
this office is
appropriate and
convenient for
students?

NO
YES

Table 4. Student Life Survey (Continued)

Please answer the following questions about the offices and agencies with which you are familiar.

Academic Advisement
Career Planning & Placement
Career Resource Library
Health Service (Infirmary)
Financial Aid
Counseling
Housing

3. If you have dealt with the agency, do you feel that the time it took to get help was

Extremely Long
Long
Fairly Long
Fairly Short
Short
Extremely Short

Below are listed most of the extracurricular activities on campus.

In an attempt to evaluate them in a general way, we are asking you to indicate *in the columns at the left* which *four* programs you would eliminate and which *four* you would retain, given the problem of financial limitations and assuming the desire to maintain a balanced programming concept. In the column marked R, indicate in priority order which four programs you would retain by ranking them 1 through 4 (1 should indicate the program you most want to retain; 2 would be the second most, and so on). In the column marked E., indicate in priority order those four programs you would eliminate.

In the columns at the right of the list below, indicate one of the following for each program.

(1) *Not Aware:* I haven't participated in this program because I was unaware it existed.
(2) *Conflict:*   I am unable to participate in this program because I have a conflict in my schedule.
(3) *No Interest:* I am not interested in participating in this program.
(4) *Would:*   I have participated in this program and would participate again.
(5) *Would Not:* I have participated in this program but do not want to participate again.

	R	E	Program	1	2	3	4	5
01	( )	( )	SAB Movies	( )	( )	( )	( )	( )
02	( )	( )	Jam Sessions and Beer Blasts	( )	( )	( )	( )	( )
03	( )	( )	Drag-Inns & Coffeehouses	( )	( )	( )	( )	( )
04	( )	( )	Night Clubs	( )	( )	( )	( )	( )
05	( )	( )	Media Lounge (Corey Union)	( )	( )	( )	( )	( )
06	( )	( )	Major Concerts	( )	( )	( )	( )	( )
07	( )	( )	Lectures and Speakers Programs	( )	( )	( )	( )	( )
08	( )	( )	Intramural Sports	( )	( )	( )	( )	( )
09	( )	( )	Lyceum and Masquers Production	( )	( )	( )	( )	( )
10	( )	( )	Life Courses	( )	( )	( )	( )	( )
11	( )	( )	Human Sexuality Program	( )	( )	( )	( )	( )
12	( )	( )	Living/Learning Programs	( )	( )	( )	( )	( )
13	( )	( )	Resident Assistant Apprenticeship Program (RAAP)	( )	( )	( )	( )	( )
14	( )	( )	Craft Fairs and Demonstrations	( )	( )	( )	( )	( )
15	( )	( )	Corey Union Craft Shop	( )	( )	( )	( )	( )
16	( )	( )	Academic Clubs (such as Biology Club)	( )	( )	( )	( )	( )
17	( )	( )	Special Interest Clubs (such as Chess Club)	( )	( )	( )	( )	( )
18	( )	( )	Professor Speaks Program	( )	( )	( )	( )	( )
19	( )	( )	Continuing Education Program	( )	( )	( )	( )	( )
20	( )	( )	Recycling Projects	( )	( )	( )	( )	( )
21	( )	( )	Career Planning and Placement Seminars	( )	( )	( )	( )	( )
22	( )	( )	SAB Travel Bureau	( )	( )	( )	( )	( )
23	( )	( )	Corey Union Bowling Alley	( )	( )	( )	( )	( )
24	( )	( )	Corey Union Games Room	( )	( )	( )	( )	( )
25	( )	( )	SAB Record Store	( )	( )	( )	( )	( )
26	( )	( )	Campus Shuttle Bus Service	( )	( )	( )	( )	( )
27	( )	( )	CCSA Charter Bus Service	( )	( )	( )	( )	( )

tended." These findings are similar to the results of studies of secondary school achievement in which the median family income and educational level of the parents were shown to be the dominant factors in the student's high school performance (Diamond, Martin, and Miller, 1969). A "good" home environment gives students an advantage at the outset of college that continues to widen during the four years. Thus the supposed value added may be more a function of an encouraging home environment where books and learning are commonplace than of any college program.

What can students be expected to learn from the collegiate experience? Dozens of lists of goals have been developed over the years, as I pointed out in the previous chapter. In addition to presenting a noteworthy catalogue of goals, Bowen (1977) also evaluated a considerable number of studies that sought to determine how going to college contributes to achieving these intended outcomes. With respect to cognitive learning, Bowen reached these conclusions:

> *Verbal and Quantitative Skills:* Students do make significant gains through the college years in verbal and quantitative skills (though comparable data for persons not attending college are scarce). We found no substantial evidence to the contrary [p. 65].
>
> *Substantive Knowledge:* The overwhelming weight of evidence is that, on the average, students make gains in substantive knowledge during the college years [p. 68].
>
> *Rationality:* A review of the data relating directly or indirectly to change in rationality suggests that on the average students do make gains but that the amount of these gains is modest [p. 78].
>
> *Intellectual Tolerance:* Seniors tend to be less authoritarian, less dogmatic, and less prejudiced than freshmen and more open to new ideas, and more able to deal with complexity and ambiguity. Numerous studies amply confirm this conclusion and reveal relatively large degrees of change [p. 81].
>
> *Esthetic Sensibility:* There is evidence of moderate success in the attainment of this goal, at least for many students [p. 82].
>
> *Creativeness:* Change during college with respect to creativeness has not been fully revealed in any studies be-

cause this complex phenomenon cannot be addressed by use of any single scale. . . . The evidence on creativeness is so scanty and so nebulous that educators should be cautious in making claims about the effect of college in enhancing this quality in its students [p. 84].

Intellectual Integrity: Though intellectual integrity is part of the basic creed of the academic world that educators seek to impart to students, we have been able to find no evidence or even opinion about the success of higher education [in producing it]. . . . One disquieting recent development is the apparent increase in cheating and plagiarism in the academic work of students and the collapse of many of the traditional honor systems [p. 85].

Wisdom: Though there is almost no evidence that higher education helps students to develop into *wise* men and women . . . comparisons of college-educated persons with others . . . suggest that the college-educated may be somewhat more prudent than others in their savings and investments, consumer choices, mobility, practices relating to health, and so on [pp. 85–86].

Intellectual and Cultural Pursuits: The available information on the intellectual and cultural pursuits of students indicates that college has some impact, but how significant or lasting is hard to say [p. 88].

Lifelong Learning: Our judgment [based on the residue of a college education and the cognitive abilities of alumni] is that the goal is attained to a moderate degree [p. 97].

Finally, Bowen presents estimates of what his summary of the research says about changes in cognitive learning (Table 5), emotional and moral development (Table 6), and practical competence (Table 7). And Bowen's summary of the overall changes is given in Table 8.

Getting a handle on student outcomes at the campus level presents some problems, considering the data base, available instruments, and political sensitivities. Generally speaking, cognitive changes are easier to measure than affective ones but still cannot be assessed as accurately as psychomotor outcomes.

Additional instruments are being developed for assessing mental aptitude or achievement, including the certification or licensure examinations required or recommended by the profes-

Table 5. Summary of Estimated Average Changes in Cognitive Learning Resulting from College Education

	Descriptive Term	Estimated Overall Change Expressed in Standard Deviation Units
Verbal skills	Moderate increase	.50
Mathematical skills	Small increase	.20
Substantive knowledge	Large increase	1.00
Rationality	Small increase	.35
Intellectual tolerance	Moderate increase	.60
Esthetic sensibility	Moderate increase	.60
Creativeness	Small increase	.20
Intellectual integrity	Not ascertainable	
Wisdom	Not ascertainable	
Lifelong learning	Moderate increase	.40

Source: Bowen, 1977, p. 98.

Table 6. Summary of Estimated Average Changes in Emotional and Moral Development Resulting from College Education

	Descriptive Term	Rough Estimates of Overall Change Expressed in Standard Deviation Units
Values and aspirations	Small increase	.20
Personal self-discovery	Large increase	.90
Psychological well-being	Moderate increase	.40
Human sympathy		
Toward groups in the abstract	Moderate increase	.60
Toward individuals	No change	0
Morality	Not ascertainable	–
Religious interest	Moderate decrease	– .50
Refinement of taste, conduct, and manners	Small increase	.20

Source: Bowen, 1977, p. 134.

**Table 7. Summary of Estimated Average Changes in Practical
Competence Resulting from Higher Education**

Citizenship	Moderate qualitative gain
Economic productivity	Moderate increase
Family life	Large qualitative gain
Consumer behavior	Small qualitative gain
Leisure	Small qualitative gain
Health	Moderate improvement

Source: Bowen, 1977, p. 218.

**Table 8. Summary of Estimated Average Changes in Individuals
Resulting from College Education**

Descriptive Term	*Personality Dimension*	*Estimated Overall Change Expressed in Standard Deviation Units*
Not ascertainable	Intellectual integrity, wisdom, morality.	
Negative change	Religious interest.	−.10 or less
No change	Human sympathy toward individuals.	−.09 to +.09
Small increase	Mathematical skills, rationality, creativeness, refinement of taste and conduct, consumer behavior, leisure.	.10 to .39
Moderate increase	Verbal skills, intellectual tolerance, esthetic sensibility, life-long learning, psychological well-being, human sympathy toward groups, citizenship, economic productivity, health.	.40 to .69
Large increase	Substantive knowledge, personal self-discovery, family life.	.70 to .99
Very large increase	None.	1.00 or over

Source: Bowen, 1977, p. 221.

sions. The Law School Aptitude Test, the Aptitude Test for Graduate Schools of Business, the Medical School Admission Test, and the Graduate Record Examination are examples. The wide array of devices available is indicated by Buros' *Mental Measurements Yearbooks*, the seventh edition of which lists standardized instruments for the following fields: accounting, biology, business, business education, chemistry, computer programming, dentistry, economics, education, engineering, English, fine arts, foreign languages, geology, geography, health and physical education, history, home economics, industrial arts, law, mathematics, medicine, nursing, philosophy, political science, psychology, physics, reading, religious education, selling, skill trades, sociology, speech and hearing, supervision, and transportation.

These rather specific outcome evaluations do not, however, address the larger issue of the overall cognitive competence that should accrue from the collegiate experience, and scholars and education officials increasingly are looking at this more general result. The American College Testing Service is working on a College Outcome Measures Project (COMP), which is to develop assessment instruments and procedures for evaluating the general education—the broad knowledge and skills—acquired by undergraduates.

Two existing instruments that seek to appraise these more general, less easily measured, outcomes (attitudes, beliefs, values) have been developed by the National Center for Higher Education Management Systems. The first shown in Table 9 is a modification of a procedure developed by Newcomb and Wilson (1966), which asked students two basic questions: "As you reflect upon your college experience, what do you see as significant changes in yourself which have occurred during this period?" and "How did these changes come about?"

As Table 9 shows, a number of "agents of change" can be inserted, such as courses, faculty, other students, general maturity, cultural environment, and community image. One box could be left blank so students can insert their own agent of change.

The second procedure (National Center . . . , 1975), given in Table 10, is designed to obtain students' perceptions about how much the institution has influenced their progress or change and how significant that progress is to them.

Table 9. Student Perception of Change in College

Directions: For each of the *Types of change* listed along the left-hand side of the page, please rate how much you have changed *Overall* and then rate how much influence each *Agent of change* has had in causing that change. In each column, please check (√) the space below the number that most accurately reflects the amount of change.

Key: 3 = Very much change
2 = Some change
1 = Little/no change

	A. Overall Change			B. Agents of Change																	
Types of Change	3	2	1	3	2	1	3	2	1	3	2	1	3	2	1	3	2	1	3	2	1
1. Development of a world view and personal philosophy	—	—	—	—	—	—	—	—	—	—	—	—	—	—	—	—	—	—	—	—	—
2. Development of an interest in new fields of learning	—	—	—	—	—	—	—	—	—	—	—	—	—	—	—	—	—	—	—	—	—
3. Development of general thinking skills	—	—	—	—	—	—	—	—	—	—	—	—	—	—	—	—	—	—	—	—	—
4. Development of an identity and sense of self-confidence	—	—	—	—	—	—	—	—	—	—	—	—	—	—	—	—	—	—	—	—	—
5. Development of social skills	—	—	—	—	—	—	—	—	—	—	—	—	—	—	—	—	—	—	—	—	—
6. Development of career plans and skills	—	—	—	—	—	—	—	—	—	—	—	—	—	—	—	—	—	—	—	—	—
7. Development of a positive attitude toward this college	—	—	—	—	—	—	—	—	—	—	—	—	—	—	—	—	—	—	—	—	—

Source: National Center for Higher Education Management Systems, 1975.

Table 10. Student Perceptions of One Change Agent: the Institution

1. There are many reasons for pursuing education, some of which are listed below. In thinking over your educational experience, how much do you think this institution contributed to your progress in each area? (Check the appropriate box to the right of each category.)

	No Progress (1)	Little Progress (2)	Moderate Progress (3)	Much Progress (4)	Very Much Progress (5)
A. Intellectual Growth: Your ability to understand and use concepts and principles from several broad areas of learning.					
B. Social Growth: Your understanding of other people and their views; your experience in relating to others.					
C. Aesthetic and Cultural Growth: Your awareness and appreciation of the literature, music, art, and drama of your own culture and of others.					
D. Educational Growth: Your understanding of a particular field of knowledge; your preparation for further education.					
E. Vocational and Professional Growth: Your preparation for employment in a particular vocational or professional area.					
F. Personal Growth: Your development of attitudes, values, beliefs, and a particular philosophy of life; your understanding and acceptance of yourself as a person; your ability to be realistic and adaptable and to make decisions about your own future.					

2. How important is that progress to you? (Check the appropriate box to the right of each category.)

	No Progress (1)	Little Progress (2)	Moderate Progress (3)	Much Progress (4)	Very Much Progress (5)
A. Intellectual Growth: Your ability to understand and use concepts and principles from several broad areas of learning.					
B. Social Growth: Your understanding of other people and their views; your experience in relating to others.					
C. Aesthetic and Cultural Growth: Your awareness and appreciation of the literature, music, art, and drama of your own culture and of others.					
D. Educational Growth: Your understanding of a particular field of knowledge; your preparation for further education.					
E. Vocational and Professional Growth: Your preparation for employment in a particular vocational or professional area.					
F. Personal Growth: Your development of attitudes, values, beliefs, and a particular philosophy of life; your understanding and acceptance of yourself as a person; your ability to be realistic and adaptable and to make decisions about your own future.					

Source: National Center for Higher Education Management Systems, 1975.

The use of these and other outcome measures can be helpful; however, the institution should raise a number of questions
before undertaking such an effort. First, what is the purpose(s) of
the undertaking? Is it to revamp the curriculum or to learn more
about the student body or to change the student-body mix, for
example? An answer to the first question should significantly influence what evaluation procedures are chosen. Second, what are the
estimated costs, both direct and indirect? Third, who is to interpret
the data? The biases and skills of the analysts and interpreters will
determine the direction and effectiveness of the report. For example, will the conclusions reflect a strict or liberal interpretation of
the data? Will the conclusions express the position of the "it doesn't
exist if we can't measure it" school, or will they try to take into
account other factors, such as "side effects." Medical models of
evaluation address both the discovered outcomes and a wide range
of possible outcomes. If studies of students' learning adopted a
similar model, they would consider not only the results but also the
process and the context. This approach would recognize the importance of multivariate analytical procedures that take into account student-process-environment interactions.

We should not expect definite answers from research on
goals or outcomes; approximations or strong inclinations are more
realistic. On the basis of what we do know, however, we can conclude that the collegiate experience in general does have a lifelong
and significant impact on its principal consumers, the students.

The central reason for having institutions known as colleges
and universities is the education of students, a simple truth that is
often overlooked thanks to day-to-day pressures, the rapid flow of
events, and faulty perceptions of just what students are like. One
hears such comments as "Students are much different today" or
"Students want to party rather than study." Such generalizations
contain some truth, although most of them are developed from a
small sample, sometimes from one's own daughter or son, and are
therefore suspect. One systematic longitudinal study reported by
Stern (1971) covers student attitudes at Syracuse University in
1926, 1958, and 1968, using a comparable attitudes inventory. He
concluded: "In some important respects students today are not
unlike their cohorts in 1926. Students then and now are pragmatic

in their educational and vocational outlook, although not without intellectual curiosity, politically conservative, religious but suspicious of the church, and convinced that they are in a minority of enlightened participants, most others being neither one nor the other" (p. 9). Stern's respectable work covers only one university and a particular type at that, but his conclusions are worthy of careful consideration. They do illustrate an important point: Any evaluator of student learning needs to begin from as solid a data base as possible, to be open-minded with a minimum of preconceived conclusions, and to develop inventories and procedures that will result in evidence relevant to the questions asked.

4

Examining
the Effectiveness
of Faculty

In his address at the first meeting
of the North Central Association in 1896, President Richard H.
Jesse of the University of Missouri, in naming the essential characteristics of a college, said: "A college must have . . . at least eight
good instructors who devote their whole time to teaching in the
freshman or higher classes" (Zook and Haggerty, 1936). His modest prescription bespeaks an era that is almost beyond comprehension, yet it does indicate that the quality of an institution has been
inextricably related to the quality of the faculty for a long time.
(The influence of effective teaching was recognized by those good
Athenian citizens who tried Socrates!)

Faculty members are at the heart of the collegiate enterprise and constitute an institution's most stable component. Professors with tenure remain, while deans and presidents come and go. Inasmuch as the teaching and learning of youth and adults are the essence of a college or university, the quality, dedication, and morale of the faculty are crucial to the whole effort. Yet the faculty's influence is interwoven with that of other campus groups. When there are fewer students, there are fewer faculty members; and when administration is weak or incompetent, the teaching and learning enterprise becomes less effective—and the result may be disaster for weak, small colleges. Higher education, then, is a cooperative endeavor in which each group has a distinct and significant role.

What are the characteristics of faculty members? The stereotype of an absent-minded professor, shabbily dressed and with insufficient common sense to come in out of the rain, probably never was very accurate and is less so today. In a recent speech, a former liberal arts dean at the University of Texas told about visiting his friendly neighborhood stockbroker in Austin and usually finding university faculty members busily following the electronic tickertape.

Extensive data exist on the characteristics of faculty members. Table 11 is based on 60,028 responses gathered as part of a Carnegie Commission on Higher Education study and reported by Trow (1975). The survey was completed in 1969 and therefore some data, such as the salary figures, have obviously changed; teaching and learning have gained emphasis since then also. Further, because the study was done near the height of the turmoil on campuses, it may be suspect in its undue influence by the confusion, uncertainty, and defensiveness of those times. With these caveats, the study is an extensive and competently designed effort that is worthy of careful consideration.

Some findings in Table 11 seem especially noteworthy. For instance, the consistency of the average age across all types of institutions is a bit surprising. One would expect the community colleges, the most rapidly growing type, to have younger faculty members and the high-ranked universities hold faculty members and therefore to have a somewhat higher average age. The sex of the respondents in the various institutions is also interesting. With

Table 11. Background Information on Faculty Members

| | Quality level and type | | | | | | | |
| | Universities | | | Four-year colleges | | | Two-year colleges | |
	High (I)	Medium (II)	Low (III)	High (IV)	Medium (V)	Low (VI)	All (VII)	All institutions
A. Highest degree attained (percent)								
Ph.D.	59	59	51	58	38	28	5	40
Professional (law or medicine)	15	11	4	2	1	1	2	5
Other professional	10	10	14	12	18	21	14	15
Master's	11	16	26	22	39	45	63	33
Other or none	5	4	5	6	4	5	16	6
	100	100	100	100	100	100	100	99
B. Percentage whose highest degree was earned at a large, high-quality university	70	40	34	49	29	24	18	35
C. Percentage who are male	90	87	83	84	78	71	74	80
D. Average (mean) age	42	42	42	42	41	41	42	42
E. Father's occupation:* percentage whose fathers are/were manual workers	15	19	24	19	27	30	30	24
F. Average (mean) hours per week spent in classroom teaching (includes part-time staff)	5.4	6.4	7.9	8.1	10.3	10.9	13.4	9.0

		1	2	3	4	5	6	7	8
G.	Percentage teaching less than 25 students in courses this term	40	30	22	22	15	16	12	22
H.	Percentage who teach exclusively undergraduates	17	24	36	61	69	78	99	55
I.	Percentage whose interests lie primarily in research rather than teaching	50	40	28	26	12	10	5	24
J.	Number of professional writings published or accepted for publication in past 2 years (percent) 0	21	29	42	47	63	73	87	53
	1-4	52	51	47	44	33	25	12	36
	5 or more	27	20	11	9	4	2	1	11
		100	100	100	100	100	100	100	100
K.	Percentage who have worked outside the academic profession for at least a year since obtaining their bachelor's degree.	57	62	67	62	69	72	80	68
L.	Average (median) salary (thousands of dollars)	14.5	13.9	12.3	12.6	10.6	9.7	10.1	11.5

*The response categories for this question varied slightly between samples. Comparisons between types of institutions are valid, but comparisons among faculty members, graduate students, and undergraduates may be misleading.

Source: Trow, 1975, p. 293.

the faculty members in so-called elite universities being 90 percent male, as compared with somewhat lower percentages for all other categories, one can see why more class action suits have been brought against the elite universities than against any other type of institution. Many other findings in Table 11 are about what one would expect. With the exception of average salaries, the figures can be useful benchmarks to institutional evaluators.

In 1975 Ladd and Lipset (1976, pp. 1, 12) surveyed a national sample of the 1969 Carnegie respondents to see what changes had taken place. Their report included this summary:

> On the surface, things appear to have changed greatly. Academe has moved from an era of protests and activism to an era of retrenchment and quiescence. Faculty members' concerns today are quite different from those during the Vietnam years. But the underlying structure of professorial opinion has been little affected. The nature and configuration of divisions among academics are unchanged, and the relationship of their views to those of other groups in the society has remained constant.
>
> The most striking elements of the opinions of the American academic community remain these: . . . A strong commitment to egalitarian goals within the university and in the larger society. . . . A deeply etched pattern of divisions, most notably organized by type of institution and academic discipline. . . . An intense professional self-criticism.

In addition to considering these general characteristics of faculty members, the evaluator must assess specific aspects of their performance, such as workload. Numerous studies have delved into this matter, and a beginning point might be the 1919 study by Koos, which found that the average faculty member said he worked 8.5 hours a day, 5.5 days a week, or 46.75 hours a week. The volume on *The Faculty* in the six-volume North Central study (Haggerty, 1937a), reporting a survey of nearly four thousand teachers, states that the average college teacher devoted approximately 40 hours a week to his instructional responsibilities. Approximately 16.5 hours were spent in class and laboratory instruction, a little more than 12 hours in immediate preparation, and somewhat more than 6 hours in reading. This survey excluded time given to research, administration, and public relations. After a survey of more than one hundred studies, Yuker (1975, p. 26) concluded that "faculty members typically work more than 50 hours per week. . . . On the average, faculty members claim that they work approximately 55 hours per week during the academic year. Figures close to this have been cited in study after study at many different situations, which would seem to provide evidence of convergent validity." (Yuker also did a comprehensive study himself in 1974.) The conclusion, then, is that faculty members put in a full day's work by any normal definition of the term.

The teaching load of faculty members is a related and sensitive issue, and one that is sometimes misunderstood by the general public and legislators, as some state legislative actions to mandate teaching loads have shown. Such efforts most often are counterproductive, providing an impetus for sub rosa attempts to circumvent the system. Higher education agencies in most states are in a position to monitor teaching loads if requested to do so. But here again, the connotation of distrust and duty shirking by faculty members may make the monitoring counterproductive. Most efforts of this nature were initiated around 1972 with the advent of statewide data systems, and they have served to alert institutions to the increasing use of management models and to the erosion of monetary support. Many, if not most, institutions have therefore undertaken internal analyses and have made some reallocation decisions based on these findings. The soft spots in terms of teaching loads are known to those inside the system, as well as to persons at the state level if they have developed analytical procedures and good institutional relationships.

As we saw in Table 11, the average instructor taught three three-hour courses for a total of nine hours per week in 1969, although the figures vary across institutional types. The figures on teaching load at the major universities probably have increased slightly since 1969, whereas the figures for four-year and community colleges have remained relatively constant, since they were higher initially. Despite some slight changes, then, the figures in Table 11 can serve as bases of comparison.

11. **Are current policies and procedures for evaluating individual faculty members satisfactory?**

Every college and university has some system for evaluating faculty members' performance, and most institutions have examined their policies and procedures within the past five years. These efforts have tended to focus on students' evaluation of teaching and learning, the most important single element in appraising teaching effectiveness. Considerable evidence indicates that students, if asked questions that relate to their frames of reference, are valid and reliable judges of teaching effectiveness (Miller, 1972, 1974). And the 1975 AAUP "Statement of Teaching Evaluation," in advocating the use of students' appraisals to evaluate classroom performance, states that "student perceptions are a prime source of information from those who must be affected if learning is to take place. Student responses can provide continuing insights into a number of the important dimensions of a teacher's efforts: classroom performance, advising, informal and formal contracts with students outside of class." One can reach a similar conclusion using common sense, although there are times when nothing is more uncommon than common sense. College students are exceedingly experienced teacher watchers, having had twelve years' experience before they came to college. They learn early or late that academic success is related to their ability to analyze the strengths and weaknesses of their teachers—and countless peer discussions assist in these analyses. In college, a class of twenty-five students, meeting for fifty minutes three times a week for twelve weeks (with 10 percent absenteeism), watches an instructor for 565 hours per course. Each student has about twenty-three hours' watching time in addition to conference periods and peer analyses, which is quite an extensive basis for judgment.

The overriding purpose of faculty performance evaluation should be improved performance. Better instruction comes about through using the results from an evaluation to assist those who are faltering, to encourage those who are tired, and to direct those who are uncertain. An institution of higher education employs professional teachers in good faith and with the expectation that their performance potentials will permit progression up the professorial ladder to tenure. Evaluation for improvement, then, is a logical extension of this initial expectation and evidence of institutional good faith in working toward better performance.

The evaluation begins by determining which of several components should be assessed: classroom teaching, advising, faculty service and relations, administration, performing and visual arts, professional services, publications, public service, and research. Each professor should be judged on those components that relate most directly to his or her professional responsibilities as well as to departmental and institutional needs—and this decision should be made cooperatively with the professor. (I have discussed these categories and a procedure for evaluating each one in *Evaluating Faculty Performance*.)

For most colleges and universities, classroom teaching is the most important of these nine components, and it can best be appraised through the following six means: student evaluation, classroom visitation, evaluation of teaching materials and procedures, examination of the course's content, special-incident analysis, and self-evaluation. Though more than one mode should be used, the single most important, as I said, is student evaluation. A number of excellent survey forms are available, and several are given in *Developing Programs for Faculty Evaluation* (Miller, 1974).

Data on faculty members' performance should be used for making personnel decisions as well as for bringing about improvement. Those who would gather and use a separate set of data for each kind of evaluation are placing an excessive burden on information management and utilization, and this extra workload will probably require additional administrative assistance to manage the two systems, not to mention additional time by faculty members to cope with the increased flow of information. Many effective systems using one set of data have been developed that both evaluate faculty performance and make promotion and tenure decisions—and I strongly recommend this approach over the dual-approach.

The following questions can assist in judging an institutional system of faculty evaluation:(1) Does the current system provide for instructional improvement when evaluation indicates this need? (2) Do students take seriously the form(s) used to evaluate their teachers? (3) Is the system administratively manageable? (4) Have internal research studies been undertaken to better understand and to improve the system? (5) Is the cost of the system as low as possible? And (6) Is it time to evaluate the effectiveness and efficiency of the current program for evaluation of faculty performance?

A system of faculty evaluation should be carefully designed yet simple enough to be manageable, and it should be modified as needs for improvement become evident. A perfect and completely equitable system never will be created; nor will one be developed that is pleasing to everyone and devoid of problems. And any system should be kept in perspective: the primary mission of colleges and universities is the education of young adults. Most faculty members are serious students of their respective disciplines and are doing a professionally competent job. But improvement is always possible, and an excellent teacher is constantly seeking ways to become better. Evaluation can help improve performance by allowing one to see himself or herself as others do. When the purpose of one's life work is to influence others, it is altogether fitting that the views of others count.

12. **Are current instructional improvement/faculty development programs serving their purposes?**

Faculty development (or improvement) can be defined as an organized institutional effort to increase professional competence. Its basic aims are better courses, professional improvement (or updating), higher-quality instruction, and personal development. These four goals may be pursued through a variety of related activities, as Table 12 indicates.

Faculty development is probably the most pressing academic need in small colleges and universities, and it is an item of considerable importance also to larger institutions. Professors in small institutions have the greatest need because they have the fewest opportunities for professional development and mobility. With respect to the pedagogical component of faculty development, two modes of improvement are most commonly used: a center or program to encourage innovation and to work with those who need help with their teaching, and individual enrichment activities.

Many institutions have established programs or centers for

improving instruction, or at least designated an individual who can assist others with their teaching problems and ideas. For example, whom does a professor see who wants to put some lectures on videotape or to set up a research design for testing a hypothesis about large- and small-group teaching? Institutions should have a program staffed by at least one person who is respected academically and who knows the campus well enough to know where to turn for specific help. Such avenues for improvement provide tangible evidence that the evaluation of faculty performance does have the positive purpose of improving instruction.

The individual enrichment activities that can help to bring about better teaching include sabbatical leaves, apprenticeships, summer and year-long institutes, short-term workshops, individual grant programs, faculty retreats, professional meetings and conventions, visits to other institutions, packaged programs such as an ITV course or a PLATO course, and professional reading. These sorts of activity should be among the array of opportunities offered at any one campus. The extent of their usage will depend on a variety of factors, not the least of which.is monetary support. All activities, however, should be coordinated by the office that is responsible for the overall direction of faculty development on the campus.

To get off the ground, a campuswide faculty improvement program will need the following: support at the top, planning by the faculty and administration, support from successful and visible faculty members, positive emphases, a direct administrative relationship with the vice-presidential level, and some money and people allocated by the institution. Once the program is flying, its success will be influenced by at least these factors—tangible results, diversified programming, institutional visibility, evaluation (with subsequent modifications), and the resources allocated to it.

The current circumstances of tight money and stabilized or declining enrollments may bring some professors and administrators to view faculty development as a fringe benefit and to mark it as an early casualty in the "management of decline." But a lot of money is not required to initiate and maintain many useful faculty development programs, and if policy makers realize that it is likely that professors "will be spending the next thirty years where they

Table 12. Use and Estimated Effectiveness of Institution-Wide Policies on Practices in Development (N=756)

	Percentage of institutions following the practice				Percentage of respondents indicating practice effective or very effective[a]				Percentage of respondents considering practice essential though not in use[b]
	All (N=756)	Two-Year (326)	Four-Year (315)	University (93)	All	Two-Year	Four-Year	University	
1. Annual awards to faculty members for excellence in teaching	38	20	44	79	28	37	24	27	6
2. Circulation of newsletter, articles, and so on that are pertinent to teaching improvement or faculty development	68	71	65	67	27	32	22	25	3
3. A specific calendar period set aside for professional development	44	62	33	14	52	52	55	38	5
4. Periodic review of performance of all faculty members, tenured or not	78	87	71	77	59	63	56	49	4
5. Sabbatical leaves with at least half salary	67	60	72	82	66	60	73	61	5
6. A policy of unpaid leaves that covers educational or development purposes	72	70	73	80	51	47	55	49	1

7. Lighter that normal teaching load for first-year faculty members	21	15	23	25	53	64	51	45	6
8. Temporary teaching-load reductions to work on a new course, major course revision, or research area	61	58	59	81	64	68	63	59	8
9. Travel grants to refresh or update knowledge in a particular field	52	46	56	61	64	67	64	57	4
10. Travel funds available to attend professional conferences	93	95	92	95	62	69	59	51	1
11. Visiting scholars program that brings people to the campus for short or long periods	55	37	65	86	57	60	57	54	3
12. Summer grants for projects to improve instruction or courses	58	61	56	62	70	72	66	74	5
13. Campus committee on faculty development	61	63	60	62	50	55	48	46	5

[a]Percentages based only on institutions at which practice existed.

[b]Percentages are based on all institutions (N=756)

Source: Centra, 1976, p. 12.

are now" (Freedman and Sanford, 1973, p. 14), the overall program might well gain a higher priority as an important element of the future.

Questions such as the following ones can serve as guidelines for evaluating the faculty development program: (1) Who is served by the program? (2) Is the effort given to the four general components—course improvement, professional development, better pedagogy and personal development—apportioned satisfactorily? (3) How are individuals identified who may need faculty development or renewal? (4) How are faculty members encouraged to concern themselves with faculty development? (5) Does the level of administrative support allow some innovation? (6) Do communication procedures result in widespread knowledge about the program? (7) Has the faculty improvement program been evaluated recently?

13. **Are faculty personnel policies and procedures considered satisfactory?**

This question cannot be answered by observing and talking; it requires systematic comparison of current practices by someone or some committee that is conversant with the institution's statements as well as with developments elsewhere. In making the assessment, the evaluator(s) might consider the following items for examination (Knowles, 1970, chap. 6, pp. 29–30).

- Personnel records
- Faculty recruitment
- Faculty appointments
    First appointments
    Terms of appointments and reappointment
    Appointment of visiting professors and other special
        appointments
    Appointment of administrative personnel
- Termination of employment
    Faculty resignations
    Retirement policy
    Termination for cause
- Faculty orientation procedures

- ˙ Policies regarding academic rank
        Use of special titles and ranks
        Faculty status of graduate teaching assistants
        Academic rank for administrators
        Combination of appointments
        Faculty equivalencies
        Part-time faculty
            Responsibilities
            Remuneration
            Qualifications
        Policies regarding ROTC faculty
- Promotion policies
        Consideration for promotion
        Procedures for recommending promotion
- University-faculty relations
        Use of university property for private purposes
        Purchasing through the university for private purposes
        Regulations governing outside consulting
        Faculty support of university functions
        Regulations governing smoking and alcoholic beverages
- Community-faculty relations
        Use of university name
        Faculty political activities
        Off-campus speakers
        Faculty-legislative relations
        Faculty religious activities

Tenure is one dimension of personal policies and procedures that deserves special attention. Tenure was developed initially to protect and support academic freedom, and this purpose
remains a crucial one, but tenure has become increasingly related
to job security as money concerns become more pressing. Those
who have earned tenure have served the institution well and longer
than those without it, and therefore they can reasonably expect
greater economic security. Length of service (seniority) is a recognized criterion for selection in most occupations (including politics,
as in congressional chairmanships).

Tenure in colleges and universities had almost become an

"immovable object" by the time it came up against the "irresistible force" of diminishing funds. Institutions faced with severe money problems usually must reduce personnel costs, which account for 60 to 80 percent of most institutional budgets. If only nontenured teachers are released to meet financial exigencies, an institution risks losing the vitality and new ideas that are so crucial to its future; yet to disregard tenure and base termination decisions on the value of the individual to the institution raises questions about institutional tradition, the criteria for selection, and campus politics. Some institutions have skirted the issue by making decisions in terms of programs rather than individuals. But they cannot get around it completely, because the elimination of programs usually does involve releasing (or retraining) some tenured faculty members. The so-called erosion of tenure will likely continue into the 1980s, particularly in those institutions that have not planned in the 1970s for declining enrollments in the next decade.

Tenure quotas (limits) are being developed to an increasing extent. El-Khawas and Furniss (1974, pp. 39–40) found that the percentage of institutions with some limit on tenure increased from 5.9 percent in 1972 to 9.3 percent in 1974—or a 35 percent increase in two years. Chait (1976, pp. 39–40) summarizes the advantages and then the drawbacks of a tenure limit:

> 1. Flexibility. Some slots will always be available to introduce new faculty, to respond to market changes, to add instructors with the most up-to-date preparation, or to appoint persons with particular expertise not now represented on the faculty.
> 2. Diversity. Vacancies assured by a tenure limit afford occasions to build or maintain a diverse faculty as measured by sex, race, age, and ethnicity.
> 3. Selectivity. A tenure limit forces discerning judgments, and helps thwart inclinations to be charitable or to avoid definitive comparisons.
> 4. Economy. A tenure quota ensures a certain percentage of untenured faculty, presumably at the lower academic ranks. Furthermore, the money "saved" may be used to appoint additional faculty or to provide very competitive salaries for senior appointments.

The advantages offered by a tenure limit may seem quite attractive. However, tenure limits are not without drawbacks that also should be weighed.

1. Inequity. A tenure guideline adversely affects (at least directly) only untenured faculty. The inequity is compounded when a university adopts a tenure limit effective immediately. The untenured faculty already aboard will protest that the rules have been changed after the game has started.

2. An end to meritocracy. A tenure limit introduces to tenure decisions mathematical as well as qualitative considerations. Indeed, the issue may be numbers without regard to merit, since theoretically tenure limits may preclude permanent faculty status no matter how well qualified the candidate may be.

3. Reordered faculty priorities. With chances for tenure severely limited, faculty members may devote attention to activities designed to enhance their mobility rather than their value to the immediate college community, for example, research and publication instead of classroom teaching and public service.

4. Competitive disadvantage. Able faculty people with more than one offer may not accept an appointment at a school with a tenure limit.

5. Discontinuity. With few vacancies in the tenured ranks, most junior faculty will only be transients, a condition that may breed low morale and hinder cohesion.

The institution that wants to avoid a tenure quota might increase selectivity, minimize "instant tenure," minimize credit for prior service, lengthen the probationary period, permit "holding patterns," appoint faculty members outside the tenure track, evaluate tenured faculty, separate tenure and promotion decisions, and facilitate early retirement (Chait, 1976, p. 41).

The current tendency is to establish quotas rather than seriously explore the options, such as these outlined by Chait. Because the quota system is simpler, gives the illusion of equity, and is easier to administer, it appeals to administrators considering the issue's sensitivity.

Decisions on tenure should be based on a clear institutional picture of the promotion-and-tenure status of each faculty member, and the situation five years ago and five and ten years hence should be known also. Evaluators can draw on the annual AAUP "Report of the Economic Status of the Profession," usually published in the August issue of the *AAUP Bulletin*, which provides institutional data on each rank of the professoriate as well as the percentages of tenured persons by rank.

In summary, the following questions about an ideal situation might assist in evaluating one's own faculty personnel policies and procedures. (1) Has the institution recently updated its policies and practices? (2) Does the faculty handbook treat most of the items cited by Knowles (referred to earlier)? (3) Do faculty procedures allow a more or less continuous updating and modifying of policies and procedures? (4) Has the institution developed detailed statistical data on tenure—adequate to assist in making policy decisions? And (5) Do personnel policies and procedures relating to promotion and tenure reflect the operational rewards system?

14. Are faculty salary scales and fringe benefits competitive?

Salaries and benefits can be compared (1) by using data from benchmark institutions, state higher education agencies, and the National Center of Educational Statistics and (2) with the annual AAUP "Report on the Economic Status of the Profession" and other AAUP findings. Detailed salary and benefit information by rank, by increase per rank, by fringe benefits as a percentage of average salary, and other breakdowns are given for each reporting institution. For their own institution, administrative officials should have salary and benefit analyses by rank, department, and college, and a trend line beginning five years earlier. These data can be particularly helpful to private colleges in making salary decisions.

The economics of scarcity weigh heavily on contemporary salary considerations, and matters are likely to be more difficult in the 1980s. The broad dimensions of the problem can be understood by glancing at Table 13, which shows salary increases in terms of purchasing power. (The AAUP quite appropriately entitled its 1974–75 Economic Status Report "Two Steps Backward.") Although some professors are doing a better job than others, and this conclusion can be established, current salary increases often are

Table 13. Increases in Average Compensation, Unadjusted and Adjusted by the Increase in the Consumer Price Index[a]—Institutions Reporting Comparable Data for Each of the One-Year Periods Since 1967-68[b] (Standard Academic-Year Basis)

Academic Rank	1973-74 to 1974-75	1972-73 to 1973-74	1971-72 to 1972-73	1970-71 to 1971-72	1969-70 to 1970-71	1968-69 to 1969-70	1967-68 to 1968-69
			Unadjusted				
Professor	6.5%	5.9%	5.0%	4.0%	5.8%	7.1%	7.0%
Associate	6.6	6.0	5.0	4.0	6.2	7.1	7.5
Assistant	6.3	5.7	5.0	4.3	6.3	6.9	7.2
Instructor	6.1	5.7	5.0	5.3	6.6	7.6	7.0
Lecturer	5.4	7.7	3.4	6.3	6.9	10.8	9.3
All ranks	6.4	5.9	5.0	4.3	6.2	7.1	7.2
		Adjusted by the Consumer Price Index					
Professor	−4.1	−1.5	0.2	0.2	0.7	1.2	2.0
Associate	−4.1	−1.4	0.2	0.2	1.0	1.2	2.5
Assistant	−4.3	−1.7	0.2	0.5	1.1	1.0	2.2
Instructor	−4.5	−1.7	0.2	1.4	1.4	1.7	2.0
Lecturer	−5.1	0.2	−1.3	2.4	1.7	4.7	4.2
All ranks	−4.2	−1.5	0.2	0.5	1.0	1.2	2.2

[a]Consumer Price Index obtained from the *Monthly Labor Review* for each one-year period. The academic-year increases in compensations were adjusted by the average increase in cost of living also computed on an academic-year basis.

[b]In calculating these figures, we used what amounts to a Paasche Index, since numbers of persons who are currently in the various ranks were employed as weights. Thus, we computed as base what average compensation would have been last year if relative numbers in the different ranks had been what they are currently.

Source: American Association of University Professors, 1975b.

inadequate just to keep abreast with inflation. Administrators used to have more flexibility in setting faculty salaries, and merit raises were more appropriate when salaries were increasing 5 to 8 percent per year.

Another reason administrators have less flexibility now— other than less money to disperse—is that union contracts and state-level salary decisions have a significant impact on the public-sector salary picture. In some states with strong faculty unions, salary negotiations bypass the governing systems and coordinating boards and are handled directly by the governor's office. In other states the coordinating board recommends to the state legislative body and governor a salary figure for each system and institution. In recent years, and particularly in the major industrial states, the figures recommended by the state educational agency have been reduced substantially by governors and legislatures. Some restoration of cut funds usually is accomplished, but not through articulate, factual presentations, although these efforts are necessary and occasionally helpful; rather, the restoration results from political negotiations.

The funding picture is significantly influenced also by the fact that higher education no longer enjoys the high status it had before the student upheavals in the 1960s. Higher education would be in financial trouble today because of pressing economic problems even if student campus protests had never taken place, but the students' actions gave legislators an emotional rationale for cutting budgets that they would not have had otherwise: "If college administrators can't control the students and if students cannot behave and keep from destroying state property, then they do not deserve much." We are still overcoming this view among public officials. Nevertheless, because we are coming out of a mild recession, salaries can be expected to take a modest turn upward, at least for the remainder of the 1970s.

Several questions may be useful in applying criterion 14, such as (1) Are comparative data on salaries from benchmark institutions used for making salary decisions? (2) Are fringe benefits analyzed regularly to determine their currency, adequacy, and cost? (3) Do salaries for women and minority persons have equity? (A method for determining equity can be found in Scott, n.d.) (4) Do institutional policies and procedures for salary adjustments function adequately?

15. **What is the overall quality of faculty members' performance?**

Presumably every mission-and-scope statement will mention the importance of high-quality faculty performance, but verification of such an objective requires standards. The North Central Association (Haggerty, 1937a) developed an elaborate system for appraising faculty competence. The fifty-six North Central institutions were first rated on institutional excellence by a complex procedure combining test-score data with expert judgment. Then this rating was correlated with faculty competence as judged by these criteria: possession of a doctoral or master's degree, graduate study, experience, publications (books, articles, monographs, reviews, nonprofessional writing), and participation in learned societies (memberships, meetings, offices held). Table 14 indicates the intercorrelations of the chosen measures of faculty competence, the correlations of each measure with a composite of the ten measures, and then the correlations of each measure with criterion VIII, which is an overall rating of institutional excellence.

As the table indicates, each chosen measure of faculty competence was positively correlated with the composite faculty rating, and the composite faculty rating correlated .40 with criterion VIII, institutional excellence. The high correlation (.50) for attendance at meetings is surprising. Perhaps attendance at the considerably fewer meetings during the Depression years had a different status from the social and position-seeking activities that are significant aspects of today's many and diversified conventions.

Bayer (1975), selecting from data in a Carnegie Commission survey, used five aggregated measures of faculty quality: the percentage of the faculty who had received their highest degrees from one of the nation's top twelve institutions, as rated in the Cartter study (1966); the percentage of Ph.D.s on the faculty; the percentage subscribing to three or more professional journals; the percentage with at least one published article or book; and the percentage expressing primary interest in research rather than in teaching. These measures then were correlated with ratings of concern for the individual student as judged by the Inventory of College Ac-

Table 14. Coefficients of Intercorrelation of the Measures of Faculty Competence, Correlation of Each Measure with a Composite of the Ten, and Each with Criterion VIII

	Doctor's Degree	Master's Degree	Study	Experience	Books	Articles	Membership	Meetings	Office	Program	Composite Faculty	Criterion VIII
Doctor		−.06	+.58	+.40	+.29	+.52	+.71	+.57	+.49	+.49	+.78	+.30
Master			+.05	−.21	−.002	−.20	+.03	−.03	−.16	−.01	+.12	+.11
Study				+.14	+.07	+.27	+.35	+.35	+.09	+.14	+.43	+.01
Experience					+.26	+.23	+.44	+.41	+.51	+.27	+.52	+.29
Books						+.65	+.21	+.22	+.44	+.58	+.49	+.13
Articles							+.48	+.58	+.53	+.71	+.73	+.41
Membership								+.74	+.69	+.60	+.86	+.39
Meetings									+.51	+.56	+.80	+.50
Office										+.59	+.77	+.27
Program											+.77	+.43
Composite faculty												+.40

tivities by Astin (1977). All five measures of faculty quality were negatively associated with concern for the individual student, and three measures (journal subscriptions, publications, research bias) reached statistical significance in their negative correlations. Bayer concluded (pp. 562–563) that many faculty attributes, including "quality," have only moderate and indirect effects on college climate—at least that aspect of the environment having to do with undergraduate students' evaluations of the institution's concern for them as individuals.

Balderston (1974, pp. 135–136) writes about some indicators of faculty distinction that would be more applicable to the larger universities than to other types of institutions:

> Research funding reflects the reputation and the aggressiveness of faculty (and getting it may be facilitated by helpful support on the mechanics of proposal writing). There are other measures of faculty distinction, both for the scientific fields for which research funding is a signal and for those fields where there is little or no outside funding. One indicator is honors received and evidence of prominence in the scholarly societies of a field. Another is service on editorial boards of the scholarly journals. Still another is the receipt of honorific fellowships and appointments— Nobel Prizes, Guggenheims, appointments to the Institute for Advanced Study in Princeton or to the Center for Advanced Study in the Behavioral Sciences in Stanford, and memberships in such organizations as the National Academy of Sciences and the National Academy of Engineering. These kinds of recognition are frosting on the cake of scholarship that is primarily based on research productivity.

How, then, does one measure the quality of a faculty? Is not quality in the eyes of the beholder—the students, the administrators, the board members, or the general public—and does not each constituency march to a different drummer? The Ph.D. degree, for example, is not positively correlated with institutional concern for students or with institutional excellence, according to Bayer, yet a high Ph.D. percentage among the faculty is viewed by the general public, professors, and administrators as an indication of high quality.

I suggest eight criteria for judging overall faculty quality: professional preparation, teaching effectiveness, student retention, faculty retention, professional activities, research and publications, vitality, and administrative support.

Professional preparation, as evidenced by the number of Ph.D. and other advanced professional degrees, does not seem related to the quality of teaching but should be used as a quality indicator because it is an element in the institution's own self-image and in the public image of the institution. And it is also a factor in securing external funding.

Teaching quality can be determined fairly well, and therefore some overall judgment about it can be made. (See criterion 14 in this chapter.)

Student retention is discussed in the chapter on students' learning. As mentioned earlier, some student attrition is normal and desirable, but an institution needs to monitor carefully the causes of attrition. Genuine and personalized faculty concern for students remains one of the most effective deterrents to student attrition. The reasons for student attrition can be related to faculty interest and assistance both in and out of the classroom. Of course insufficient money is a major factor as well.

Faculty retention relates to several factors, some positive and some negative. Some colleges and university administrators recruit outstanding young faculty members, knowing they will not stay much beyond three years; some professors in small colleges have nowhere to go; and in some states the insufficiency of monetary support for higher education causes marketable professors to move. These and other factors considered, if an institution still has a higher attrition rate than comparable institutions, then causes should be sought. A high rate usually indicates that poor financial support or working conditions, poor morale, excessive bureaucracy, incompatible personalities, or antiquated programs are driving away the mobile faculty members.

In his study of eleven "better" private liberal arts colleges McGee (1971) compared why professors left for better positions and why professors stayed who had firm offers to leave. He found that 54 percent of those who elected to leave "Shadyside" in favor of "Fairlawn" rated Shadyside as either "good" or among "the very best," whereas 74 percent of those who remained at Shadyside gave those ratings. Professors who elected to remain gave "best" ratings to their own college five times as often as those who decided to leave (pp. 141–152). The McGee study indicates that, at least for his sampling, the retention of faculty members who had an opportunity to leave but chose to stay was significantly related to a positive perception of institutional quality.

Professional activities (papers given and offices held) indicate interest in keeping abreast with a particular field and in wanting to assist its growth. A form for rating the professional status and activities of faculty members can be a useful aid in evaluation. The sample on page 55 of my book, *Evaluating Faculty Performance* (1972) asks the appraiser to rate the individual by a seven-point scale on seven characteristics: (1) activity in professional associations and societies; (2) offices in such organizations; (3) papers or other presentations before professional groups; (4) evidence of efforts toward professional improvement; (5) professional status, as viewed by colleagues; (6) professional status, as viewed by the profession; and (7) professional recognition in terms of awards or honors.

Research and publications tell something about the person's zeal to communicate what he or she believes should be said, to share the results of research with colleagues elsewhere, and to keep options open for professional mobility. These two aspects of faculty members' performance can also be assessed by means of rating forms. Thus, a publications appraisal form, such as illustrated on page 58 of *Evaluating Faculty Performance*, can identify a publication and have appraisers rate it on these characteristics: (1) the reputation of the publisher in the academic field of the publication; (2) rating by departmental colleagues of the publication; (3) rating of colleagues outside the institution; (4) rating by the head of the department; (5) response to the publication in reviews; (6) extent of citations to and quotations from the publication; and individual rating of the publication. Colleagues can also rate a faculty member's research by using an adaptation of this publications appraisal form, and the researcher can complete a self-evaluation form regarding the project (see Miller, 1977, p. 71), describing the research project and answering these questions: Are the goals of the project well defined? Are they realistic with respect to time and resources? Which obstacles have been overcome, and how was this achieved? What resources have been more available and useful? What resources have been lacking? Has the institution been receptive to the work? Have colleagues expressed interest in it? Has the research changed, modified, or strengthened the investigator's theoretical position? If students were involved, what was their reaction to the project? And what plans exist for publishing the results?

Vitality is a state of mind, an aspect of one's attitudes toward work, colleagues, institution. Faculty members are critics by the nature of academe and by professional preparation; as Ladd and Lipset pointed out, abundant self-criticism is characteristic of professors. The tone and nature of the self-criticism is the key to judging institutional vitality. Generally speaking, a dynamic faculty, although concerned about salaries and retrenchment, exhibits a positive, constructive tone. An astute and experienced observer can discern something about a faculty's vitality by visiting and talking, and some survey instruments may be helpful in this respect. (For further discussion, see the chapter on institutional vitality.)

In discussions of faculty quality, *administrative support* usually is not mentioned as an indicator, yet its importance is evident in two ways. First, support and understanding at the top is crucial for building a dynamic and innovative faculty. By making statements and doing things for faculty betterment, giving high priority to faculty development and evaluation, encouraging experimental teaching and academic programs, and making the strongest case for good salaries and benefits, the chief administrative officer and his staff can do much to influence the quality of the faculty — especially if he is persistent and remains in one place long enough.

Second, administrators affect faculty quality by the extent to which they take part in recruitment. Recruitment may seem like an anachronism in the current era of austerity and retrenchment, but some recruitment is always necessary as new directions are taken and as essential faculty replacements must be made. Most chief executive officers do not spend adequate time on recruitment, especially in the current "buyer's market." Their influence will be relatively indirect in a university of thirty thousand students where the respective academic colleges have considerable independence, but chief administrators should set the tone and find ways of seeing that the recruitment of professors and administrative personnel follows their general guidelines. Here again, persistent interest—overtime—can make a difference.

Finally, one might ask: Are faculty members sufficiently aware of the severe problems that may confront higher education and possibly their institution in the 1980s? Do they realize the extent to which their professional existence, not to mention the opportunities for high-quality performance, is threatened? Faculty members use the words of scarcity, decline, and reallocation, but their hearts are not in it. (And they are not alone!) A number of factors may be responsible for their attitudes. Perhaps the abundant *self*-criticism that Ladd and Lipset have found among the professoriate is a factor; perhaps stories in the *Chronicle of Higher Education* about administrators crying "wolf" have added fuel to inherent problems between professors and administrators and have thereby caused faculty members not to believe in, or care about, scare talk; or perhaps a certain otherworldliness found on some residential campuses and in classrooms tunes out undesirable realities. Professors, like most of us, are prone to the "I'll think about that tomorrow" syndrome. For these and other reasons, administrators need to search for more ways to work cooperatively with faculty members on matters of mutual concern.

An example of the difficulties that may lie ahead is the case of a public university with sixty-five hundred students, situated in a nonmetropolitan area but near several smaller cities. The institution grew rapidly in the 1960s and developed residence-hall space for eight thousand students, and all rooms were filled in 1972. But then a number of factors converged to sorely affect enrollment, the recession, the shrinkage in the potential student pool, aggressive recruitment by a new community college nearby, the "stop-out" phenomenon, and the fact that students view college education as less essential to later-life success than they did five years ago. Another significant influence was that because the new interstate highway provided better access, more local students chose the much larger state university seventy-five miles away, with its stronger and more diversified academic programs. Consequently, the institutional research unit did an extensive and excellent projective study. Demographic information from census data and elsewhere was analyzed; and local and regional occupational trends were examined to find out what needed programs the university might initiate and what programs should be phased down or out. The university's enrollment in 1985, according to a number of projections, should stabilize at about fifty-five hundred students.

What courses of action are open to this and other universities and colleges, and especially to their faculties, in the next few years? But a prior question may be: What mental attitude will set the tone for attempted adjustments? Several alternatives come to mind: Ignore the matter; pretend things are as they always have been and will be. Resist change, supporting a situation that is not as good as it could be for fear things may become worse than they are now. Rationalize, developing solutions that are unrelated to reality but consistent with desired outcomes. Fake it, moving back and forth like a rocking chair but going nowhere and accomplishing nothing. Or face the matter and act:

> The life of the faculty member today, then, is not easy—not as easy, at any rate, as it used to be. The well-trodden paths and the signposts that directed his or her professional ways have become blurred and in some cases obliterated. Tradition, custom, and convention no longer serve to organize his life. A young faculty member must forge his own role, and many an older faculty member must fix a level gaze on the beliefs and activities of decades. This experience may be an exciting challenge, but it is likely to be trying as well. In all events there is no way around it. Faculty members have no choice but to examine themselves and their social and professional situation. They can attain control over their professional lives and the society and organizations in which they live only to the degree that they can understand what is happening to them and to the world they inhabit [Freedman and Sanford, 1973, pp. 2–3].

5

Evaluating Existing and Planned Academic Programs

A college is three things: people, programs, and places—and in that order of importance. Curricular and instructional matters should be a key concern of faculty members and administrators, yet these areas too often are left to chance or not considered sufficiently important to warrant continuous monitoring or renewal. What Dressel and DeLisle (1969, pp. 76–77) concluded in their study of 322 colleges and universities ten years ago is pertinent today: "Many critics of the current higher education scene concentrate on the deficiencies of instruction and of institutional climate. In this view the curriculum is relatively unimportant. Clearly, both instruction and curriculum are important. A motley but uncoordinated array of good teachers does not yield a sound and unified four-year experience. A well-planned curriculum, of which an essential part is a statement of objectives and a rationale for the experiences provided, is a necessary structure in which instruction can be appropriately defined in relation to the learnings desired. If a faculty cannot or has not been able to agree on a comprehensive curricular design, good instruction will surely be fortuitous. It will also be individualistic in that it will be based on personality factors, and it will be isolated in that each 'good' instructor becomes such by becoming a 'character' rather than by becoming a contributor to a grand design."

There are some overriding curricular issues that are as relevant today as they were when Plato established his Academy. Mayhew and Ford (1971, pp. 2–4) discuss six of these transcendent issues: culture versus utility, or what Muller (1974) calls "higher education or higher skilling"; the general versus the specific; the elective versus the prescribed; egalitarianism versus elitism; a student orientation versus a subject orientation; the discipline versus the interdisciplinary; and science versus the humanities. An institution may want to examine its academic programs in terms of where it stands on the continuum that each of these issues represents. For example, the egalitarianism/elitism issue is controversial yet not openly debated on many campuses. An occasional campus tussle with such a topic can be useful in sharpening the focus on the curriculum.

Four other potential problems or opportunities should also be kept in mind during curricular review. Emerson once said that "nothing great is achieved without enthusiasm," but too much of a good thing can create problems. A professor who is determined to have his new course approved may be creating proliferation problems for the department; and the curriculum is in trouble if enough zealots are able to move their special-interest courses through the institution's maze of policies and procedures. Yet the reason for this zealous enthusiasm should not be ignored, because the individual professor may have had an insight into a curricular need or had an important idea about a new course that the curriculum designers missed.

Departmental inertia may impede the forward movement

that is essential for any discipline or professional field to stay abreast or ahead of academic developments. Science curricula, for example, should be reviewed fairly regularly, because fundamental changes in most fields of science take place every few years. And also, the review needs to mesh new science with better ways of teaching and learning in order to attract students.

Institutional indifference to curricular matters manifests itself in several ways. If the institution has not carefully developed its policies for producing and improving programs, if it does not have effective internal procedures for program review and evaluation that result in the addition and deletion of courses, and if faculty members and administrators have not created a campus environment conducive to curricular innovation, then the institution may not care much about its curricula, even though it perceives itself otherwise.

Statewide coordinating and governing bodies can create problems or opportunities with respect to programs. Through access to state and federal funds, state agencies can encourage needed developments, such as environmental studies, interinstitutional cooperation, health services, and lifelong learning. Or the state coordinating board can be perceived as the ogre that prevents an institution from being able to offer the Ph.D. degree that it requires (in its own eyes) to enhance its prestige. Several states have a preprogram review process through which academic programs are presented early to the staff of the state board—at the idea stage—to see whether the institution should be encouraged to do further work on the program request.

A positive residue of the traumatic campus experiences of the late sixties is a greater emphasis on teaching and learning and on academic programs. Most colleges and universities examined their instructional and curricular commitments at the time and some made constructive changes (although others used the cosmetic approach). The events of the sixties resulted in three other changes: modified entrance and grading standards, more diversified curricula and teaching methods, and greater attention to evaluating instruction and curricula. The easing of admission standards was evident in permitting increased enrollments of minority students and economically poor students. These modifications continue to serve useful educational purposes *provided* that special programs in counseling and learning are available. Student unrest on some major campuses stemmed largely from the universities' admitting students with marginal academic backgrounds and then not offering special counseling and learning opportunities to help them cope with the social environment of the campus and its academic requirements.

In the sixties many colleges and universities moved to some sort of pass-fail grading system, and many campuses eliminated failing marks on transcripts. At one midwestern private liberal arts college with about twenty-six hundred students, there were some faculty pressures to move massively in this direction. This effort was led primarily by professors in the philosophy, English, and history departments and resisted by those in the natural and physical sciences. An experimental program was established in philosophy, and some other disciplines also were permitted to try out this approach, but without much administrative encouragement. The administration did not, however, permit eliminating failing grades on transcripts despite some faculty advocacy. Recently, opinion has turned 180 degrees, and many pass-fail grading experiments of the sixties have been replaced by standard letter grades.

The movement toward diversifying the curriculum continues to have a salutary effect on college programs, but there is a point at which diversification can weaken impact and diminish quality. Independent study, the granting of credit by examination and of credit for experiential learning, off-campus credit courses (which have been available at the University of London since 1848), and university and college acceptance of credits from other institutions such as community colleges and proprietary schools are current examples of diversification. It is possible—and necessary—to develop quality controls for each of these developments. High quality and standards are not necessarily incompatible with planned diversification. Thus we come to the first of the criterion questions relating to program evaluation.

16. **Does the institution have effective policies and procedures for developing new programs?**

Those who seek to keep ahead in a field of knowledge need sound subjective sense, based on thorough factual knowledge, of what is fad and what is real. This is true also of curriculum planners, who must try to figure out which subjects will interest potential and actual students. Current estimates show, for instance, that lifelong learning, environmental studies, health-related services, managerial sciences, and some service occupations are likely to be popular for the next few years, whereas teacher education and agriculture will not be fields of growth in the near future, although some new programs are essential in both growing and declining fields to keep abreast of new knowledge and pedagogy.

Continuing education, or lifelong learning, is an example of an existing domain of the curriculum that will be enlarged in the future. Lifelong learning is becoming a major educational theme as more individuals retire early and develop new interests and careers, as more individuals seek to escape the routine of a highly structured environment, as job obsolescence requires more or less continuous education, and as economic austerity and severe competition for the public funds foster more delivery systems that are not placebound. Institutions considering new outreach programs for adults should find two publications useful: *Educational Brokering* (Hefferman and others, 1976) and *Programs for New Clientele* (American Association of State Colleges and Universities, 1976b). The new clientele includes "such groups as senior citizens, returning women, ex-offenders, handicapped students, and many others" (p. *ii*).

An important aspect of new-program development concerns the policies and procedures for moving program proposals through the institution's organizational structure. A balance is needed between a process that provides only token scrutiny of new programs and courses and one that takes an inordinate amount of time and places unnecessary obstacles before new offerings.

A proposal has a better chance of moving smoothly through the approval process if its planners have considered all the necessary elements. One useful proposal-development model, designed by Southern Illinois University at Edwardsville, follows very closely the "New and Expanded Program Request Form" created by the Academic Affairs Staff of the Illinois Board of Higher Education, which is adaptable to undergraduate or graduate programs. Some adaptations have been made in the model as presented here.

1. Description of the Program
   A. State the program objectives. Present them so that they can be related to the criteria in the evaluation plans.
   B. Summarize the important features of the program and include a full catalogue description. This section should contain the following. (1) Admission and retention procedures and standards and their relationship to the program objectives. (2)Degree requirements. Include course requirements, majors and specializations, credit-hour requirements, research-tool requirements, examination procedures, and requirements for a research paper, thesis, or dissertation; also include field work or other similar training requirements and any other information that helps to describe the program of study. (3) Course offerings. Include here the titles of present course offerings, proposed new courses, courses that may be added during the first three years of the program. For each course title, indicate which faculty member or members are likely to teach it. (4) Typical students' program of study.
   C. List the principal FTE faculty members to be utilized. Group them by faculty category, and provide the following information for each: (1) name; (2) education, including highest degree earned; (3) relevant teaching experience; (4) active research interests related to proposed programs; (5) recent publications; and (6) percentage of his/her time to be allotted to the program.
   D. Indicate the expected results of the program and, if this is a proposal for an expanded or modified program, specify how the proposed change may achieve results different from those produced by the current program.
   E. Evaluate the adequacy of the library resources and the available instructional materials for the proposed program. Include library personnel (subject librarians as well as other staff members with relevant specialties) and library materials.
   F. Describe other institutional resources that will be needed, including laboratory, research, and training facilities. When appropriate, submit an evaluation of these facilities, with information about anticipated needs and costs.

2. Rationale for the Program
   A. Describe the clientele to be served and state which of their specific needs will be met by the program. Indicate any special characteristics, such as age, vocation, or academic background. Present a factual (and preferably quantitative) assessment of the potential clients' demand for this program.
   B. Present a factual assessment of the employment opportunities that are likely to be available to program graduates. Include data and references supporting this assessment. Indicate the types and numbers of jobs for which such a curriculum is appropriate. If listed manpower needs resources appear inadequate to meet objectives of the program, provide justification for this apparent discrepancy.
   C. Describe the impact of this program on other programs that it will support or that will be supported by it. Give the past three years' data on majors and graduates of these programs. Describe how the projected enrollments and majors will affect those programs. Indicate whether this program will reduce the need for existing programs at your institution.
   D. Indicate the history to date of the development and submission of this program. What resources, personnel, financial equipment, and so on have already been invested in this program? What planning activities have supported this proposal? What past grants, research, or public service activities have contributed to the development of this program?
   E. Describe any alternatives to the development of this program that have been considered and why they were rejected.
   F. Relate this program to the institution's goals and objectives and indicate any similar programs in the region or state.
   G. Describe any cooperative arrangements (including clinical affiliations, internship opportunities, personnel exchanges, and equipment sharing) that have been explored.
3. Evaluation of the Program
   A. Indicate the evaluation or review guidelines and procedures that will be used for this program. Note when it will be internally evaluated.

B. Indicate what accreditation agencies exist for programs in this field. If there are any, state when this program will be reviewed for accreditation.

C. If this is a new program that will be administered by a unit with an established program, summarize the major findings of reviews by external consultants or accrediting agencies of the established program.

D. If this is an expanded program, summarize the criteria, procedures, and results of internal reviews of this program that have occurred to date. If this is a graduate program, summarize the internal reviews of the undergraduate program(s) which support this program.

E. Summarize the results of any external evaluation of this proposed program (such as preliminary discussions with accrediting agencies, consultants, and so on).

4. Program Implementation and Projected Resource Requirements

A. Indicate the maximum size the new program or expanded program is likely to achieve during a six-year period, using a form like that in Table 15.

B. If the program will not be fully developed within six years, indicate the maximum planned size of the program in terms of degrees and majors or clients served and the target year for full development of the program.

C. If the administrative unit that will be responsible for the proposed program offers academic programs at off-campus sites, indicate those programs by site. If plans and projections are being considered for moving the proposed program to these or other sites, also indicate these programs by site.

Program Location and Plans

Site	Title of Existing Program	New Program at Site

Table 15. Five-Year Projection of Program Size (Fall Semester Headcount Data)

	Historical Years		Current Year	Budget Year	Second Year	Third Year	Fourth Year	Fifth Year
	1976–1977	1977–1978	1978–1979	1979–1980	1980–1981	1981–1982	1982–1983	1983–1984
Number of students served through course offerings of the program (for service programs, indicate number of clients served)	——	——	——	——	——	——	——	——
Number of credit hours generated by courses within the program	——	——	——	——	——	——	——	——
Number of program majors	——	——	——	——	——	——	——	——
Credit hours generated by majors in the program (for service programs indicate the number of client contact hours)	——	——	——	——	——	——	——	——
Number of degrees granted (annual total)	——	——	——	——	——	——	——	——

D. Indicate whether the proposed program will require an expansion of any support services on campus. If the program is adopted or expanded, describe any special library, laboratory, or computational facilities, equipment, or materials that would have to be established. Include the expected costs, and describe how such expansions will be incorporated into the budgeting of the institution.

E. Indicate whether the program will require the addition of new space or facilities or the remodeling or renovation of existing space. If so, provide a statement detailing such plans and space needs and their funding implications.

F. Present information, on a form like the one in Table 16, on the operating resource requirements by object expenditure. Identify here what resources the institution has committed or will need to commit to this program if service levels reach those set forth in this proposal. Funds allocated to either the development or the implementation of a new or expanded program should be identified on this form. If the institution plans to reallocate resources to the program in the budget year or in the subsequent five-year period, such reallocation also should be reflected.

G. Determine and report how much faculty time and other resources are committed to existing programs in the same department, or other division, as the proposed program. If the proposed program is confined to a school in a university, then the school should be responsible for determining these faculty and resource commitments. But if it involves more than one school, then other provisions must be made for finding out what human and other resources are already committed. Help may be obtained, for example, from the Department of Institutional Research. Once these present commitments have been ascertained, they should be reconciled with the demands on faculty and other resources by the new program.

In recent years the state coordinating and governing bodies for higher education have developed policies and procedures for reviewing and approving new programs. The processes vary considerably from state to state, although a consistent trend since about 1972 has been toward more rigorous and detailed reviews. In general, the reviewing body requires these elements: (1) A program description with a minimum of rhetoric and expletives. (2) A statement of goals and objectives, and probably one that shows how the aims of the proposed program are related to those of the institution. Increasingly, state-level guidelines are asking for such expanded statements. (3) A statement of both the needs and the demands for the program. Institutional, state, and regional needs are described, along with anticipated enrollments. It is quite conceivable to have a need for developing more individuals with particular expertise yet there may be little actual student demand for the program; or the popular demand for some programs may have diminished the need for it or caused an oversupply of available personnel. (4) A cost analysis. (5) A statement about what personnel the program will require. Even in the current era, when staffs are expanding very little, institutional representatives should continue to seek new programs in order to keep the curriculum abreast of new needs and developments. State-level officials are becoming increasingly skeptical, however, of the ability of institutions to absorb new programs without dropping old ones. The answer, which institutions generally reject, is that "fat" in the personnel area may allow such absorption.

Responses to questions like the following may be helpful in appraising the adequacy of the new program. Are the instructions and requirements for developing new programs sufficiently clear and comprehensive? Does the institution have well-established policies and procedures for initiating, reviewing, and making decisions about new programs? Do these policies and procedures provide adequate safeguards against course proliferation and against courses being developed in isolation? Although program development and curricular matters are primarily the responsibility of the faculty, does the administration have enough ways to influence the process if faculty policies and procedures do not result in adequate self-discipline? Do the faculty and the administration give more than verbal deference to the importance of responsible new-program development? What are specific instances of their activity or lack of it? Finally, does the process of creating new programs at

Table 16. Five-Year Projection of Total Operating Resources

	Historical Years 1976–1977	1977–1978	Current Year 1978–1979	Budget Year 1979–1980	Second Year 1980–1981	Third Year 1981–1982	Fourth Year 1982–1983	Fifth Year 1983–1984
Positions (staff years)								
Administrators								
Faculty members								
Graduate assistants								
Nonacademic personnel								
a. Clerical workers								
b. Professionals								
Operating Costs (appropriated funds only)								
Personnel services								
Administrators								
Faculty members								
Graduate assistants								
Nonacademic personnel								
a. Clerical workers								

b. Professionals					
Contractual services					
Equipment					
Library materials					
Other support services (specify)					
Nonrecurring expenses (for equipment, and so on)					
Total Costs					
Sources					
State government (appropriated funds only)					
Federal government (non-appropriated funds only)					
Institutional budget (if private university)					
Other					
Total of All Sources					

public institutions give adequate attention to state policies and procedures? And also to state politics?

17. Does the institution have effective policies and procedures for the review and evaluation of existing programs?

The assessment of existing programs is a relatively recent arrival on the scene stimulated by economic austerity and pressures from state agencies. The lack of money has forced institutions to make decisions about priorities and quality. A number of systems for establishing priorities have therefore been created. One excellent procedure, developed by the Pennsylvania State University, is primarily a self-study by faculty members in the program. The Undergraduate Academic Program Review (UAPR), as it is called, has eight basic principles. First, qualitative review is considered necessary for effectively maintaining high-quality educational programs. Second, such qualitative evaluation requires competent faculty members, in most cases including some who are skilled at a range of activities in a particular college, as well as outside that college. Third, the responsibility for UAPR is shared by the academic administration and the faculty. Fourth, the "maximum appropriate involvement" of the faculty in the program under review is a vital aspect of the appraisal process. This involvement takes the form of self-description and assessment. Fifth, although the use of consultants from outside the college or university may sometimes be appropriate, the fundamental responsibility for qualitative judgment belongs inside the university. Sixth, at all stages of the assessment, faculty members, students, and appropriate academic officers have opportunities to give their advice or to participate. Seventh, the UAPR is not concerned with cost effectiveness or other fiscal measures of academic programs; instead it is intended to fill the void left by such quantitative assessments, that is, to provide reasonably structured reviews of the quality and societal relevance of existing undergraduate programs. And finally, the UAPR should be flexible enough to deal with diverse programs.

Another useful resource is a compilation entitled *Program Evaluation* (American Association of State Colleges and Universities, 1976a), which examines "the organized and continuing efforts of an institution to examine the several dimensions of its educational program for purposes of improving it" (p. *ii*). Case studies of two different approaches to evaluating existing programs are given here. The University of Illinois COPE program is a continuing endeavor that initially was undertaken by intracampus teams of faculty members and administrators outside the programs being evaluated and by an inside team of members within the program. Later, COPE moved to using only inside teams. The second approach detailed in *Program Evaluation*, that of the State University of New York at Buffalo, was developed by a campuswide committee, and its recommendations to the president focused on the very sensitive issue of reducing faculty and staff positions.

Council on Program Evaluation (COPE). The Council, which was formed at Urbana-Champaign in 1973, consists of nine faculty members, including five without administrative appointments, and three students. The Council is chaired by the associate vice-chancellor who directs the Office of Planning and Evaluation. During the first academic year of operation (1973–74), faculty members and administrators were appointed to seventeen academic task groups, each with seven to twelve members. From 1973 to 1975, thirty task groups analyzed and reported on programs and centers on the Urbana campus.

The evaluation of each academic program has three identifiable parts: a statement of the program's mission and its relation to institutional objectives; definitions of the assessment criteria and of more specific indicators that measure how well the program attains its mission; and the procedures for using these indicators, scoring the criteria, and applying the results to decision making.

Each academic task group employs, in addition to cost data, five criteria for evaluation, each of which is accompanied by a number of quality indicators according to the results obtained from examining the criteria. The group rates the components, as well as the whole program, as outstanding, strong, adequate, or marginal. The weights attached to these criteria, the format for presenting the results of the evaluation, and to whom, the extent of the supporting analyses and commentary, and the actions appropriate for particular circumstances are important aspects of the process. Following are the five criteria and their indicators, as well as the means used to determine the program's productivity and cost effectiveness.

1. Quality of instruction in individual courses and of the instructional program as a whole.
   A. Students' assessments of the courses, teachers, and overall program
   B. Recent graduates' appraisals of the quality of the program
   C. Standards for admission to and retention in the program
   D. Availability of adequate space and facilities
   E. Institutional commitment to and concern for the instructional program, as determined by (1) the effectiveness of student advising, (2) the distribution of instructional load by faculty rank, (3) the institution's responsiveness to the changing needs of the program, (4) a faculty reward system to promote quality instruction, and (5) the institution's willingness to assess students' attitudes and to respond to their views
2. Quality of research, creative activity, scholarly work, service, or professional performance
   A. ACE ratings
   B. Accreditation or other ratings by professional societies
   C. Outside support received by the program compared to that received by other programs in the field
   D. External recognition of staff members, as demonstrated by (1) a listing in *Who's Who* and similar honors; (2) exhibits, commissions, prizes, and awards; (3) lectureships, visiting appointments, job offers; (4) advisory appointments and consulting; and (5) offices held and professional activities
   E. Publications and other evidence of creative productivity
   F. Productivity of and recognition of program graduates
   G. Creative and efficient use of space and facilities
3. Centrality of the program—its contribution or importance to other campus programs
   A. Relation of the program to the institutional mission
   B. Instruction of students from other programs
   C. Contribution of the program to people in other programs
   D. Redundancy—unnecessary and nonproductive overlap with other programs on campus.
4. Value of the program to society or its uniqueness in the state's program of higher education

A. Contributions to the solution of societal problems.
B. Value to society of its graduates, as determined by (1) the placement of current graduates, (2) the projected needs of society for its graduates, (3) the suitability of the program's content, (4) the availability of similar programs of comparable quality, and (5) the role and fraction of foreign students in the program
C. Recent graduates' assessments of the value of the program
5. Potential and future expectations
    A. Prospects and potential of program, according to (1) statements by those in the program, (2) analyses of statements by those in related areas, and (3) analyses of statements by outside experts
    B. Quality of the leadership and intellectual life of the program, as viewed by (1) those in the program and (2) others on campus
    C. External trends in financial support and societal needs

The costs and cost effectiveness of the program, though not one of the five criteria of quality, are nevertheless analyzed carefully in COPE. These aspects of the program are determined by the number of students majoring in the program; the number of instructional units taught by the program's staff; the number of FTE staff members, by level and type of assignment; the number of degrees granted by the program; the failure rate of students; the average length of time required to complete the program; and the state and nonstate money used by the program.

After making their evaluations, the task groups write three types of reports. They give a Summary Report, which presents their major findings and recommendations, to the unit being evaluated after consulting with the unit at the end of the interviewing period. The Summary Report and the unit's response to it, along with a more detailed Task Group Report, are shared with the vice-chancellor for academic affairs. The contents of this detailed report have confidential status. The third type, the Action Report, constitutes COPE's public statement to the campus. It describes the findings, actions recommended, and actions taken in the case of each evaluated unit.

In 1975–1976 COPE shifted to the use of self-evaluations by individuals within the unit only, as I mentioned earlier. The university gives three reasons for this policy change. First of all, the outside task groups, although a necessary part of the early, experimental COPE operations, entailed a major commitment of resources to evaluation that the campus does not believe it can afford on a long-term, across-the-board basis. Second, the original document that established COPE provided guidelines that emphasized the role of self-evaluation as a continuing process on the Urbana-Champaign campus. And third, the university has a statutory obligation to replace its annual financial reports with planning and evaluation reports. An "unofficial" reason for the policy change stems from strong criticism of some task-group reports and some unfortunate "leaks" to the news media. These political factors reflect the nervousness of most people when evaluation is taking place rather than reflect on the commendable quality of the reports. Some COPE reports did make hard recommendations that some individuals preferred not to believe or to face.

What are some findings from COPE? The top-rated academic departments on the Urbana-Champaign campus, although they run the gamut of ways in which academic departments can operate, show unmistakable characteristics, according to the evaluations of COPE:

> They are impressively systematic in managing unit functions. Self-evaluation efforts are prominent. Faculty report each year about their activities in teaching, research, and service. After consideration by peers, faculty are rated annually along one or more dimensions of professional activity. Top-rated units characteristically assign explicit functions to a number of standing committees. Among these functions are committees on undergraduate and graduate admissions and education, on planning, and on promotions and personnel. Usually undergraduate advisement and the training of graduate students are matters of considerable concern, and resources are devoted to both. It may seem a trivial matter, but it is true also that our top-ranked departments tend to have by-laws that set forth explicitly many of the details of departmental operations as well as of the sub-units within the department. Major committee operations are described, and responsibilities for departmental functions are explicitly detailed.

State University of New York at Buffalo. President Ketter of SUNY at Buffalo announced in spring 1975 that during the 1975–1976 academic year an intensive effort would be made to develop an academic plan for the university. The committee established for this purpose, headed by the dean of the Graduate and Professional Education Division, consisted of eleven administrators (including deans and chairpersons), four faculty members, and one student. The president charged the committee with deciding which programs should be given the highest priorities. These decisions would be based on the assessed strengths and weaknesses of the various programs and on their compatibility with the institutional mission-and-scope statements.

After the committee was appointed, however, three external events occurred that effectively changed and limited its activities. In June 1975 the university was told by the SUNY system office that its required savings for the 1975–1976 SUNY fiscal year (the amount contained in the approved budget that must be held in escrow) would be increased by one million dollars to $2,835,000—and the mandated increase in savings was requested when Buffalo was already one quarter into the fiscal year. A revised savings plan, which was made in a very short time, used only vacant lines (positions), put a freeze on almost all new appointments, and reduced temporary services and other personal service funds. These cutbacks permitted the university to meet the imposed reductions without laying off individuals.

But a short time later, Buffalo officials were informed that their base budget for the next academic year (1976–1977) would be decreased by $1,150,000. This reduction involved the specific identification and elimination of 59.76 FTE positions. Again the plan developed at Buffalo relied primarily on the use of vacant personnel lines or on personnel lines that were predicted to be vacant.

Then the other shoe dropped: the 1976–1977 executive budget submitted by New York's governor to the legislature required the elimination of an additional 133.08 FTE positions, a figure that was subsequently increased to 143.08 by the legislature. In brief, the university had 4507.55 authorized full-time-equivalent positions at the beginning of the 1975–1976 fiscal year; and this number was to be reduced to 4304.71, or a reduction of 202.84 FTE positions.

This series of events meant that the Academic Planning Committee turned from its original more leisurely charge to the onerous task of making these reductions. Guided by institutional statements of mission and priority, the committee established *quality, need,* and *promise* as three criteria for determining priorities. The committee then translated its mission statement and other university statements of goals into criteria for judgment, with the purpose of ascertaining the degree to which any program supported the goals. These seven criteria were adopted by the committee:

1. Need for the program: student demand (taking into account programs in which certain courses are required and programs in which this is not the case); graduate employability; essentiality for this university's profile; essentiality for SUNY profile; the support it provides to other programs.
2. Type of clientele served: minorities and women (especially at graduate level); preprofessional, professional; general education (includes credit SS and MFC clienteles); continuing education.
3. Quality of program: external evaluations (including accreditation ratings); student quality (particularly at graduate-professional level); faculty quality (inclusive of individual and overall productivity, creativity, or innovation).
4. Public service activities related to program mission: professional association activities of major visibility; consultation with public and business firms; public lecturing, and so on.
5. Participation in multidisciplinary programs: unit participation in or affiliation with colleges, centers, and institutes, on this or other campuses.
6. Program efficiency: program profile data as described; unnecessary overlap with other programs; unnecessary course offerings; ability of program to monitor and evaluate its own activities.
7. Resource needs: what is required to maintain or bring the program more in line with priorities given to it.

An interim report of the committee published on February 12, 1976, met a heavy squall line of faculty resistance at a March 4,

1976, faculty meeting, and there was a vote of "no confidence" on the report. Although the faculty was negative, it could not suggest a more equitable approach, and thus the committee moved ahead with concrete recommendations for personnel reductions.

The President's Report on Resource Reductions and Reallocations was printed on May 3, 1976, and the final report of the Committee on Academic Planning, entitled *Report on the Future of the University*, was released on June 9, 1976.

The Buffalo experience is instructive in that a committee established for one purpose was given a different, and highly controversial, assignment. It was a no-win, can-lose situation for the committee, and yet the assignment needed to be done. The task was handled well, although the final decisions on personnel reductions were based more on political considerations and intuition than on the established criteria and data.

Course evaluation. Since programs consist of a number of courses, the institutional evaluators may well want to appraise individual courses. Unfortunately, they will find few comprehensive models designed for this purpose, perhaps because some individuals assume that the evaluation of classroom teaching is synonymous with course evaluation. Some survey instruments for judging instruction encourage this view in that they have two parts: part one on the teacher's performance and part two on the course. Although assessing a course is related to assessing classroom teaching, it may be quite different also. An introductory psychology course, for example, with twenty sections using the same book and same syllabi, needs to be evaluated independently of individual teaching performance.

One excellent model for course evaluation is outlined in Table 17. In discussing this approach, Hastings and associates contend that a comprehensive evaluation of an educational program must consider many effects. Such an assessment does not begin and end with a consideration of students' achievement in the program, for many students seem to succeed regardless of (or in spite of) the particular instruction to which they are exposed. Thus a systematic appraisal should consider the complexity of costs, such as the cost of teacher preparation, supplementary materials, and additional instructional time, such products as better student-parent-

Table 17. Framework for Evaluation of Introductory Geography Courses

Classes of Information			Sources of Data			
Focus	Exemplars	Illustrative Variables	Public Facts	Instructor Impressions	Observer	Instruments
A Environmental Conditions	1. Student characteristics	Background, aptitude, aspirations		*		*
	2. Instructor characteristics	Experience, style, personality				*
	3. Instructional setting	Physical plant, intellectual climate		*		*
	4. Departmental accommodation	Support by colleagues, administration		*		
	5. Interest by other departments	Curricular context, discussion of course		*		
B *Instructional materials	1. Rationale	Utility, ideals, assumptions	*	*		
	2. Instructional objectives	Points of view, student changes	*	*		*
	3. Reference works, study aids	Library, handouts, models, maps	*	*		
	4. Subject-matter coverage	Emphases, concepts, structure	*	*		*
	5. Sequence and time allotment	Concept development, review	*	*		*

C	Instruction-learning acts	1. Instructional strategy	Teaching styles, assignments	*	*
		2. Student-instructor exchange	Information flow, counseling	*	
		3. Student-student exchange	Discussion, social climate		*
		4. Reinforcement, grading	Motivation, utility, tests	*	*
		5. Lab experiences	Involvement, coverage	*	
D	Outcomes	1. Student competence	Knowledge, understanding, skill	*	*
		2. Student interest and attitude	Commitment, prejudice, course demands	*	*
		3. Effects on instructors	Extra work, insights, expanded interests	*	
		4. Side effects	Prestige, social reaction	*	

Note: Asterisks denote sources.

Source: Hastings and others, 1970, p. 4.

teacher attitudes and more interest and greater achievement by students.

The course evaluation should be modified to fit the inevitable limitations on time, money, and personnel. But something less than ideal is much preferable to nothing or to impressionistic data.

Some questions can assist in the assessment of existing programs. For instance, does the institution have a clear policy on the criteria and processes to be used in evaluating existing programs? Is the institution regularly evaluating at least some of its existing programs? And have program reductions or modifications taken place as a result of the evaluation committee's work?

18. **Is the general education component an intellectually stimulating and integral part of the curriculum?**

Most academic programs are tripartite, consisting of one-third general education courses, one-third major courses, and one-third electives. Of these three, general education fares most poorly. With some shining exceptions, general education has been eroded by the steady gain of postsecondary career education, the simultaneous proliferation and specialization of academic programs, unfavorable institutional reward systems, campus "turf" considerations, full-time equivalencies and retrenchment, national economic problems, and administrative anomie. Or to express it another way: since general education is in everyone's interest, it ends up being no one's responsibility. The Carnegie Foundation for the Advancement of Teaching (1977) called it "a disaster area" (p.11) and entitled its chapter on general education "An Idea in Distress" (pp. 164–185). "An idea in distress" seems closer to the mark than "a disaster area," but both descriptions, as well as this excellent chapter, point to some problems.

Levine (1976, pp. 24–25) found general education plagued with several difficulties. For one thing, the rewards and incentives to faculty members for participating in general education are meager. Indeed, teaching general education courses, even outside university settings, frequently serves as a negative factor in faculty evaluations for promotion or tenure. It is so treated because general education involves service outside the discipline, because general education teaching demands a disproportionate amount of faculty time, time that could be used for other more positively perceived activities, such as publication or committee work, and because the average faculty person does not usually excel at general education teaching and thus does not wish to tackle something that might produce a blot on his or her teaching record. Further, the background and training of most instructors do not prepare them well for broad, cooperative, interdisciplinary teaching. Not surprisingly, then, the turnover rate of faculty members in general education is high, and participation is sometimes involuntary. Another difficulty is that the academic departments have not utilized their most able and most senior faculty members and graduate students to teach general education courses. In addition, departments are fond of transforming a general education course into an introduction to the department or into the first course in the major, inasmuch as such a transformation is an effective way to recruit students for the discipline. And finally, required general education is unpopular with students. In the 1960s students opposed requirements, and in the 1970s they appear to be more favorably disposed to practical or career-oriented study.

Despite these obstacles, however, Levine did find some successful models. One of these, the General College at the University of Minnesota, owes its success, he believes, to the following factors. The college's reward system is closely linked to the general education commitment; promotions and tenure are tied primarily to excellence in teaching; young faculty members were brought to the university for teaching in the General College; and today most of the college's key administrators and division chairpersons are products of this system. General College faculty members are separated from the more research-oriented disciplines of the university, and very few have joint appointments in the university academic departments. And, not least, the General College spends much time and effort on evaluating courses and teachers.

The decided decrease in the number of required general education courses (or their relatives) has been documented by several researchers. Blackburn and associates (1976) found that the percentage of institutions requiring English declined from 90 to 72 percent between 1967 and 1974, from 73 to 53 for a foreign language, from 33 to 20 for mathematics, and from 86 to 55 for

	1969-70	1975-76
Professions	38%	58%
Social sciences	18	8
Humanities	9	5
Biological		
sciences	5	7
Physical sciences	7	8
Arts	6	6
Other	17	8

physical education (p. 34). These figures, drawn from a national survey, reflect the continued decline in social science and humanities majors that is shown in a survey conducted by Trow (1977, p. 7), which also indicates a sharp increase in professional areas and a slight increase in the sciences.

One should not have to make a case for general education; it has been made eloquently and often. (For example, the 1945 Report of the Harvard Committee on *General Education in a Free Society* and the 1977 Carnegie Foundation report on *Missions of the College Curriculum* are important contributions to the literature.) And there are various case studies of successful curricula in the literature and practice of general education. A general education component may consist of some required skills, such as in reading, writing, and computation, and some broader understandings that may involve a number of academic areas. Bell (1966, p. 173), for instance, argued for history as a central subject, saying that "the senses of the past and the knottiness of fact are the necessary means of transcending contemporaneity and 'actualizing the universe.' " Dressel and Mayhew (1954, pp. 272–286) wrote in favor of "critical thinking as a possible principle of integration." And perhaps general education got its greatest boost from the "Contemporary Civilization" course or core of courses that was initiated in 1919 at Columbia University. In short, we know enough about the desirable components of general education to develop an academically sound and intellectually stimulating program on any campus.

And now for the good news: in spite of all the negatives cited above, one senses a national resurgence of interest in general education. C. P. Snow has written much about the problems of communication among men of goodwill with different specialities. As specialized education continues to teach more and more about less and less, some common elements should transcend the increasing tendency toward communication isolation. This view is resulting in more attention to some interlacing fabric such as general education.

A national rekindling of interest in ethics and values is evident, too. And general education is the best-equipped means for helping people probe and clarify their own values as well as analyze, understand, and evaluate societal and cultural values and norms. This interest in values is related also to the increasing national concern about the purposes of a college education, which is probably a Hegelian counterreaction to the rapid increase in vocationalism and career education.

Even retrenchment may be contributing, if only modestly at present, to a resurgence of general education. Those academic fields suffering the greatest enrollment declines because of changing student interests are those that are integral to general education. A well-developed general education thrust, therefore, may provide the best avenue for the continued academic employment of young faculty members in vulnerable disciplines.

Several questions, such as the following ones, may be useful in evaluating the general education component:

1. Has the overall general education program been studied carefully within the past three years?
2. Are the objectives of the general education program clearly enunciated?
3. What is the impact of the general education program on the individual student? In answering this question, one might consider a series of subordinate questions adapted from Dressel and Mayhew (1954, pp. 22–23). (Recent discoverers of behavioral objectives will note this orientation in these questions.) A. What does general education mean in terms of definite and concrete action, feeling, or behavior on the part of the individual student in the program? B. What are some of the specific situations, problems, or experiences which confront individuals

and for which the types of behavior described by the objectives of the general education program are necessary or desirable? C. Does the conjunction of various kinds of behavior and the possible inability to separate one kind in order to evaluate it suggest a redefinition of the original objectives or a grouping of several related aims? D. What kind of record is to be kept of the student's behavior in the program? How is the record to be analyzed, and what is to be done with the results? E. What specific classroom experiences—readings, demonstrations, discussions, activities, or lectures—are thought to contribute to the growth of the individual with respect to the objectives of the program? F. Do the general education experiences add to the growth of the individual as compared with other individuals who have not had these particular experiences? G. Do the analyses of the program's objectives and the overall program suggest additional activities that might be carried on in the classroom, or different ways of teaching?

4. Have current campus problems with general education been openly and carefully considered?
5. Does the general education program have the active support of key administrators?
6. Are persistent and creative attempts being made by general education personnel to work cooperatively with other academic units?
7. Does the institution have an established procedure for evaluating the general education program fairly regularly?

19. Are the quality and size of the graduate program consistent with institutional goals and objectives?

Strong and creative graduate programs are critical to the national welfare and to technological advancement. These programs lead to significant advances in basic and applied research that are essential for scientific progress, and they provide technical and professional skills that are necessary to maintain and improve the standard of living. According to Jencks and Riesman (1968, pp. 513–514), "the American graduate school has become the envy of the world, a mecca for foreign students, and a model for foreign institutions. It has also become one of the central institutions of American culture. Both the best and the worst in undergraduate education emanate from it, and the overall quality of American intellectual life depends more on it than on any other single institution."

Yet all is not well here. The sixties saw a very rapid growth in graduate education due to the same factors—a large potential pool of students and increased state aid—that caused undergraduate enrollment increases, plus a substantial infusion of federal money into graduate-level research. But the seventies have seen a dramatic change in national needs, in state and federal support, and in the vitality of the national economy. With respect to federal support, a Ford Foundation report (1978) noted that between 1945, when the federal government assumed prime responsibility for basic scientific research, and 1968, American basic science attained first place in the world. By 1968 federal support was at an annual level of $2.3 billion, accounting for 70 percent of all support for graduate school research. By 1976, however, the government's support, measured in constant dollars, had declined by nearly 15 percent. So now other countries, such as the Soviet Union and West Germany, surpass the United States in the percentage of gross national product devoted to scientific research.

The results of this expansion and contraction have been complex. For one thing, the large graduate enrollments of the sixties produced a glut of Ph.D.s, a good number of whom could not find employment either in academe or in business because of the economic recession. Katz and Hartnett (1976, p. 13) put it this way: "Clearly, the picnic is over. . . . Students with doctorates, who were in such demand in the mid sixties that they often had their pick of numerous job opportunities, now find that there is an excess of Ph.D.s and that jobs are extremely scarce." (A useful analysis of the Ph.D. market is given in Cartter, 1976.) This excess not only discouraged potential graduate students but contributed to the decline in government support for graduate education.

And what effect have reduced enrollment and support had on the quality of graduate programs? The answers differ dramatically, depending on what type of institution one is examining. The titular public and private universities remain largely unchanged in their ability to maintain strong graduate programs. Clark (1976, p. 89), for example, found that "when universities with high overall standings in the ACE [graduate] surveys are compared with the lists compiled by Hughes in 1925 and Keniston in 1957, university reputations are exceedingly stable." Because the institutions are firmly rooted in their states and in the minds of their graduates, in addition to their long history of significant contributions, they have been able to maintain high quality. However, the erosion of federal research funds in recent years threatens to have long-term effects on the quality of certain programs. In contrast, regional state universities in many cases have greatly curtailed their graduate programs; in others the size has not changed much but the quality has eroded considerably. These institutions are struggling to maintain high-caliber graduate education in spite of declining student enrollments and rising costs, not to mention the high cost of graduate education in general.

Whichever category—prestigious or struggling—the institution is in, however, if it is a public college or university, it is increasingly being influenced and controlled by the state. Some of the reasons for this declining autonomy can be traced again to the periods of expansion and contraction referred to above. The production of excess Ph.D.s contributed to the public's view that graduate education is developing specialists for jobs that do not exist. The national economic downturn, coupled with a new public sophistication about the costs and productivity of education, has aroused a general concern about accountability and encouraged the idea that education, particularly graduate education, is inefficient. Consequently, legislators, especially their staff members as well as the state budget offices, are taking a much harder look at graduate schools. A few states have mandated a minimum enrollment figure for graduate classes, and others have declared a one-or two-year moratorium on new graduate programs. Such states as Illinois, Louisiana, and New York have introduced more rigorous procedures for reviewing doctoral programs, and more will do so. Indeed, in some states, the quality and size of graduate programs are influenced as much by the state's plans and policies as by those of the institution.

Thus, certain external forces are having a good deal of impact on the nature and quality of graduate education. A more internal problem that divides some graduate schools is disagreement about the proper mission of various doctoral programs. In the study by Clark (1976), fifty-seven graduate deans ranked each of three purposes—preparing researchers, preparing teachers, preparing practitioners—in their own institutions' doctoral programs for the physical sciences, biological sciences, social sciences, and humanities. The results are shown in Figure 1. It turned out that the deans assigned quite different missions to the four curricular areas. Most deans rated the goal of developing researchers as the most important in the physical and biological sciences. Developing college teachers was rated the most important task of the humanities program, and for the social sciences the two aims of developing teachers and researchers were rated about equal. These differences might affect the quality and size of a graduate school or of individual doctoral programs in several ways. For one thing, the costs of achieving these goals and of supporting each kind of pro-

Figure 1. Major Tasks of Ph.D. Programs, as Ranked by Graduate Deans.

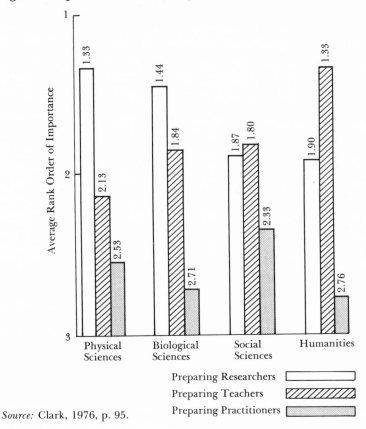

Source: Clark, 1976, p. 95.

gram differ. Developing researchers requires greater expenditures for equipment and supplies, library materials, and computer facilities; and the teacher-pupil ratios are lower, and therefore more expensive to maintain, in the physical and biological sciences. So if a graduate school gave the highest priority to, say, preparing researchers in the physical sciences, it might (given a fixed amount of money to be distributed) have to accept lower-quality programs in the other three curricular areas or to curtail its programs or enrollments. Or it might decide to eliminate one program in order to boost the quality of another.

And what of the quality of students' experiences and training in graduate school? These, too, must be evaluated, and past assessments have revealed a number of problems. Many graduate students tend to be less than enthusiastic about their doctoral education, but apparently only a few are now interested in improving it. Writing about his experiences in graduate school, Sanford (1976) cites the predominance of two groups of students: the "grinds"—those who plod along doing what is expected of them and believing what the professor professes—and the "system beaters." Sanford observes: "Unlike the student activists of the 1960s, students who are system beaters do not openly question the educational system or otherwise take risks which might jeopardize their educational careers. System beating is a covert activity, and those who engage in it want to give an appearance of conforming to established academic regulations. . . . System beaters are interested only in circumventing the system, not in changing it. . . . Graduate students, on the whole, feel that they have very little power, and system beating is a way of asserting power in spite of the rules and regulations" (p.3).

In their book-length study of the development of graduate and professional students, Katz and Hartnett, (1976, pp. 261–263) have a good deal more to say about the quality of graduate education and students' attitudes toward it:

> 1. Graduate student relations with members of the faculty are regarded by most graduate students as the single most important aspect of the quality of their graduate experience; unfortunately, many also report that they are the single most disappointing aspect.

2. Conditions crucial to the optimum development of productive scholars and scientists are neglected in graduate education. Among these conditions are cultivation of the imaginative capacity, encouragement of cooperative inquiry, discouragement of undue allegiance to a specific "school of thought," and security of expectations.

3. In spite of many advances since the 1930s, there has been a loss in graduate training of theoretical breadth, community of inquiry, and civility.

4. The very training that graduate students receive and the professional transformation they undergo generally tend to decrease the likelihood that they will become effective teachers of undergraduates.

5. Both for developing relationships with others and for developing autonomy, the graduate and professional experience often has an inhibiting effect on students' growth and development.

6. Though graduate students are not generally regarded as individuals who are particularly vulnerable to emotional disorders, there is convincing evidence to the contrary. Loneliness, severe anxiety, role confusion, and alienation are common maladies among graduate students.

7. In spite of changes in certain demographic characteristics of new graduate students—for example, more women, more minorities—students attending graduate school in the early 1970s were basically the same types as those attending ten years earlier.

8. Though graduate and professional education for minority students is no longer separate, it still is unequal. Directly and indirectly, minority students have less access than white students, particularly to the informal aspects of training.

9. Women are still discriminated against institutionally and individually, but their influx into graduate school is beginning to lead to the exploration of hitherto neglected research areas, to more cooperative modes of inquiry, to more interdisciplinary work, and to more emphasis on teaching.

10. Though the number of institutions awarding the doctorate has been steadily increasing, approximately half the doctorates are still granted by only thirty institutions and more than one fifth of the doctorates are granted by just ten institutions.

11. Graduate school students are not professional school rejects; nor is the opposite the case. [For] only about

5 percent of both graduate and professional students [does] their field [represent a] second choice.

12. Though graduate departments base their choice of students on a great deal of information about the students, the opposite is not the case. Students' choices of graduate departments are often based on scant information about characteristics and features that subsequently turn out to be very important to their performance and satisfaction in graduate school.

13. Departmental reputation—in the eyes of deans and faculty members, but not students—has often been viewed as being synonymous with departmental quality. Extended definitions of quality and of how it is to be measured are necessary.

The foregoing information on the problems besetting graduate education and on previous assessments of its quality should help institutional evaluators design an effective plan for assessing their doctoral programs. Also useful is the section of Clark's study (1976) that asked the fifty-seven graduate deans to rate ten characteristics of doctoral programs (on a four-point scale from essential to not important) and to estimate the adequacy and availability of several indicators. The number in parentheses after each characteristic below is the deans' average rating.

Characteristic: General academic ability of students entering the program (3.61). *Indicators*: Undergraduate gradepoint averages, scores on graduate aptitude tests, and scores on appropriate advanced tests were rated as good indicators, and most deans said this information was available at their universities. Rated unacceptable: student self-ratings.

Characteristic: Achievements, knowledge, and skills of students at the time of completing the advanced degree (3.61). *Indicators*: The deans thought the best measure would be the excellence of recently accepted dissertations as judged by external experts, but almost no one had access to such information. Other good indicators: the percentage of recent graduates doing work related to their fields of specialization, and the percentage of recent graduates who published prior to the degree. Poor indicators: scores on standardized tests, evaluations of internship or assistantship performance, oral and licensing examination performance.

Characteristic: The university's financial support for the program (3.60). *Indicators*: None of the suggested financial indicators received very enthusiastic endorsement. Most acceptable was the amount budgeted per full-time-equivalent (FTE) student for education and general expense. Least acceptable was the median faculty salary by rank.

Characteristic: Library facilities (3.60). *Indicators*: Good indicators were judgments of the adequacy of relevant holdings by faculty members and visiting experts, but less than one third of the deans indicated that such information was available. Measures not endorsed: circulation figures, self-reported library use by students or faculty members, number of books in the collection.

Characteristic: Academic training of the faculty (3.57). *Indicators*: Good and available indicators: the percentage of the faculty with Ph.D.s or the equivalent, percentage of Ph.D.s from "top" programs in each field. Least adequate measures: average grades in graduate school, ratings of excellence by enrolled students.

Characteristic: Purposes of the program (3.49). *Indicators:* Good indicators were judgments of the clarity of the program plans and purposes by recent graduates, faculty members, or visiting experts, but almost no university collected this information. Available but unacceptable: the ratio of graduates to undergraduates, the number of specializations within a program.

Characteristic: Laboratory equipment and facilities (3.47). *Indicators*: Good indicators were ratings of adequacy by faculty members or outside experts. Such ratings, however, were seldom available. Measures of space were judged least helpful.

Characteristic: Courses and other educational offerings (3.45). *Indicators*: Acceptable measures: faculty/student satisfaction with courses and other offerings, judgments of these offerings by visiting experts. Few deans reported collecting such information. More available, but less adequate: the number of new or revised courses, the percentage of student credit hours devoted to seminars and tutorials, faculty-rated ease of introducing new courses.

Characteristic: Admissions policies (3.43). *Indicators*: Acceptable: the percentage of qualified applicants admitted, judgments by outside experts of whether admission standards should be higher or lower. Unacceptable: the cost of admissions recruiting and processing per FTE student.

Characteristic: Provision for the welfare of faculty members (3.42). *Indicators*: Most acceptable: median salary by rank, faculty satisfaction with freedom to plan courses and conduct research, provision for assistance to new and young faculty members as judged by the faculty. Least adequate measures: turnover rate, percentage on tenure, percentage ranked full or associate professor.

Other issues to be addressed by the evaluators are suggested by the following questions.

1. Has the institution arrived at the most desirable "balance" between graduate and undergraduate education? Does the institution have the human and material resources to conduct quality programs at both the undergraduate and graduate levels?

2. In considering new graduate programs, have the planners given sufficient thought to its "ripple effect" on other institutional programs?

3. Has a *vigorous* review of existing graduate programs been undertaken recently? Did the review cover need, demand, quality, productivity, and the compatibility of the programs' mission and scope with those of the institution?

4. To what extent do graduate students become victims of the system rather than its beneficiaries?

5. To what extent is the possible conservatism of the graduate school excessively impeding needed institutional reforms?

6. In the case of public institutions, is sufficient attention paid to state activities related to graduate education?

20. **Does the library or learning resources center provide good service to the academic community?**

The basic purpose of a college library is to provide students and faculty members with materials, assistance, and an environment that facilitate teaching and learning. How important is the library to the academic enterprise? A measure of its importance would be to imagine a residential campus without one.

Another measure may be gleaned from one volume of the

1930s North Central study (Waples, 1937), which made one of the few careful statistical efforts to correlate the quality of the library with a criterion of institutional excellence. It used six measures for judging the library's educational caliber: the number of general reference books; the number of periodicals; the average annual expenditure for books and periodicals during the past five years; the annual expenditure for library salaries, weighted for the size of the enrollment; the average annual number of free loans per student; and the average number of loans to faculty members. A composite of these factors correlated positively with institutional excellence—a .64 correlation.

Yet the role of librarians remains unclear on many campuses. Though libraries are an integral part of academe, the consideration of librarians as academicians has developed more slowly than is justified by their contributions. Farber and Walling (1974, p. 17) state the case in this manner:

> The teaching faculty's lack of confidence in their librarians as colleagues in the educational process has another unfortunate consequence: the librarian's role is viewed as a passive one, one devoted to housekeeping, to getting materials quickly and making them accessible with dispatch and efficiency, and to being available when needed for putting materials on reserve. Deans and presidents, most of whom have come from faculty ranks and are prone to the same attitudes, want their librarians to "run a tight ship"—to keep their accounts balanced, to make sure all student assistants and clerical help are working hard, and to answer the needs of the academic departments. Whether the college's students are really deriving much benefit from the library is rarely questioned. Lip service is paid to the library's being "the heart of the college," but as long as faculty members don't complain, as long as the size of the collection and other standards meet a level acceptable to accrediting agencies, the administration is happy to let the library alone. And, unfortunately, too many librarians like it this way.

Some basic principles of library evaluation should be developed before the appraisal. Lyle (1971, pp. 294–295) has suggested three such principles: "(1) The librarian must have a clear conception of its purposes in relation to the major objectives of the college. In the final analysis each library must be judged by how well it performs the services required to meet the needs of its particular college. . . . (2) Evaluation of any one segment of the college should involve a total commitment on the part of the administration, faculty, and student body, as well as the library staff. . . . (3) Evaluation must be a continuous process of appraisal and improvement, of reevaluation and reimprovement."

Detailed library standards have been established by the Association of College and Research Libraries, a division of the American Library Association. These standards are well known and used by librarians. In addition, a number of questions can be used to assist in the assessment.

1. To what extent do librarians teach students library use and the procedures of library research? And how effective is this program, according to evaluations by students and faculty members?
2. To what extent is the library an active environment rather than a passive one? Is the environment pleasant and conducive to learning? Environmental conditions are discussed by Lynch, 1974.
3. What is the effectiveness of the library's administrative staff? Is the library work well organized; are professional and non-professional duties clearly recognized? And to what extent is authority as well as responsibility delegated to the library staff? Does the institution have an established system for evaluating the effectiveness of professional librarians and other library staff members? A series of administrative policy decisions are outlined by Morse (1968). Also see McAnally and Downs (1973), Johnson (1972) and Holley (1973) for further discussions of the administrative aspects of library operations.
4. To what extent are library personnel helpful and pleasant to students and faculty members? The self-study committee for the Regenstein Library at the University of Chicago reported: "One of the biggest surprises . . . was the discovery of the depth and breadth of hostility toward library policies and staff. Again and again faculty members and students have expressed not simply annoyance but anger because of some experience of

mistreatment or injustice, imagined or real. . . . Interestingly enough, the staff members most frequently accused of offense in this respect are those on the circulation desk, and they are usually themselves students" (Booth, 1976). For one approach to library self-study, see Webster, 1974.

5. How closely does the library budget approach 5 percent of the educational and general budget? This figure may be low for new or developing institutions. Within the library budget, about 60 percent should be allocated for salaries and wages and about 40 percent for books, periodicals, supplies, equipment, and travel.

6. Is the library planning for the future? Obviously future plans are related directly to new resources, yet short- and long-range plans must be made today if improvements are to be realized tomorrow. Several future possibilities need to be considered.

What library adjustments are desirable to meet the needs of new clienteles? For example, as lifelong learning becomes a more common practice, more part-time adult learners will use campus facilities.

What plans for interinstitutional library programs are being developed? Many such arrangements have been made already, and more can be expected and should be encouraged.

To what extent are plans being made for the possible use of media other than books, for facsimile reproduction, and for easily portable teaching machines? In the near future libraries can expect greater use of small-unit, highly specialized data in the physical sciences, references for legal briefs, and bibliographical information.

The computerization of almost every hand operation done in a library is possible; the question is whether it is cost-effective. Greater use of the computer is inevitable and desirable; it is a matter of when, for what, and at what price. But the book will continue to be a primary teaching device: it is portable, reviewable, markable, personal, and relatively economical, and it can be retrieved as easily as memory will allow.

Conclusion

Improving the curriculum likely will become a more prominent concern of faculty members and administrators in the next three to five years and beyond. An excellent statement of what needs to be done is given in the Carnegie Foundation report (1977, pp. 264–265).

> The major tasks are few but important. They are (1) to formulate more clearly the advanced learning skills necessary in college and provide better training in them; (2) to give more attention and use greater ingenuity in improving distribution requirements; (3) to make integrative courses a more central feature of intellectual activity —concentrating on broad structures of thought as well as on areas of more specific analysis; (4) to assist the primary and secondary schools in teaching basic skills and providing compensatory training in them, when necessary, at the college level; (5) to bridge the gap between thought and action and create more opportunities for students to understand the world of work; (6) to clarify and apply more precisely the essential moral principles of academic life for the sake of the integrity of campus life and for the contribution that can be made to the skills of citizenship more generally; and (7) to assert the corporate interests of the academic community in the quality of the curriculum in its totality as well as in its component parts.

"The curriculum alone cannot bring wisdom, but it can help." Perhaps that one sentence from the report (p. 12) sums up in a quiet way the importance of programs. Campus plans for the flamboyant sixties called for adding, building, and giving; now they must modify, evaluate, and economize. Austerity tends to inhibit innovative approaches when the opposite is often needed. Institutions that choose to sit out current financial problems may be in for a long session. Others are choosing to undergo intensive analysis and study, with innovative action as the outcome. These colleges and universities will be moving through the rough seas ahead in a surer and more effective manner than others that choose to ignore Cassius' admonition: "The fault, dear Brutus, is not in our stars, but in ourselves."

6

Determining the Adequacy of Support Staff and Facilities

It takes many people to make a college or university function effectively. The crucial roles of professors, students, and administrators are more obvious, but many others also are integral parts of the academic community. Those who maintain the grounds, type letters, provide security, repair faucets, clean buildings, and make renovations and repairs perform services that are essential to the institution. Generally the work of these people goes unnoticed and is often not fully appreciated until something goes wrong.

Institutions should not wait until something goes wrong before noticing the support staff. The student paper at the Oregon College of Education, for example, carried this editorial on September 23, 1976: "Mr. Bill Neifert, director of the physical plant, came to OCE last December and in less than a year has organized the physical plant crew into a hardworking and energetic bunch of people. One of the most noticeable accomplishments has been the completion of the New Grove. Before Neifert's crew got busy on the grove, most of us began to wonder if it was ever going to be anything more than a lot of dirt. In just a short time, it has been developed into a beautiful park, a welcome addition to the physical appearance of any campus." And President A. B. Bonds of Baldwin-Wallace College has an annual luncheon in midyear where service to the college is recognized, and the college also sponsors a fall luncheon picnic for employees. These are but two of many ways that institutions can honor the essential services performed by these employees.

The institutional support services should be reviewed periodically to keep it current with changes in the college's mission and scope, as well as with developments in the institutional support area and the surrounding community. Some of the more or less enduring objectives relating to employees, as developed by the American Council on Education's former Committee on the Preparation of a Manual on College and University Business Administration (1955, p. 80), are to establish and maintain a fair classification and pay plan, treating all employees consistently and uniformly; to provide the best possible working conditions; to promote economy and effective service; to help operating departments recruit, select, train, and promote personnel; to encourage sound employer-employee relations; to encourage effective employee communication and participation at all levels; and to help department heads and supervisors understand and accept their administrative and supervisory responsibilities.

Good personnel policies are a key element within the institutional service area; they should contribute to the effective operation and management of the institution. The conditions of employment, as a minimum goal, should be at least equal to the acceptable conditions of employment in the surrounding community. Marks (1970, chap. 6; pp. 8–9) has identified these characteristics of a quality personnel program: (1) Personnel administration should be centralized in one department. (2) The personnel program should include all personnel functions. (3) Institutional personnel policies should be developed as a joint effort of management and employees. (4) Personnel policies should be clearly defined, they should be reduced to written form, and they should be made known to everyone affected by them. (5) The personnel program needs strong support from the administration. And (6) a high-quality personnel program depends on effective management, adequate resources, and adequate facilities and equipment.

21. **Are the physical plant and facilities adequate for the size of the student body enrollment and for the nature of the academic program?**

Little new construction of campus buildings can be expected in the next five or so years, and most of what is done will be in the private sector. Glenny and his coauthors (1976) asked one thousand college and university presidents about their building programs for 1968, 1974, and 1980. The results showed that in 1968, 53 percent of their institutions were funding substantial building programs; the figure for 1974 dropped to 18 percent; and by 1980 a majority (51 percent) expect to be doing little, if any, building. Only one out of ten institutions expects to have a substantial building program by that time. Bowen and Minter (1976), reporting on the financial and educational trends in one hundred private four-year institutions representing a universe of 866 institutions, concluded that "capital spending has been erratic in recent years, and no clearly defined trend is evident—though 1975–76 will prove to be a relatively low year." This conclusion is somewhat contrary to that of Glenny, who found capital spending to be steadily diminishing.

To accommodate some new programs and some enrollment increases without additional bricks and mortar, institutions will have to use their space more efficiently. Wood (1970, chap. 4, pp. 112–114) makes the following recommendations: Centralize the scheduling of room use in a key official who reports directly to the president and is backed up by him. Eliminate proprietary ownership of rooms by a particular department. Require an annual analysis of room utilization for year-to-year comparative purposes within the institution (this is much more realistic and meaningful than comparisons with other institutions). Consider using academic space on a twelve-month basis. Promote the use of Saturday classes; this will usually increase room use on Tuesdays and Thursdays as well. Increase the use of the class hour of 4 to 5 P.M. Eliminate the fixed lunch hour. Examine individual buildings and departments in which utilization is low to make sure that it is either justified or correctable. In locating new buildings, keep the campus plan compact to make it easy to get from one building to another. If possible, connect the buildings or provide covered passages between them. This promotes good utilization. Avoid building small buildings even if you must locate several departments in a larger one. This not only reduces capital costs but improves utilization and reduces operating costs. Use "special" rooms for "general" purposes when they are not in use as "special" rooms.

Wood makes further suggestions: Use wall storage lockers in chemistry laboratories rather than "under bench" lockers, which usually limit the bench use to two students. Change laboratory periods from two and a half to two hours. Encourage greater use of "special" rooms in the mornings, and of "general" rooms in the afternoon, when their use is usually low. Consider using "multipurpose" laboratories, which have been successfully adopted in several medical schools. The laboratory equipment for each special use is moved into the room as needed by a specially trained crew who operate on a tight schedule—almost like stagehands in the theatre. Keep "available" space always on the short side; this pressure always promotes good utilization. Consider eliminating courses that enroll fewer than ten students; this will improve not only the utilization of teaching space but the use of faculty time. Establish a percentage of utilization that seems to be reasonably attainable and push for that goal.

The Space Officers of Washington state have developed physical analysis forms that are being used in each of the state's public colleges and universities for a preliminary survey of its buildings (1977). One form is the Physical Analysis Rating System (quality evaluation) presented in Table 18.

22. **Does the institution have a relevant and current long-range plan for developing and maintaining its physical plant?**

The long-range planning of capital expenditures has become commonplace in higher education, but there is still much room for improvement. The Carnegie Commission (1972, p. 120) recommended "(1) that long-range plans for capital expansion be continually revised to meet changing circumstances, (2) that adequate allowance be made for meeting increased debt service and maintenance costs on the basis of several alternative and relatively conservative estimates of the behavior of future income, and (3) that capital and operating budgets be consolidated (with the capital budget converted to a rental costs basis), so that shifts can be made from one allocation to the other at the discretion of the board of trustees."

The costs of maintenance currently are being handled more realistically by many institutions, probably nudged along by the findings of several studies. For example, the Jenny and Wynn study (1970, p. 5) found "little if any evidence in the financial records of the forty-eight colleges suggesting either *how* these institutions will cope with the plant problem in particular or *that* they will be able to tackle the renovation and replacement problems when they arise."

Many colleges and universities, however, are still skirting the consequences of deferred maintenance. This is particularly true for private liberal arts colleges. Pressures for increases in faculty salaries as the highest institutional priority have been instrumental in postponing maintenance, and now the problem looms on a number of campuses. It is easier to take care of current demands for salaries and programs than to allocate dollars for upkeep, but delaying repairs increases the eventual costs geometrically rather than arithmetically—as some colleges are finding.

The National Commission on the Financing of Postsecondary Education (1973) looked into the financing and costs of physical plants. Although the building boom of the 1960s was over, the Commission found that because of inflated building costs, large sums of capital were still required for the declining volume of construction. The Commission sounded this warning about funding patterns for maintaining physical plants and equipment: "Colleges

Table 18. Physical Analysis Rating System

I. BUILDING DESCRIPTION

_____
Institution

_____
Building Name

Year of construction: _____
Year of latest renovation[a]: _____

Year of construction for each addition:
_____
_____
_____
_____

Gross area: _____
Assignable area: _____
Number of floors: Total _____
           Below ground only _____

Ownership:
_____ Fee simple
_____ Title held but payments being made
_____ Lease/purchase
_____ Leased or rented
_____ Other (shared or available at little or no cost)

Type of Construction: Designed to be relocated or demountable? _____ Yes _____ No

_____ Woodframe with exterior stud walls
_____ Woodframe with masonry walls
_____ Reinforced concrete (fireproof)
_____ Structural steel frame (fireproof)
_____ Other (identify)_____

Estimated 7/78 replacement cost: _____ $ per GSF $ _____
                       GSF times $ per GSF $ _____

II. PHYSICAL ANALYSIS

Institution _____

Building Name _____

Component	Satisfactory[b]	Deteriorating[c]	Unsatisfactory[d]	Estimated 77/78 Costs to Improve Deteriorating Condition[c]	Estimated 77/78 Costs to Improve Unsatisfactory Condition[d]	General Description of Problems and Proposed Repair/Improvement
Primary Structure						
Foundation	☐	☐	☐	$_____	$_____	_____
Exterior and bearing walls	☐	☐	☐	$_____	$_____	_____
						_____
Secondary Structure						
Roof	☐	☐	☐	$_____	$_____	_____
Windows	☐	☐	☐	$_____	$_____	_____
Partitions, ceiling, floors	☐	☐	☐	$_____	$_____	_____
						_____
Service Systems						
Ventilation/air-conditioning	☐	☐	☐	$_____	$_____	_____
Heating	☐	☐	☐	$_____	$_____	_____
Plumbing	☐	☐	☐	$_____	$_____	_____
Electrical	☐	☐	☐	$_____	$_____	_____
Fixed equipment and communications	☐	☐	☐	$_____	$_____	_____

[a] Renovation means an expenditure for remodeling or improvement of an existing structure equal to 25 percent or more of its then-current replacement value; renovation excludes new additions.

[b] Requires no repairs or improvements.

[c] Repairs, restoration, remodeling, or improvement required in the next six to ten years.

[d] Repairs, restoration, remodeling, or improvement required in the next six years.

Table 18. Physical Analysis Rating System (Continued)

II. PHYSICAL ANALYSIS

Institution _____

Building Name _____

Component	Satisfactory[b]	Deteriorating[c]	Unsatisfactory[d]	Estimated 77/78 Costs to Improve Deteriorating Condition[c]	Estimated 77/78 Costs to Improve Unsatisfactory Condition[d]	General Description of Problems and Proposed Repair/Improvement
User-Related Factors						
Building accessibility	☐	☐	☐	$ _____	$ _____	_____
Fire safety	☐	☐	☐	$ _____	$ _____	_____
Handicapped accessibility and accommodation	☐	☐	☐	$ _____	$ _____	_____
						_____
Efficiency Factors						
Source of energy for HVAC	☐	☐	☐	$ _____	$ _____	_____
Efficiency of HVAC systems	☐	☐	☐	$ _____	$ _____	_____
Lighting efficiency	☐	☐	☐	$ _____	$ _____	_____
Net/gross area ratio	☐	☐	☐	$ _____	$ _____	_____
Insulation of exterior surfaces	☐	☐	☐	$ _____	$ _____	_____
						_____
Site Factors						
Utility lines/extensions	☐	☐	☐	$ _____	$ _____	_____
Cost effectiveness of maintenance of building and site	☐	☐	☐	$ _____	$ _____	_____
						_____
TOTAL COST				$ _____	$ _____	_____
Cost as a Percentage of Replacement Cost				_____	_____	_____

III. BUILDING CONDITION

Institution _____

Description of building condition in terms of
    (a) the need and appropriateness of improvement,
    (b) the immediacy of the need, and
    (c) the relative cost of the improvement.

Building Name _____

____ 1.A   SATISFACTORY: The building is suitable for continued use with normal maintenance.

____ 1.B   Same as 1.A, but will require repair, remodeling, restoration, or improvement in the next six to ten years.

____ 1.C   Same as 1.A, but should be razed or removed from service in the next six to ten years.

____ 2.A   REMODELING A: During the next six years, the building requires repair, remodeling, restoration, or improvement costing less than 25 percent of building replacement cost.

____ 2.B   Same as 2.A, but will require additional repair, remodeling, restoration or improvement in the next six to ten years.

____ 2.C   Same as 2.A, but should be razed or removed from service in the next six to ten years.

____ 3.A   REMODELING B: During the next six years, the building requires repair, remodeling, restoration, or improvement costing 25-50 percent of building cost replacement.

____ 3.B   Same as 3.A, but will require additional repair, remodeling, restoration, or improvement in the next six to ten years.

____ 3.C   Same as 3.A, but should be razed or removed from service in the next six to ten years.

____ 4.A   REMODELING C: During the next six years, the building requires repair, remodeling, restoration, or improvement costing more than 50 percent of building replacement cost.

____ 4.B   Same as 4.A, but will require additional repair, remodeling, restoration, or improvement in the next six to ten years.

____ 4.C   Same as 4.A, but should be razed or removed from service in the next six to ten years.

____ 5.   DEMOLITION: During the next six years, the building should be razed because of its unsafe or unsound condition. (Takes precedence over 1, 2, 3, 4.)

____ 6.   TERMINATION: During the next six years, the building should be removed from service for reasons other than unsafe or unsound character. (Takes precedence over 1, 2, 3, 4.)

and universities normally do not include charges for depreciation of plant and equipment as a cost of current operations. Equipment replacement and renovations, if not funded out of current income, must be financed from outside sources. One consequence of this practice has been a perennial lack of capital to take care of major plant renovation and expensive equipment replacement. The absence of reserves for these purposes is a fundamental weakness in higher education finance and poses a serious long-range problem in all but the few institutions that do maintain depreciation reserves or are wealthy enough to have capital when they need it. [Table 19] shows the estimated annual addition to depreciation reserves that collegiate institutions should be accumulating just to pay for new plants and equipment" (pp. 212–213).

The cumulative effect of these annual increments represents a future capital requirement that has significance for long-range planning. A number of questions can be useful in evaluating the adequacy of that planning. For instance, are there institutional policies and procedures for developing and updating long-range plans for physical plant development and maintenance? Are these plans closely coordinated with the institution's overall long-term goals? Are the long-range needs for physical facilities and programs adequately communicated to all members of the academic community?

Table 19. **Estimated Capital Requirement for Additions to Plant and Equipment Resulting Only from Depreciation of New Assets Acquired in 1971–72 (in millions)**

Year	Total		Public		Private	
Approximate Depreciation Rate	*4.7%*	*2.7%*	*4.8%*	*2.4%*	*4.6%*	*2.3%*
1969–70	$197	$113	$137	$67	$57	$28
1970–71	198	115	146	71	42	26
1971–72	200	115	152	73	51	25

Note: Straight-line depreciation method. The smaller of the two annual estimates for depreciation in each case excludes new land.

Source: National Commission on the Financing of Postsecondary Education, 1973, p. 215.

23. **Are the salaries and other benefits for support personnel sufficient to attract and retain competent individuals?**

The foundation of an effective personnel program is the development and maintenance of a classification and compensation plan. The plan needs to be understandable and equitable, and it should include complete and current information on each position. And clear differentiation should be made between the job description in the classification plan and the qualifications of the individual currently in this position.

The salary and benefits package should be competitive with those received by employees in similar positions in the surrounding community. (There are exceptions related to specialized jobs, such as providing financial-aid assistance, that may not have counterparts in the community.) The current trend in union contracts, in the automotive industry, for instance, is to emphasize fringe benefits rather than salaries, and this direction can be expected in postsecondary education as well.

Griffin and Burks (1976, pp. 149–151) have developed these questions (guidelines) for use in appraising salary administration and staff benefits.

Salary Administration. Is the position-classification and salary-determination system clearly understood and usable? Is it perceived as fair and equitable and does it satisfy the needs of both line managers and employees? Is the system subject to reasonable and timely adjustments to meet changing conditions and operating requirements? Is there an effective merit pay program that is equitably administered? Are the results carefully monitored? Are requests for the reclassification of positions processed in a timely and equitable manner? Are individual reclassification actions evaluated in relation to other positions and the total staffing pattern for the organization unit involved? Is the salary-administration and position-classification system effectively coordinated with other phases of personnel work, such as recruitment and performance evaluation, to meet campus needs? Is there an operative program to assure compliance with the requirements of the Fair Labor Standards Act and related legislation and regulations?

Staff Benefits: Is information about employee benefit programs effectively communicated to employees in a timely manner?

Is the counseling staff that handles employee benefits large enough and sufficiently well informed to provide effective advisory services both to the departmental administrative staffs and to employees with special benefit problems? Is a systematic effort made, with significant advice from employees, to evaluate the adequacy and deficiencies of the staff-benefit program and to initiate changes in it for the consideration of campus management? Are adequate safeguards in effect to avoid abuse in connection with such staff-benefit programs as workmen's compensation, unemployment insurance, medical disability and sick and vacation leave?

Another type of benefit to be considered is providing opportunities for professional and personal growth to support personnel. Employee development, as a significant aspect of benefits, is receiving greater attention now, and additional emphasis can be expected in the future. This activity is consistent with the trend toward greater developmental opportunities for both faculty members and administrators. An institution of higher education, if it has not done so recently, should examine the developmental policies and procedures for its support staff. The "employee development" policy for the University of California at Berkeley (n.d.) might be useful in this respect:

> This policy encourages departments to work out the interested employees' mutually agreeable career development plans designed to increase their opportunity to serve the University. Where departmental budgets permit, they are authorized to provide financial support (both in terms of payment of course fees and time off with pay).
>
> Because of the wide variety of types of training which may benefit different employees, and because training programs rely to a considerable extent on support from departmental funds, departmental supervisors have the major responsibility for developing comprehensive development programs with each interested employee.
>
> The concurrence of the Personnel Manager in authorizing time off with pay to attend *work-related courses* requires the review of a formalized employee development plan, one which has been jointly developed by the department and the employee.
>
> 1. A basic criterion for acceptability is that the plan clearly states the career objectives to be achieved and relates

them to upgrading skills for the person's present job, and for future advancement within the University.

2. The development plan should include courses or other types of education to be taken to achieve the objective, specified as to title, content, relationship to the developmental objective, and the school at which to be taken. Additional related special work assignments or other on-the-job training, if any, that are part of a career development objective should also be specified.

3. Note that there is no definition of "other educational sources." Purposefully, this definition is left to departmental discretion, as long as it is "work-related." Thus, a speed-reading course could well be appropriate for one individual and not for another; a specialized correspondence course might be the only appropriate educational course available in a technician's area, etc.

4. Where approval is desired to take only one course for one quarter in one academic year, no development plan is required. Send a note to your departmental Personnel Representative giving the employee's name, job title, course title, educational institution where the course will be taken, relationship of the course to present or future University work, and amount of time off with pay required.

5. Affirmative action programs may require a combination of on-the-job training, work, and more than six hours per week course attendance. For approval of the latter, direct requests with specific details to the Special Training Coordinator, Personnel Office, who will be responsible for obtaining the Chancellor's review.

It is the department chairman's responsibility to determine whether all, part, or none of the fees will be paid by the department. Factors entering into such a determination include departmental finances, the relevance of the course content to the development plan, the size of the course fee, and the availability of other sources of similar course content at lower cost or during nonworking hours.

Reimbursement is made *after* the course has been concluded, since written proof of acceptable course completion is required. Acceptable course completion is (a) C grade or better in a "grade course," (b) pass grade in a pass/fail grading course, (c) satisfactory grade in a satisfactory/unsatisfactory grading course.

Books and other course-related materials are not subject to reimbursement, unless the cost is included in the fee.

Employees are reimbursed for fees for educational purposes in accordance with Staff Personnel Policy 260, by entering the following on a Form 5:
"Reimbursement for course fees (receipt attached) for the following course:
          (Description)   (Amount)
In accordance with Staff Personnel Policy 260.3, I certify that this course is related to the employee's work, and written proof of acceptable completion has been submitted.

Department Chairman (or comparable Administrative Officer)"
          The Personnel Office Training Section functions to provide internal training programs requested by departments which have substantial value for numbers of employees and which do not duplicate courses otherwise available; for example, supervisory techniques, budget work sessions, and refresher shorthand. In addition, it provides current information on pertinent non-University educational opportunities, stimulates programs of individual employee development, and is available to departments for counseling and assistance in the training area. The Special Training Coordinator in the Personnel Office has the prime responsibility for establishing with departmental cooperation special preemployment and on-the-job training programs as part of the campus' affirmative action program.
          The work of the University staff is a reflection of the competency of its supervision. The Personnel Training section has available a series of training programs especially designed for new supervisors. We strongly urge that department chairmen insist that their supervisors participate in them. While operational skills are taught, the emphasis is on training for effective supervision.
          This section of the rule emphasizes the continuing need for periodic goal-centered work appraisals, as called for in Staff Personnel Policy 255—Reviewing Employee Performance. Consult the department Personnel Representative for information on techniques and forms.
          Time spent outside regular working hours by an employee at a conference or in an educational program is

not counted as hours worked unless the employee is required to attend.

A determination of whether participation in associations outside regular working hours is considered to be
hours worked is to be made by the cognizant dean or vice-
chancellor. Normally, such work should be considered as
voluntary and not reimbursable.

The Personnel Office will prepare such reports as
are required, requesting a minimum of information from
departments.

Summary. Employee development is one of management's primary responsibilities. Within departmental plans
and programs individual supervisors have certain responsibilities which include (a) Establishment of identifiable
career ladders within their departments. (b) Assignment of
training situations—either training positions or cross-
training opportunities for employees from other departments. (c) Granting of release time to employees for classes
and other educational opportunities. This is especially
necessary in departments where intradepartmental opportunities are limited. (d) Preparation of career plans for
employees. Individual employees must show initiative, but
equally managers must provide an atmosphere which encourages employees to think in terms of their potential. (e)
Promotion of employees on the basis of (natural) talent
rather than just prior education and experience.

A number of questions can be used as guidelines for evaluating whether salaries and other benefits are adequate. For example,
have salaries and benefits been analyzed recently? Do support personnel have enough opportunities to comment on or participate in
the process? Have employee-development possibilities for support
personnel been reviewed recently? Does the development plan reflect a balanced concern for the needs of the units, the employees'
interests, the legal ramifications, institutional policies, and the
necessary human and material resources, including costs?

24. **Are systematic procedures used for evaluating the perfor-
    mance of support personnel?**

As appraisals of faculty members and administrators have
increased greatly in the past few years, so have evaluations of the
support staff. Many larger colleges and universities have been as-

sessing these employees for a number of years, and the current upswing of interest has caused them to analyze and update their policies and procedures. Many other institutions recently have entered this arena for the first time.

The performance appraisal should develop mutual understanding, help people improve, and let people know where they stand. In essence, evaluations of support personnel should analyze productivity, prepare personnel for changes in position, justify pay increases, provide feedback for organizational change, contribute positively to achievement motivation, and discover new employee talents. The overall goal, as I said earlier, should be to improve performance as well as evaluate it. The following six approaches to assessing support personnel, including their advantages and disadvantages, are adapted from Mali (n.d., pp. 2–5).

Trait appraisal (graphic rating scale). The most widely used performance evaluation technique is the trait appraisal. The evaluator (supervisor) is presented with a series of traits or work-related characteristics and asked to rate employees on each trait or characteristic shown. Examples of traits are the quantity of work, the quality of work, cooperation, dependability, initiative, leadership and personality. The advantages of this technique are that it (1) is simple, easy, and uncomplicated; (2) reaches for human qualities we know are important in getting results, and (3) recognizes that all organizations where people are banded together are social organizations requiring certain characteristics to make them work. It also has these drawbacks: (1) Supervisors are reluctant to label deficiencies and make criticisms without foolproof evidence. (2) It is unilateral; the employee is not involved. (3) The evaluator tends to remember recent or negative incidents. And (4) the meanings and definitions of the traits are difficult to arrive at.

Critical-incident appraisal. This technique, which is not used very often, requires the evaluator to write an essay or report describing important experiences or incidents, positive and negative, involving the employee. The incidents are recorded in a log of some type, often daily, so that they are not forgotten. For example, if an employee has a disastrous experience with a client and hostility was exchanged, the superior records the incident. This approach has these advantages: (1) Compared to the trait appraisal, it is more closely related to the job's elements. (2) It records work incidents that would otherwise not be known about in detail. And (3) it overcomes a partial remembering and the tendency to recall the latest incident. The disadvantages are that the log tends to have a judgmental, "police" quality, and the log writer commonly identifies more negatives than positives. In addition, the employee usually is not involved in this appraisal method either.

Standards-of-performance appraisal. Many organizations are showing great interest in this technique, which requires a series of descriptive and quantitative statements that represent standards of performance. For example, a standard for a supervisor might be this: The amount of overtime is equal to not more than 4 percent of scheduled hours. This technique is advantageous in that it is very directly related to the requirements of the job; it specifies the level and consistency of effort necessary for effectiveness; and it keeps subjective judgments to a minimum. On the negative side, the employee once again is allowed little or no participation in setting the standards or making the evaluation. Second, not all important aspects of performance can be quantified. And third, the technique can only be used where work does not change frequently.

Process-standards evaluation. This approach is gaining in appeal because of the "due process" requirements of laws governing civil and individual rights. The method is based on a series of descriptive and quantitative statements that represent standards of effective behavior on the job. Unlike the standards of performance described earlier, process standards have to do with the behavior of the person rather than the quality of his work and the resources of the job. Absenteeism, tardiness, alcoholism, violation of rules concerning such activities as coffee breaks, accidents, failure to observe safety precautions, and insubordination are examples of the kinds of behavior that are treated in these standards. This technique has these pluses: it helps to control behavior, such as being on time and following rules, that must be managed if the job is to get done. It specifies the behavior that will lead to effective performance. And it provides information and data that are critically needed for "due process" procedures. The minuses are that human behavior is too broad to be described in terms of levels of effectiveness, that not all behavior can be externally controlled, and that skillful workers can have terrible behavior patterns.

Appraisal based on a management-by-objectives approach. This means of evaluation is increasingly attractive to organizations because of their need to be accountable for their use of resources and to motivate people to achieve certain results. The method requires the supervisor and subordinate to sit down during a planning period and agree on the objectives to be reached during the operating time. At the end of this period, they again sit down and evaluate the results achieved. An example of an objective is to reduce costs during the current operating year by 24 percent of the approved budget, at a rate of 6 percent per quarter. This approach has the advantage of being future oriented; it does not have to follow past practices. In addition it is not passive or unilateral, since it involves both supervisor and subordinate. And thus the evaluator becomes more like a counselor than a policeman or judge. This technique is also closely connected to the results needed and expected by the organization. And when used properly, it will motivate staff members. Its disadvantages are that the targeted results can be influenced and changed by so many uncontrollable factors; it ignores personal traits, activities, and work habits that are deemed important; and under such a system, linking pay to performance is difficult.

Eclectic appraisal. What is probably the most effective method for most organizations is to select elements from a number of evaluative techniques and fit them to the purposes and needs of the situation. A careful definition of what the appraisal is expected to accomplish obviously should precede the selection of appropriate elements. The advantages of an eclectic approach are that it does not slavishly follow preconceived ideas and methods; it tailors evaluation to an already tailored situation; and it handles effectively purposes that are many and complex. But it can only be used by people who are competent and skillful, and it makes comparisons between and among groups more difficult. A further disadvantage is that it may require a systems approach in which the entire organization participates.

Most systems for evaluating support personnel in colleges and universities use either trait appraisals or eclectic approaches. But the system itself probably is not as important as the procedures used to administer it, or the ways in which the results are used. An example of a thorough system is depicted in Figure 2.

The University of Illinois at Urbana-Champaign has developed two forms for employee appraisal: one for nonsupervisory personnel and another for professional, supervisory, or administrative personnel (Tables 20 and 21). The following general instructions are printed on the back of each form:

Purpose of Program. It is the aim of the Performance Appraisal Program to encourage and facilitate the efforts of all staff members to grow professionally and to reach their full potential in their work. Using actual job performance as a basis for discussion, the program provides supervisors and employees with an opportunity to identify performance goals and developmental needs on a mutual basis. In addition, the program supplies a means of defining work objectives and the most appropriate courses of action to pursue in order to increase competency, improve performance, and attain career aspirations.

Method of review. The immediate supervisor has the basic responsibility for the provision of information and guidance through periodic performance reviews. This review, which utilizes the Performance Appraisal Form, calls for an exchange of comments and ideas related to the employee's current job performance. To be constructive, the performance review ought to include, as a minimum, a discussion between the rater and the employee regarding (1) what is expected of the employee, (2) the supervisor's evaluation of performance, and (3) corrective or developmental activities called for by the review. The employee may comment on the results of the review and must acknowledge that the review has been read and discussed by signing the form. The employee should, in turn, receive a copy of the review.

When to review. Supervisors should complete all applicable factors for each employee and meet with the employee to discuss performance work objectives and actions to be taken to meet performance and developmental needs and goals at the following times: the four-month

Figure 2. Employee Performance Appraisal Flow Chart

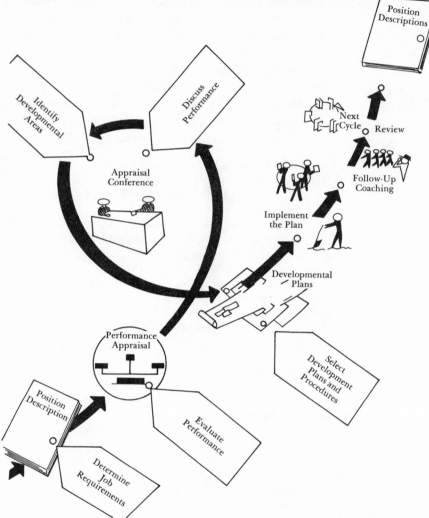

Source: University of Illinois at Urbana-Champaign (n.d.).

Table 20. Appraisal Form for Nonsupervisory Personnel

NAME _____ DEPARTMENT _____ DATE _____
CLASSIFICATION _____ TIME IN CLASS _____ TOTAL YEARS EMPLOYED _____
TYPE OF REVIEW: ☐ PROBATIONARY ☐ ANNUAL ☐ OTHER: LEARNER-TRAINEE-APPRENTICE

A. JOB DUTIES AND RESPONSIBILITIES: Describe the *key* duties and responsibilities.

_____

_____

_____

B. ACCOMPLISHMENT: Please use the space provided to clarify the rating given as well as list any mutual goals which were established.

1. JOB KNOWLEDGE: Consider knowledge of the information, procedures, materials, equipment, techniques, etc., required for current job.

☐ Exceeds Requirements COMMENTS/GOALS _____
☐ Meets Requirements _____
☐ Needs Improvement _____

2. QUALITY OF ACCOMPLISHMENTS: Rate the *accuracy* and *completeness* of work.

☐ Exceeds Requirements COMMENTS/GOALS _____
☐ Meets Requirements _____
☐ Needs Improvement _____

3. PRODUCTIVITY: Rate the *volume* and *timeliness* of work.

☐ Exceeds Requirements COMMENTS/GOALS _____
☐ Meets Requirements _____
☐ Needs Improvement _____

Table 20. Appraisal Form for Nonsupervisory Personnel (Continued)

4. RESPONSIBILITY: Consider efforts to ensure the successful completion of tasks, the leading of others in various tasks, *extra efforts* made to meet work demands, general assistance and dependability.

Exceeds Requirements   COMMENTS/GOALS _____

☐ Exceeds Requirements
☐ Meets Requirements
☐ Needs Improvement

5. INITIATIVE: Consider attempts to improve unit operations, appropriate use of work time, amount of direction required, and assistance offered to accomplish tasks more efficiently.

Exceeds Requirements   COMMENTS/GOALS _____

☐ Exceeds Requirements
☐ Meets Requirements
☐ Needs Improvement

6. INTERPERSONAL RELATIONS: Consider relationships with other employees, students and faculty, and willingness to perform required duties and to help others accomplish tasks.

Exceeds Requirements   COMMENTS/GOALS _____

☐ Exceeds Requirements
☐ Meets Requirements
☐ Needs Improvement

7. ATTENDANCE: Consider punctuality and attendance.
   COMMENTS/GOALS _____

☐ Satisfactory
☐ Unsatisfactory

8. ADDITIONAL AREA(S) RELATED TO JOB PERFORMANCE:

_____
_____
_____

C. OVERALL EVALUATION OF PERFORMANCE:

COMMENTS/GOALS

☐ Exceeds Requirements
☐ Meets Requirements
☐ Needs Improvement

D. CHANGE DEMONSTRATED SINCE LAST APPRAISAL:

E. GROWTH AND DEVELOPMENT:

Possible activities which employee could utilize to increase present job effectiveness or to prepare for promotion. Consider (1) possible self-development activities, (2) areas which the supervisor and employee could work on together, and (3) development needs which can be met by training programs. (please specify)

F. EMPLOYEE COMMENTS:

G. FOLLOW-UP ACTIONS: (Actions suggested and/or taken by immediate supervisor, next level supervisor, and/or unit head)

EMPLOYEE'S SIGNATURE _____ DATE _____

SUPERVISOR'S SIGNATURE _____

NEXT LEVEL SUPERVISOR'S SIGNATURE _____

Table 21. Appraisal Form for Supervisory Personnel

NAME _____ DEPARTMENT _____ DATE _____
CLASSIFICATION _____ TIME IN CLASS _____ TOTAL YEARS EMPLOYED _____
TYPE OF REVIEW: ☐ PROBATIONARY ☐ ANNUAL ☐ OTHER: LEARNER - TRAINEE - APPRENTICE

A. JOB DUTIES AND RESPONSIBILITIES: Describe the *key* duties and responsibilities.

_____

_____

_____

B. ACCOMPLISHMENT: (To maximize the clarity and benefit of the evaluation, please use the "Comments" area to
indicate the considerations which influenced your rating)

1. JOB KNOWLEDGE: Consider knowledge of the information, procedures, materials, equipment, techniques, etc.,
required for current job.

☐ Superior   COMMENTS: _____
☐ Exceeds Requirements
☐ Meets Requirements   _____
☐ Needs Improvement   _____
☐ Unsatisfactory   _____
☐ Not Applicable   _____

2. QUALITY OF ACCOMPLISHMENTS: Rate the *accuracy* and *completeness* of work.

☐ Superior   COMMENTS: _____
☐ Exceeds Requirements
☐ Meets Requirements   _____
☐ Needs Improvement   _____
☐ Unsatisfactory   _____
☐ Not Applicable   _____

3. PRODUCTIVITY: Rate the *volume* and *timeliness* of work.

☐ Superior
☐ Exceeds Requirements   COMMENTS: _____
☐ Meets Requirements   _____
☐ Needs Improvement   _____
☐ Unsatisfactory   _____
☐ Not Applicable   _____

4. ORGANIZATION: Consider areas such as setting objectives, anticipating requirements, establishing priorities, developing efficient methods, utilizing available resources and the like.

☐ Superior
☐ Exceeds Requirements   COMMENTS: _____
☐ Meets Requirements   _____
☐ Needs Improvement   _____
☐ Unsatisfactory   _____
☐ Not Applicable   _____

5. INTERPERSONAL RELATIONS: Consider relationships with other employees, students and faculty, etc., and willingness to help others accomplish tasks.

☐ Superior
☐ Exceeds Requirements   COMMENTS: _____
☐ Meets Requirements   _____
☐ Needs Improvement   _____
☐ Unsatisfactory   _____
☐ Not Applicable   _____

6. ADDITIONAL AREA(S) RELATED TO JOB PERFORMANCE:

☐ Superior
☐ Exceeds Requirements   COMMENTS: _____
☐ Meets Requirements   _____
☐ Needs Improvement   _____
☐ Unsatisfactory   _____
☐ Not Applicable   _____

Table 21. Appraisal Form for Supervisory Personnel (Continued)

SUPERVISORY DUTIES AND RESPONSIBILITIES:

7. LEADERSHIP: Setting standards, encouraging productive and efficient performances, etc.

COMMENTS: _____

- ☐ Superior
- ☐ Exceeds Requirements
- ☐ Meets Requirements
- ☐ Needs Improvement
- ☐ Unsatisfactory
- ☐ Not Applicable

8. COORDINATION/DELEGATION: Consider utilization of resources and distribution of work.

COMMENTS: _____

- ☐ Superior
- ☐ Exceeds Requirements
- ☐ Meets Requirements
- ☐ Needs Improvement
- ☐ Unsatisfactory
- ☐ Not Applicable

9. TRAINING AND DEVELOPMENT OF SUBORDINATES: Rate aspects, such as providing information regarding work objectives and responsibilities, giving clear task instruction, providing developmental resources and offering guidance.

COMMENTS: _____

- ☐ Superior
- ☐ Exceeds Requirements
- ☐ Meets Requirements
- ☐ Needs Improvement
- ☐ Unsatisfactory
- ☐ Not Applicable

C. OVERALL EVALUATION OF PERFORMANCE:

COMMENTS: _____

- ☐ Superior
- ☐ Exceeds Requirements
- ☐ Meets Requirements
- ☐ Needs Improvement
- ☐ Unsatisfactory

D. CHANGE DEMONSTRATED SINCE LAST APPRAISAL:

E. GROWTH AND
DEVELOPMENT:

Possible activities which employee could utilize to increase present job effectiveness or to prepare for promotion. Consider (1) possible self-development activities (2) areas which the supervisor and employee could work on together, and (3)
development needs which can be met by training programs. (please specify)

F. EMPLOYEE COMMENTS:

G. FOLLOW-UP ACTIONS: (Actions suggested and/or taken by immediate supervisor, next level supervisor, and/or
unit head)

EMPLOYEE'S SIGNATURE _____   DATE _____
SUPERVISOR'S SIGNATURE _____
NEXT LEVEL SUPERVISOR'S SIGNATURE _____

point in the probationary period, and the anniversary of the employment date in the current classification.

What to do with appraisal form. After appraisals have been completed by the immediate supervisor and approved by the next level of supervision, the appraisal must be discussed with the employee, and a copy must be given to the employee. The employer's copy should be retained by the immediate supervisor for appropriate follow-up action. The Performance Appraisal Notification Card must be completed and returned as stipulated in order to indicate that the appraisal has been conducted.

Although complete appraisals are made at the time periods previously listed, the form should be treated as a working document and used for continual coaching, assessment, or performance and redefinition of developmental objectives. It is suggested further that informal appraisal sessions be held between anniversary dates to ensure accurate and timely evaluations of employee performance and development needs in view of the changing job situation and assignments.

A number of questions can be used to assist in judging the effectiveness of evaluation procedures, such as: Are support personnel formally evaluated by some criteria that are known and understood by them? Does the overall process include an employee-employer conference on the results of the appraisal? Is professional and personal development an integral part of the appraisal system? Is an assessment of results (productivity) an essential component also? And are sufficient human and material resources provided for an effective appraisal system?

Institutional-support personnel are important members of the academic community, although their contributions have not always been given adequate recognition. Carefully developed policies and procedures for college personnel are an essential *floor,* and periodic review of these statements should be undertaken. But adequate recognition involves more than policies and procedures—it means acknowledging the spirit of cooperation and the high-quality performance that characterize a significant majority of the support personnel. The chief administrative officer must set the tone and style of this recognition and do what is needed to see that others follow his or her example.

7

Judging
Administrative
Leadership and
Accomplishment

The literature on chief adminis-
trative officers in recent years has pictured them as victims of circumstances that are beyond their control and often their understanding. In a multicampus system, the chief campus administrator
is represented as being at the beck and call of the system's president. Cohen and March (1974, pp. 2–3) describe the university and
the presidency in this manner: "decision making in the university
seems to result extensively from a process that decouples problems
and choices and makes the president's role more commonly

sporadic and symbolic than significant. Compared to the heroic expectations he and others might have, the president has modest control over the events of college life. The contributions he makes can easily be swamped by outside events or the diffuse qualities of university decision making. . . . The American college or university is a prototype organized anarchy. It does not know what it is doing. Its goals are either vague or in dispute. Its technology is familiar but not understood. Its major participants wander in and out of the organization."

The role of the chief administrative officer has changed, is changing, and will change, but there are some aspects of the position that can be expected to remain relatively stable. They cluster around words such as *initiative, planning, budget, appointment, information, conflict, resolution,* and *evaluation.*

The next five or ten years will call increasingly for chief administrative officers who are effective, tenacious administrators and managers of resources and people, unlike the presidents described in the Cohen and March findings. On leadership tasks in the years ahead, Cheit (1973a, p. 33) concludes that academic leaders must "demonstrate, perhaps even in the style of the strong administrator of the pregrowth era, what it is that institutions of higher education should be doing. . . . What is needed is a renewed sense that academic men and women are willing and able to assert a large measure of control over the course of educational events." In a similar vein, Boulding (1975) has written: "One of education's first priorities . . . should be to develop a new generation of academic administrators who are skilled in the process of adjusting to decline. . . . The skills of managing a declining institution are not only different from but are probably in some sense greater than those required to manage institutional growth. There is in the former greater need for empathy and for an all too rare mixture of compassion and realism, and for the creative widening of agendas. The manager of a declining institution is required to think of more things that haven't been thought of" (pp. 5, 8).

What is the case for a dynamic leadership style? Simply stated, the times and needs favor it. The centralization of power becomes more evident when times are hard or crises arise. This is true in national affairs—particularly during wars and depressions—as well as in collegiate affairs. Current societal forces and trends are pushing multicampus and state-level systems toward greater centralization and hence a more active role for the chief administrative official. But this tendency needs to be watched carefully. Excessive centralization can lead to slower and poorer communication, inefficiency, inadequate understanding of the positions of others, distrust, and poor morale.

The difficult and sensitive nature of the major decisions that need to be made favors dynamic leadership. The retrenchment and reallocation of personnel and the increasing competition for fiscal resources require strong administrators. Faculty groups should not be expected to make difficult decisions about cutbacks or rearranging priorities, although some representative faculty group should be involved in the process.

The complexity argument that has been used by those who see the chief administrator caught in a trap with little real power can be used also by those advocating a dynamic leadership role. Because colleges and universities have indeed become complicated, someone needs to be in charge and to be perceived as such. Chief administrators may have real discretionary power over only a relatively small percentage of the budget, but they can use these funds in a catalytic manner that magnifies their influence considerably beyond the actual dollars involved. Furthermore, amid the complexity, the top campus executive has access to knowledge—and knowledge is influence and power. If this person is cognizant of this fact, he or she can have a significant influence by being able to gather, mobilize, and use knowledge to make better decisions about all facets of the operation. The "knowledge is power" argument is simple, yet according to Bogard (1972, p. 25), "the suspicion remains that many administrators are satisfied with the information received for the simple reason that they are not aware of the need for more, being content instead to deal with the day-to-day problems as they arise on the basis of personal judgment."

What are some components of dynamic administrative leadership? One, as I've just said, is the competent management of information. Another key is control and effective use of the budget. We cannot conclude that an economist with administrative experience would be an ideal choice, but college administrators do need to be fully knowledgeable about the budget and to search constantly for ways to maximize its impact and economize on expenditures—asking at least two questions, according to Meeth (1974, p. 97): "What is the point in cost below which a college cannot go without decreasing effectiveness?" and "What is the point in cost above which quality is no longer improved?"

A third component is the administrator's power of initiative, which allows the establishment of task forces, study committees, evaluation studies, and planning efforts. When used discreetly and wisely, this power can contribute significantly to dynamic leadership.

The power of appointment can also provide leverage. The chief administrative official should set a tone and level of expectation for all faculty appointments, and he or she should be the final selector of deans, vice presidents, and other senior administrators. The top executive should establish "search and screen" committees for these posts, providing appropriate representation, and also find ways of keeping in touch with the committees during their deliberations.

The chief administrative official is the final court for many conflicts. He or she is expected to make choices among almost equally plausible alternatives and sometimes when more may be lost than gained. Conflict resolution is a perennial responsibility of top management, and today only the stakes have changed—they are higher. Hard decisions formerly meant that a building or a program might be delayed; today and tomorrow they may mean the phasing out of programs and people. Accordingly, the chief administrator needs as much information as possible and as much shared wisdom as he can gain through members of his administrative team and others.

Understanding the differences between influence and power is another crucial element in administrative leadership. In the academic caldron of conflicting and murky purposes and interests, where explicit policies and procedures may not exist, the use of influence may carry the day. Power is like money in the bank: The more of it you use, the less you have. Influence comes about largely through persuasion and effective argumentation. Much of an effective chief administrator's perceived power is really influence. Those who are persuaded by him and by members of his team are not compelled to oblige, but they do so because of their respect for the individuals involved, the array of information brought to bear, and other rational and some not-so-rational reasons. The use of influence may seem inappropriate in some situations where collective bargaining has placed faculty members and administrators in hard adversary positions, yet even here one can find examples where influence is the critical element.

Another component of administrative leadership is a certain toughness (not meanness). A perceptive description of this element was written by Douglas McGregor—an early leader in management. Writing after he had served as president of Antioch College, he concluded (1966, pp. 67–68):

> Before coming to Antioch I had observed and worked with top executives as an adviser in a number of organizations. I thought I knew how they felt about their responsibilities and what led them to behave as they did. I even thought that I could create a role for myself that would enable me to avoid some of the difficulties they encountered. I was wrong! I took the direct experience of becoming a line executive, and meeting personally the problems involved, to teach me what no amount of observation of other people could have taught.
>
> I believed, for example, that a leader could operate successfully as a kind of adviser to his organization. I thought I could avoid being a "boss." Unconsciously, I suspect, I hoped to duck the unpleasant necessity of making difficult decisions, or taking the responsibility for one course of action among many uncertain alternatives, or making mistakes and taking the consequences. I thought that maybe I could operate so that everyone would like me—that "good human relations" would eliminate all discord and disagreement.
>
> I could not have been more wrong. It took a couple of years, but I finally began to realize that a leader cannot avoid the exercise of authority any more than he can avoid responsibility for what happens to his organization. In fact, it is a major function of the top executive to take on his own shoulders the responsibility for resolving the uncertainties that are always involved in important decisions. Moreover, since no important decision every pleases everyone in the

organization, he must also absorb the displeasure, and sometimes severe hostility, of those who would have taken a different course.

A colleague recently summed up what my experience has taught me in these words: A good leader must be tough enough to win a fight, but not tough enough to kick a man when he is down. This notion is not in the least inconsistent with humane, democratic leadership. Good human relations develop out of strength, not of weakness.

Now that I have given some components of effective leadership, let us look at some criteria that may be useful in appraising it.

25. Does the administration give adequate attention to planning?

The Davis and Batchelor study (1974, pp. 32–36) reports on the opinions about planning expressed by 186 presidents and 1,495 trustees representing seven types of institutions. When asked whether their institution had a long-range plan, 85 percent of the trustees and 80 percent of the presidents answered yes. These respondents were then asked how they were principally involved in the development of the plan: by formulating and deciding on it, by advising on and reviewing it, or by approving and confirming the plan. Table 22 summarizes their replies.

The very meager presidential participation in "formulating and deciding" (7 percent) is surprising; and the trustee participation (19 percent) is somewhat lower than might be expected. It would seem that the small amount of involvement in the first phase would make subsequent influence more difficult. Not only that, early and fairly extensive participation in planning by the chief campus executive seems to be an ingredient in effective management, if one judges by the successful accountability models that have been reviewed for this book.

Inasmuch as the chief administrator has final responsibility for all aspects of the institution's operation, he or she must be thinking and planning ahead; otherwise the effort will flounder or others at the system or state level will take it on themselves to provide greater "assistance." Systematic and sustained planning is not easy. Meeth (1974) writes that "this abhorrence of looking ahead seems to be rooted in our traditions," (p. 3) and Palola and others (1971) found that faculty members do not consider planning

Table 22. Percentages of Presidents and Trustees Reporting Different Modes of Involvement in Formulation of Long-Range Plans

Mode of Involvement	Comm. Coll.		State Coll.		Public Univ.		Private J. Coll.		Private Liberal Arts		Private Univ.		Black Institutions		Total	
	Pres.	Trust.	Pres.	Trust.	Pres.	Trust.	Pres.	Trust.	Pres.	Trust.	Pres.	Trust.	Pres.	Trust.	Pres.	Trust.
Formulating; deciding	3%	14%	6%	10%	0%	7%	27%	24%	9%	26%	0%	17%	15%	23%	7%	19%
Advising; reviewing	38	46	50	50	40	47	27	46	54	39	62	48	54	52	47	45
Approving; confirming	59	41	44	39	60	45	46	30	37	35	38	35	31	25	46	35

as a legitimate part of the faculty role. Busy chief administrative officers place urgent matters first and planning is often pushed back on the list of priorities until embarrassment or other pressures bring it to the front. Most are doers not planners and therefore planning takes an extra effort (pp. 587–602).

There are many models for planning, most of which were developed in industry, then adapted by higher education. Most models include goals and objectives, human and material resources for moving toward desired ends, strategies for implementation, timing, unpredictable and uncontrollable variables, and evaluation.

The chief administrative officer needs to consider these factors when planning, and also ask, When is planning counterproductive? How and when should the results of planning be used? Some colleges and universities have studied what might happen to them in the next five years, but they have not followed the logical implications of their findings because of concern about faculty and staff morale and also because they have reasonable doubts about whether the predictions will come true. If they made plans on the basis of their studies, they would have to make significant personnel reductions. But such plans might not be needed, because who knows what federal or state actions might be introduced in the future to ameliorate circumstances? And perhaps an all-out internal effort could reverse the apparent trend toward retrenchment.

Planning also can get in the way of spontaneity and creativity. The planned societies in the Communist world have brought social and educational benefits to many of their people who have not enjoyed even minimum benefits in the past, but the excesses of their planning have developed large and unwieldy bureaucracies that can stifle initiative and flexibility. In Soviet society, the role of the "fixer" (tolkach)—the go-between who finds ways of securing needed materials for industrial plants—constitutes an unofficial but tacit recognition of the bureaucratic results. As the flexible element in a clumsy and centrally planned economy, this operator is quite helpful to production.

In our society, overplanning can also take place, although, generally speaking, more rather than less planning is needed on individual campuses, although a few institutions and some state systems have made such a fetish of planning that it has become an end rather than a means.

In assessing the adequacy of the administration's attention to planning, the evaluator might keep in mind Sturner's nine principles (1974, pp. 3–8):

- Planning involves deliberately designing actions that will lead to one's goals and objectives.
- It also involves a systems approach, an attempt to understand and a perspective that affects the whole institution.
- Planning is dependent on people working together collaboratively.
- It requires wide participation.
- Planning must deal with and overcome "social habit," that "kind of inertia which requires a sufficient input of energy before movement can take place."
- An organization is not easy to change, nor is it easy to plot or quantify the changes while they are in process.
- Uncertainty and ambiguity are a way of life in the planning process.
- Planning is concerned with creating realistic images of the future.
- Planning is fundamentally an approach to management; it is a process by which one learns about one's organization and slowly but continually plans and implements actions to bring about the images desired.

26. **Do the chief campus administrator and his team have effective working relationships with other campus administrators?**

One factor that can have a significant influence on the effectiveness of these relationships is whether or not the top administrator can choose the people he will work with. The power to appoint and remove key administrative officials is one the chief campus executive should not relinquish. One president of a New York City college considered this his most undiluted power, a prerogative that he was not ready to give up. Members of search committees for deans, vice presidents, provosts, and other administrators need to understand their advisory role from the beginning, and most do. But inadvertent changes in their perceptions of their role are not uncommon as they plow through many applicant files, often spending hundreds of hours and considerable institutional money. The chief administrator should anticipate this possibility and keep tabs on their endeavors.

New chief administrators may have some difficulties with respect to deans of schools or colleges within the institution. They can appoint persons with compatible views if they choose to rotate current ones out of office or to use some other procedure for changing those with contrary views or chemistries. But some deans have developed their own power bases, and they can impede progress and sometimes create serious problems. One approach to changing the guard was suggested by Bennis (1973, p. 82): "As soon as a new president takes office, all incumbent top administrative officials should automatically turn in their resignation," thereby giving the top executive the option of appointing more compatible ones. Later in the same book, however, in generalizing about change in a university, Bennis writes: "Build support among like-minded people, whether or not you recruited them" (p. 138) and "Know the territory" (p. 142). The possible contradictions among these passages suggest some ambivalence on the matter. Generally a "know your territory" perspective would counsel against asking for early resignations.

Part of effective working relationships is working with the chairpersons and directors of special programs. To assist in identifying what might be considered successful units, one can turn to the findings of the Council on Program Evaluation (COPE) program about top-rated academic programs at the University of Illinois at Urbana. Further information on strong departments is provided by Richman and Farmer (1974, p. 248) who present the following characteristics:

> [The strongest departments] best meet the market test and satisfy the priorities, needs, and interest of those who provide the funds, of the community, and of broader society. They have the strongest external supporters, and quite possibly also the strongest supporters among the key board members. They are in the best positions to contribute to achievement of the university's goals and priorities, as well as to achieve their own. They are in a position to obtain, on their own, sizable amounts of financial support, including contributions from private organizations and individuals, research grants, and revenues from special programs. Enough jobs are available for their graduates, and most

graduates get relatively good jobs and move ahead rapidly
in their careers. . . . The external visibility and reputation of
the faculty is relatively high. [These departments] can readily redeploy faculty resources to meet changing needs and
demands for new programs, courses, research projects, and
the like. Management by objectives and performance evaluation can be applied more easily than in other faculties.
They are or could be relatively self-sufficient with regard to
various academic programs and support services.

(See also McHenry and Associates, 1977, for a discussion of departmental problems.)

In examining the effectiveness of administrators' working relationships, the evaluator might look for answers to these
questions:

1. Does the institution or the system have clearly understood procedures for the selection, retention, and termination of administrators?
2. Do the communication networks among the chief campus administrator and his key administrators serve their intended
purposes?
3. Do the networks and procedures established for communication
between the chief administrative officer and his staff and other
campus administrators serve their purposes?
4. Have the chief campus administrator and his staff created an
esprit de corps among campus administrators? Current fiscal
realities do create morale problems, but a positive group spirit is
still possible.
5. Do the appropriate administrators and others work with chairpersons in improving departmental management? For instance,
have workshops been conducted on programs, budget, personnel, and institutional policies and procedures?

27. **Do institutional governance policies and procedures allow
for effective institutional management?**

The concept of collegiality and shared authority is relatively
new, going back to around the turn of the twentieth century. The
shift by faculty members and students from subservience to participation in governance was encouraged by the Germanic model of
a research university as well as by the knowledge needs of new

sciences and technologies. Less than ten years ago the literature on governance spoke almost exclusively about faculty participation in governance; now, much literature focuses on collective bargaining—and few developments in higher education have caused "as much consternation, anxiety, and frantic activity" (Schuster, 1974).

Some erroneous views exist about what happens when power is shared, as Haire (1969, p. 36) points out in his analysis of Likert's research on leadership: "it is clear that if the leader gives his subordinates the opportunity to influence him, if he gives them some power, he does not lose power thereby. This is a thing, at least in industrial organizations, that always bothers managers. They say, 'If I give up some of my power, how the hell will I get the job done? I barely have enough to get it done now.' It is this first jump in the cold water that is hard to do. Likert's findings make it perfectly clear, and they have been replicated time after time, that the process of giving up influence, of letting the other people influence you, not only does not diminish your power but, indeed, increases it."

Similarly, the American Council on Education's study of faculty participation in academic decision making (Dykes, 1968) found that a source of tension between the faculty and the administration is the view held by many faculty members that increases in administrative power and influence must necessarily result in a decrease in their own. This view assumes that the university is a closed system with a finite power potential. The administration and the faculty are seen as adversaries competing for a limited quantity of influence. Thus any power or influence that the administration secures must inevitably reduce the influence of the faculty, and vice versa. Dykes comments: "Such a perception is both invalid and seriously misleading. Given the nature of the large university today, it is possible for administrative and faculty power to increase simultaneously. Any increase in administrative power which improves the efficiency and effectiveness of the total organization potentially increases the power of the faculty, since the total power is increased. For example, a weak administration, easily manipulated by forces from outside the university, jeopardizes the faculty's autonomy and reduces its power. In such a case, increases in administrative strength obviously enhance faculty influence.

Similarly, the centralization of certain business and ancillary functions may strengthen the administration, but, at the same time, may enable the faculty to exercise greater control by effectively influencing the policies governing the operation of such functions" (pp. 40–41).

Which responsibilities and powers should be shared and which should not? The nature of governance will vary from campus to campus, but questions such as the following can serve as guidelines for evaluating its effectiveness.

1. Do all campus constituencies understand the differences between mandated and delegated responsibilities? The board of trustees, the ultimate authority, delegates authority to the chief campus administrator to carry out general and specific responsibilities. The administration is employed to administer, and the faculty is employed to teach—and wouldn't things be easier if life were that simple! The authority and responsibilities of the board and the chief administrative official should be clearly delineated in some institutional document.

2. Do institutional governance procedures include participation by faculty members, students, and support (nonexempt) personnel? The nature of their membership and the roles of these groups in the governing body are a matter of institutional style, and no one best solution exists for the representation question. But they should have authentic and contributory roles, and the trend toward their meaningful inclusion has been quite evident for some years.

3. Are faculty governance procedures clearly set forth? In the earlier discussion of the work of the Committee on Program Evaluation at the University of Illinois, "orderly procedures" was mentioned as a distinguishing feature of top-ranked departments on the Urbana campus. One suspects that orderliness is also a prominent characteristic of an effective set of governance policies and procedures.

The governance study of the American Association for Higher Education (1967, pp. 24–25) outlined these conditions as necessary for shared authority:

> Faculty participation in campus decision making requires formal arrangements through which faculty influence may be exercised.

Faculty members should have an effective means of presenting their views to any agency with the authority to make decisions affecting the institution of higher education.

The faculty should have a voice in determining the public policies of the institution in order to ensure that these policies are designed to maintain and promote public understanding of the mission of the university.

Relationships between the faculty and academic administrators should be, to the greatest feasible extent, collegial rather than hierarchical.

Personnel policy and practices should be designed to maximize professional freedom and opportunities for professional growth.

The American Association of University Professors (AAUP) has also developed some useful guidelines on faculty governance. Most campus administrators find little disagreement with them. As one would expect, the AAUP's general statements do have a faculty bias, but this bias usually coincides with institutional interests. However, the administration, through its own careful study as well as with legal assistance, may want to make adjustments in AAUP statements to fit local circumstances.

4. Are instruction and the curriculum primarily the province of the faculty? Administrators should respect the expertise and commitment of faculty members in these areas, because normally this expertise provides sound programs. But two relatively new developments in the program area require greater administrative influence: these are establishing program priorities based on the reallocation of limited resources and evaluating programs and units. The difficult times ahead for many institutions require close faculty-administration teamwork in order to make constructive and needed adjustments in programs.

5. Are informal channels of communication available for handling problems and crises? Problems should be solved informally, if possible. Although the nature of some issues requires the use of formal campus procedures, a more casual atmosphere often helps when one is exploring positions and alternatives. Formal procedures take more time, and their public character frequently forces the involved parties to take positions that allow too little flexibility.

28. **Are satisfactory policies and procedures established for evaluating administrators and for providing professional development?**

The systematic assessment of administrators is coming rapidly into prominence—and with good reason. If faculty members and others are to be evaluated, then why not administrators? The idea is still quite new, however. As recently as 1973, my search of the literature produced very little—so little, in fact, that I placed three announcements in *The Chronicle of Higher Education* in hopes of turning up fugitive materials (still with small success). But since 1974, a number of doctoral theses, studies, articles, and workshops have been done, and continued rapid growth can be expected.

Which administrators are most frequently evaluated? A study of the assessment of administrators in 218 institutions affiliated with the American Association of State Colleges and Universities (AASCU) (1976a, p. 3) found that 17 percent *formally* evaluate academic deans, and 14 percent appraise their presidents; 13 percent evaluate department heads, academic vice-presidents, and directors; and 9 percent assess admission officers, registrars, placement officers, and others. In addition, a number of institutions *informally* evaluate their administrators: 31 percent for academic deans, 11 percent for presidents, 21 percent for divisional administrators, 29 percent for department heads, 21 percent for vice presidents, and 5 percent for other administrators. The authors of the study predicted that approximately 45 percent of all AASCU institutions would achieve systematic administrative evaluation procedures by 1977.

Yankwich (1976, p. 1) cites some pros and cons of administrator evaluation: It improves the performance of the administrative officers and consequently of the unit administered; it makes visible to each party concerned the interests and understandings of the others; it improves the credibility of the administrative process, including the process by which decisions are made, in the eyes of those affected by the process; and it provides decision makers with the necessary information to decide about the retention or nonretention of administrators who are responsible to them. But the cost in time can become serious, and excessive expectations can be raised. Further, job applicants may be deterred by this hurdle-to-be-run or by publicity about the evaluation results. And, finally, administrators' credibility will suffer if the evaluation process itself is handled badly.

These and other problems need to be considered in developing procedures for evaluating administrators. Dressel (1976, pp. 376–382) describes four more: defining exactly what administration is vis-à-vis leadership and management; the difficulty of delineating the power of administrators in light of the complicated organizational hierarchy and both internal and external sources of authority; the lack of clear and generally accepted criteria of administrative success; and the fact that administrators sometimes "purposely communicate in ambiguous ways."

Like faculty evaluations, appraisals of administrators should have two overriding purposes: to improve, as well as to judge, professional performance. The following guidelines are suggested for developing evaluation procedures. (1) The system should be rooted in the traditions, purposes, and style of each institution. (2) The procedures should be built on the premise that each administrator possesses different abilities and skills, and no one individual should be expected to perform peerlessly in all areas. (3) Performance should be compared with expectations; this means that current, reasonably specific, "job" descriptions must exist. Descriptions that are more than two or three years old usually need revision. (4) The procedures should comprise both objective and subjective measures. (5) Evaluations should be sought from persons in a position to make valid judgments—those immediately above and immediately below the individual being judged. Immediate superiors should have the major responsibility in each case. (6) The evaluation should be made in cooperation with the individual being assessed, who should have an opportunity to suggest procedures. (7) Confidentiality should be maintained throughout, and the distribution of results should be clearly understood and controlled.

A number of systematic procedures and survey instruments for evaluating administrators have been developed. An excellent summary of these has been produced by Fisher (1977a, 1977b). Other useful resources are Hillway (1973), Dressell (1976), Miller (1974), Munitz (1976), and Hays (1976a, 1976b). The criteria and procedures in these reports can be helpful, but each institution should adapt them to its own circumstances.

The AASCU study (1976, p. 12) raises a number of cautions with respect to administrator evaluation:

- Avoid developing evaluation instruments for implementation during a crisis.
- Avoid evaluation instruments issued by special interest groups.
- Avoid evaluations by individuals not competent to make them.
- Avoid the mass distribution of findings; they may be distorted and used by the news media.
- Avoid accepting evaluation as a power play in collective bargaining.
- Avoid overstressing individual items apart from the context of the whole evaluation instrument.
- Avoid assigning the same value to different evaluations— examine the background of each respondent.
- Avoid making final recommendations based on evaluation material that only represents a part of the total picture.

In addition to the guidelines and cautions listed above, the institutional evaluator might consider the following summary questions:

1. Have the policies and procedures for evaluating administrators been examined recently?
2. Do these policies and procedures allow for a fair, searching, and appropriately confidential system? And are they designed finally to improve performance?
3. Are the formal procedures carried out regularly and applied to all administrators?
4. Are the results shown to the individual who has been evaluated, and does this person have access to an appeals procedure before any results are shared with others?
5. Does the institution have a way to appraise the overall and specific effectiveness of the evaluation system itself?

Like evaluation, professional development for new as well as used administrators is a growing concern. Fisher (1977b) reminds us that college and university administrators are still selected primarily on the basis of scholarly qualifications rather than administrative experience, of which they often have had little or none. Their awareness of the need for new knowledge and skills is evidenced by the continuing success of the Institute for College and University Administrators, sponsored by the American Council on Education, and other seminars and workshops. Kauffman (1977) has written about the anxieties and problems encountered by new presidents. And Gross (1977) identifies several factors that move new and experienced administrators toward professional renewal: a new sense of management accountability or stewardship; the declining mobility of administrators due to higher education's economic depression; the growth and impact of faculty development programs; the inherent relationship between administrator evaluation and development; the necessity of administrator renewal for continuing institutional vitality; the contribution of professional development programs to the body of knowledge about administrative theory and practice; and the relief and renewal it can bring to meeting day-to-day administrative pressures.

Future developments will include more staff-development activities on campus and more sabbaticals or short-term, two- or three-month leaves. Working administrators need short leaves to escape from the daily stresses as well as to develop new knowledge, skills, and insights. For an annotated listing of seminars, workshops, conferences, and internships, see *A Guide to Professional Development Opportunities for College and University Administrators,* published annually by the American Council on Education (Galloway and Fisher). The 1977 edition describes 291 programs sponsored by 90 different institutions and associations.

Questions such as the following ones may be useful in appraising professional development/renewal programs for administrators: Does the institution have policies and procedures that govern professional development/renewal opportunities for administrators? How effective are these programs in terms of their overall objectives as well as in terms of individual cases? What improvements should be made?

29. **Does the institution have an effective affirmative action program?**

Shortly after President Kennedy signed the first executive order requiring an affirmative action effort by all federal contractors, then Chancellor Kerr of the University of California wrote that one of the "truly major changes in university life had been initiated" not from the inside but "from the outside" (1964, p. 105). Much has happened since. Various other federal laws and regulations have been enacted that prohibit employers from discriminating against employees or applicants for employment on the basis of race, color, religion, sex, or national origin.

Equitable recruiting and hiring procedures are an essential element in providing equal employment opportunities, and an early, pivotal court decision in this area is *Griggs* v. *Duke Power Company* (401 U.S. 424, 1971), which focused on the relationships among job criteria, discrimination, and methods for judging job criteria. The Supreme Court considered whether Title VII prohibited an employer from establishing a high school education or a standardized intelligence test as minimum standards for employment when "(a) neither standard is shown to be significantly related to successful job performance, (b) both requirements operate to disqualify Negroes at a substantially higher rate than white applicants, and (c) the jobs in question formerly had been filled only by white employees as part of a long-standing practice of giving preference to whites" (401 U.S. at 426). The Supreme Court ruled that the disproportionate exclusion of Negroes on the basis of educational or test-score requirements violated Title VII. (See Kaplin, 1978, for a further discussion.) This brief look at the historical picture led to Title IX of the 1972 Federal Education Amendments. The thirty-seven words that made discrimination illegal are: "No person in the United States shall, on the basis of sex, be excluded from participation in, be denied the benefits of, or be subjected to discrimination under, any education program or activity receiving federal financial assistance."

The role and actions of the federal government in these areas have been the subject of controversy and misunderstanding in higher education. Some individuals believe that imposing rules regarding the number of women and minority-group members who shall be hired or their proportions in the faculty and administration is contrary to the basic freedom of choice that is essential to excellence. Others contend that the small numbers of these persons on many faculties is irrefutable evidence of enduring discriminatory practices and that not much will change until positions are distributed more fairly. The controversy goes on. . . .

Institutions of higher education do have difficulties in equitably applying federal mandates and guidelines because of certain characteristics of the teaching profession. For instance, only about one out of three or four new assistant professors survives the rigorous teaching-research obstacle course that eventually leads to tenure. And although the bases for tenure decisions are not as systematic and as rational as those described by policy and procedural statements, they do have some validity for individual institutions. But selection based on merit may not be compatible with meeting "quotas" or with developing two sets of standards for promotion and tenure—one for those who will move along without difficulty and another in order to meet affirmative-action requirements that are placed ahead of quality standards.

Another problem is that the pool of senior professors in certain academic and professional fields who are available for posts at major universities is very small if institutions are seeking to maintain or improve quality. The field of economics, for example, can have several specialties, and a major university will want to adequately cover almost all of them. The number of women and members of minority groups that are qualified by experience and performance to fill one of these posts is very limited indeed.

Smaller colleges and universities face a different issue—competing in a market where promising blacks and women with Ph.D. degrees are in demand, and larger institutions can, and do, simply outbid smaller ones. A private institution of about three thousand students needs to work much harder to recruit promising black professionals, and success comes through much extra effort, including recruiting trips to major cities and exploring many normally untapped avenues and resources.

The cost of keeping up with the blizzard of memoranda flowing from Washington to institutions is another difficulty. The American Council on Education's study by Van Alstyne and Coldren (1976) of the expense of compliance is sobering. Using six representative institutions, the ACE study found that in 1975 the costs represented 1 to 4 percent of their operating budgets, and these costs have increased ten to twenty times in the past decade, rising much faster than total revenues. The report concludes, "The residual effects of implementing federal social, manpower, science, and tax policies have a far greater financial impact on higher education than do coherent federal education policies" (p. 15).

Just what does the government ask the institutions to do that is so expensive and difficult? In 1975 the amended Title IX regulations established the federal intention to leave to the institutions the initial responsibility for determining their compliance status and for initiating remedial and affirmative action to achieve compliance. Nevertheless, as Shulman (1977) points out, the regulations require institutions to follow several steps designed to achieve voluntary compliance:

> First, they call upon the institutions to conduct a self-evaluation " . . . in terms of the requirements of these regulations, its current policies and practices and the effects thereof concerning admission of students, treatment of students. . . . " This self-evaluation is not merely a descriptive document but an instrument for reform.
>
> Second, in keeping with its self-enforcement approach, the regulations require the institution to assign to at least one employee the responsibility for coordinating the institution's Title IX compliance efforts and for investigating any complaints of noncompliance or violation of the Title IX regulations.
>
> Third, the government has taken the unique step of requiring institutions to develop and adopt grievance procedures for students and employees to deal with complaints of Title IX violations. These institutional self-monitoring actions are the foundation of the government's Title IX compliance efforts. The government's initial contract with institutions occurs after the institutions complete and return to the Office for Civil Rights "assurance" forms, which were due by September 30, 1976. In effect, the government's involvement with Title IX enforcement does not begin until after these assurance forms are received and reviewed. The assurance form is a checklist that requires institutions to report on their progress in the areas discussed above: grievance procedures; Title IX coordinator designated; status of the self-evaluation, modifications, and remedial action requirements (pp. 3–5).

What should an affirmative action plan include? As detailed by Foxley (1976, p. 72), a statement of policy and commitment to equal employment and affirmative action is a required starting point, containing these basic elements: (1) A reiteration of the employer's equal employment opportunity policy for all persons, regardless of race, color, religion, sex, or national origin. (2) A statement that affirmative action efforts are necessary to overcome the efforts of past discrimination. (3) Policies governing all personnel actions, such as recruiting, hiring, promotions, transfers, training, compensation, benefits, layoffs, and terminations. (4) A statement establishing the responsibility for the affirmative action program. The chief executive officer or governing board has the ultimate responsibility. A top executive or administrator is assigned to direct the program. All administrative and management personnel are charged to support and implement program goals and objectives. And (5) a statement pledging the employer's continued compliance with all relevant state and federal laws and regulations and cooperation with governmental and community organizations in ensuring equal employment opportunity.

Thus, the top administrative officer is chiefly responsible for the quality of the affirmative action program and for institutional compliance with it. And within the federal mandates and guidelines, the campus administration can have considerable influence on what is done and how well it is done. A number of questions can assist in evaluating the quality of the institution's response, such as the following ones based on a study by Catlin and others (1974, pp. 69–70):

1. How does the affirmative action program relate to institutional priorities?
2. What financial resources exist for supporting affirmative action efforts?
3. Does the institution have an operational manual for deans, department heads, and other administrators to facilitate their understanding of affirmative action mandates and guidelines?
4. Have the responsibilities for monitoring and implementing affirmative action been assigned?
5. Are effective internal grievance procedures in place? Will they stand up in court?
6. What means are available to create institutional awareness of systematic discrimination and its remedies?

Burke (1977, p. 388) captures the essence of current campus malaise as well as the opportunities for administrative leadership when he writes: "The real threat to the quality of life on campus today and in the future flows less from the financial depression in higher education than from the psychological depression in the academic spirit. This psychological depression springs not so much from a lack of money as from an abatement of hope and from an abandonment of will. Presidents must work with all groups to rekindle that hope and revitalize that will. Presidents should remember that every problem also represents an opportunity . . . for change at least as large as the problem."

Many features of administration are ageless—planning, organizing, coordinating, controlling, evaluating—yet the milieus do change. Current forces and trends in the United States point toward the need for a strong, dynamic leadership by chief administrative officers on campuses. An assertive style may slightly decrease their prospects for survival in this already precarious position, but the rewards come from charting educational directions a bit better.

8

Measuring Fiscal Management and Accountability

The budget is the best single indicator of an institution's priorities and directions as well as its aspirations and self-images. A document of judgment, the budget is the means by which an institution strives to achieve what it believes to be important. In order to exercise dynamic and catalytic leadership, the chief administrative officer needs to be on top of budgetary matters. He or she must allocate or reallocate increasingly scarce resources, and these sensitive and difficult processes require detailed attention.

The rhetoric of budgeting and management in general contains numerous references to the twin goals of efficiency and effectiveness, but these two are not identical. Drucker (1967) said that efficiency is doing things right and effectiveness is doing the right things; and Meeth (1974) observes that an institution can be effective without being efficient. Efficiency, generally defined as the ratio of inputs (costs) to outputs, is the more technical term, and while difficult to measure in its own right, it is not as broad or difficult to assess as effectiveness.

The concept of efficiency has been around a long time but became a household word only recently. Efficiency was one of the aims of Taylor (1911), who put forth four basic principles of "scientific management" that revolutionized the practice of management in the early twentieth century: the development of a science to replace old rule-of-thumb methods; the scientific selection of workmen, followed by developing their skills; determining the scientific method of performing work; and close cooperation between managers and workers, with mutual recognition of the mutual benefits derived. The time and motion studies done by Frank and Lillian Gilbreth in this era also aimed at efficient work.

Causal relationships between educational costs and educational quality or effectiveness have been more assumed than researched. It has been assumed that institutions that spend more per student offer better education. Probably that assumption is correct if one compares extreme cases, as, say, institutions that spend $3000 per student and those that spend $1,000, but the relationship between cost per student and quality may be negligible when these differences are less pronounced. Meeth (1974) studied six private liberal arts colleges ranging in size from 469 to 1428 students and in cost per student from $1447 to $2469. Institutional effectiveness was judged by an alumni questionnaire, by the Institutional Functioning Inventory developed by the Educational Testing Service, and by traditionally accepted input and output assessments (the number of FTE students and faculty members, credit-hour production, faculty salaries, freshmen SAT scores, high school class rank, UGRE scores, GRE scores, library size and costs, faculty development funds, and so on).

Although this study dealt with a small sample of a particular type of college, its basic conclusion should be considered by other kinds of institutions: "Saying that cost and quality do not always stand in a cause-effect relationship among institutions does not preclude cost and quality from being directly related in a single college. . . . Nevertheless, it is no longer possible to make categorical statements that higher cost means greater effectiveness among private institutions of similar type and purpose. It is not so. A single college may spend more and increase effectiveness or spend less and hold or increase effectiveness. It can also spend more and not affect effectiveness at all. This entire study suggests that colleges are more likely to spend more and not add to effectiveness than they are to spend less and detract from effectiveness" (pp. 97–98).

Sometimes trustees who are business executives look for similarities between commercial and university management procedures—and there are similarities, but there are also fundamental differences, as is pointed out in the useful volume on *College and University Administration* developed by the National Association of College and University Business Officers (NACUBO) in 1974. The overriding objective of a commercial enterprise is to increase the economic wealth of those who provide resources to finance its operations, and these resources are intended to generate revenues that not only replace the resources consumed but provide a profit margin for the investor. The objective of a college or university is to provide services that fulfill societal needs without regard for financial gain; thus resources are consumed to attain service objectives rather than to make a profit. To provide its services the institution must continually obtain new resources. These differences are reflected in academic accounting principles, which depart from commercial practices in fund accounting, in the form and content of basic financial statements, in the application of accrual accounting, in the treatment of depreciation, and investments, and in handling institutions operated by religious groups.

With this background in mind, we come now to the first of the forty-five criteria that has to do with appraising the effectiveness of financial management.

30. Is the tuition and fee structure compatible with the institution's needs and with the student's ability to pay?

Meeth found that the sixty-six private liberal arts colleges in his study were covering 67 percent of their educational costs through tuition and fees, although the figures ranged from 33 percent to 98 percent. In the literature of higher education there is no optimum percentage of these costs the students should be paying. But Meeth concludes that "a healthy percentage would range somewhere between 65 and 80 percent of income to the institution from student fees. If the figure is lower than 65 percent, the institution would suffer radically from a tight economy, particularly if it had a small endowment and had to depend upon gifts and grants and government funding when these resources were more limited than normal. Likewise, 80 percent seems to be maximum; otherwise, an institution is in financial jeopardy if students do not materialize. A decrease in enrollment means that the college must gear itself for either drastic cutbacks or great increases in outside funding after commitments have already been made for the bulk of the potential income" (1974, p. 41).

Every president of a private college has agonized over whether to raise tuitions—again—and almost all have reluctantly (publicly anyway) agreed to increases. Public institutions find that tuition increases become political footballs that are tossed back and forth among university presidents, state education officials, state legislatures (and legislators), and governors. In the community colleges, Wattenbarger and others (1973, p. 58) found that "there is a discernable trend toward increasing these tuition charges even though the open-door philosophy of community colleges would suggest a lowering or elimination of such charges. To assess this trend we examined the 1966 and 1971 editions of the *Junior College Directory*. The median tuition fee listed for each state's community colleges in 1965 was compared with the median tuition fee given for 1970. . . . To summarize those data: there were ninety-six increases . . . sixteen decreases . . . , and fourteen no-changes."

Also increasing on the other side of the ledger are outlays for financial aid, as Jenny and Wynn (1970) found. The authors analyzed a group of private liberal arts colleges from 1960 to 1968 and completed a follow-up study in 1972. The colleges in their sample showed a 6.4 percent annual increase in the rate of income growth per student, and a 6.8 percent annual rate of growth in student expenses (tuition, books, and so on)—or a -0.4 gap between income growth and student expenses. The 1968–70 data show a gap of -1.4 percent between an income growth rate of 6.8

and a 8.2 yearly growth rate for student expenses. Moreover, student aid expenses grew more rapidly than any other expense category. In 1960–61 about eight cents of each dollar of tuition and fee income went to student aid, and by 1969–70 the figure had increased fourfold to thirty-two cents. Clearly, student aid is a significant factor in private colleges, and many presidents have pondered over the point of diminishing returns where expenditures for financial aid would amount to buying a student body (1972, pp. 26–27).

A good deal of support for students has come from the government as well as institutions. Fife (1975) reminds us that federal student aid started from virtually nothing before the G.I. Bill in 1944 and increased to more than over $6 billion by 1976. State scholarship and grant programs, also virtually nonexistent twenty years ago, spent nearly $200 million in 1970 and $500 million in 1976. Fife estimated the total 1975–76 funds available for student aid to be more than $8.3 billion. The myriad aid programs established in the past decade have had the same goals, according to Fife: to "provide the financially disadvantaged with access to some form of postsecondary education, allow these students some freedom to attend the college of their choice, provide aid over a period of years to allow students to achieve their educational objectives, provide a freer flow of students in the educational marketplace, and help preserve the diversity of higher education" (pp. 4–5).

Each institution that has some control over its tuition and fee structure should examine carefully these items as well as its financial aid programs. Some college presidents in their budget-making process have computed the income and expenditures columns and have given tuition the burden of making up the difference. Others have held the line on tuitions and fees and made up deficits in other ways. In many states, however, state-level decisions have taken this prerogative from individual public institutions. The costs of administering financial aid programs have been considerable, causing some institutions to skimp on financial aid personnel since their salaries come out of institutional funds. This approach has often backfired and caused unnecessary student attrition because of unsympathetic and incompetent assistance.

The person evaluating these aspects of the institution's financial operation will want to think about at least the following questions. (1) Does the institution have a purposeful and functional data base concerning tuition and fees and financial aid? (2) Does the decision-making process relative to tuition include developing projective models for various tuition alternatives? (3) Do other organizations, such as student affairs and admissions, sharing responsibility for financial assistance matters cooperate with the financial aid office in coordinating all campus assistance programs?

31. **Does the institution have an efficient management system for accounting and financial reporting?**

Answering this question is beyond the competence of the general academic community and most board members, although sometimes a trustee has a special expertise and interest in these matters and can participate in their assessment. The administration or board will want to use an external consultant team for in-depth evaluation of this operation. Excellent guidelines are given in the extensive and practical book *Appraising Administrative Operations* by Griffin and Burks (1976). Their work, drawing on the experience of the Quality and Management Program initiated at the University of California and field tested on a number of U.C. campuses, raises key questions about controls, reporting, recording, accounts receivable, disbursements, payrolls, cashiering, petty cash flow, fixed assets, and supply inventories.

The evaluation team should probably pay special attention to cash management, which can be the source of substantial savings or income. For instance, Ohio University increased its yearly return on short-term investments by more than $100,000 by using five cash-handling procedures described by Lykins (1973): consolidating checking accounts, determining the surplus cash available for investment by examining bank balances in conjunction with the cash book, selecting a minimum bank balance to maintain in the consolidated checking account, investing a greater percentage of surplus cash in short-term investments offering a higher yield than treasury bills, and obtaining a telephone report of the checking account at the beginning of each business day.

Questions such as the following, taken from Griffin and Burks (1976, pp. 134–135), can assist in evaluating the institution's financial management system.

1. Are there complete, written policies guiding the effective disbursement of funds?

2. Are there effective policies providing for the recording of budgetary and financial transactions? Are these policies in accordance with recognized professional accounting principles and technical and operations requirements?

3. Does the chart of accounts represent adequately the organization of the campus, lend itself to revisions with a minimum amount of time and effort, including the facility for expansion, and facilitate the preparation of financial reports?

4. Do institutional policies provide for adequate financial and budgetary control over all accounts?

5. Do institutional policies provide for effective internal audits?

6. Do the financial reports effectively meet management needs?

7. Have adequate provisions been made to assure adherence to federal contract and grant requirements?

8. Are processes in effect which assure compliance with special fund restrictions?

9. Are there adequate communications between the accounting office and all the units it services?

10. Is the financial management exercised by departments and schools effective? Is it well coordinated with the accounting office?

11. Are campus departments and outside vendors satisfied with the disbursement process?

12. Are government agencies satisfied with the financial management exercised by the institution?

13. When appropriate, does the accounting office provide useful financial advice and assistance to departments?

32. **Are institutional costs and expenditures comparable with benchmark institutions?**

Making comparisons among similar institutions can be useful in a variety of ways, such as to determine whether one's salaries are competitive. For example, the president of the University of Illinois compared his institution's salaries with those of other "Big 10" universities in order to make a case against reductions proposed by the legislature (Table 23). The results clearly show that the university's ranking had been sinking gradually during the six-year period. The Georgia University System made a similar study of salary increases in comparable southern institutions by means of a telephone survey (Table 24).

A number of carefully developed comparative cost studies are available, and these can be useful yardsticks. The "Sixty College Study," sponsored by the National Association of College and University Business Officers(1956), included sixty liberal arts colleges in various sections of the nation, ranging in size from two hundred students to more than fourteen hundred. In a report of a follow-up study (National Association . . . , 1960), the researchers stated "that approximately 50 percent of the operations of any college are routine and thus subject to direct comparison without regard to academic individuality." The findings of the 1956 study showed that (1) common patterns of sources and expenditures of funds can be identified; (2) medians or averages of classes of income and of expenditures are reliable as guiding principles; (3) deviations from medians and averages occur quite infrequently and in these cases explanations can be found; and (4) allocations of funds to various college activities are influenced by socioeconomic conditions, the characteristics of the student body, the economic resources of the college, regional habits, climatic conditions, and other special circumstances (1960, pp. 4–5).

The 1960 follow-up study, which compared 1953–54 and 1957–58 figures, revealed that whereas the total educational and general expenditures in the participating colleges increased 37 percent during the four-year period, expenditures (expressed in percentages) in the eight categories into which they were divided did not vary by more than a single percentage point in the significant areas, and rarely more than that in the less significant ones. Two conclusions were drawn from this "quite unexpected fact." First, such benchmarks as "the percentage allocations of funds into specific areas of college operation, which were accepted as isolated phenomena in the original study, can now, because of their general

Table 23. University of Illinois Ranking of Big 10 Salary Levels

Fiscal Year	Professor		Associate Professor		Assistant Professor		Instructor	
	Cash Salary	Big 10 Ranking	Cash Salary	Big 10 Ranking	Cash Salary	Big 10 Ranking	Cash Salary	Big 10 Ranking
1972	21,300	4	15,300	4	12,400	5.5	9,900	4
1973	22,100	3	15,800	4	12,900	5	10,300	6.5
1974	23,000	3	16,300	4	13,300	5.5	10,800	6
1975	23,800	3	17,100	4	14,000	5.5	11,000	8
1976	25,200	4	18,400	6	14,700	8	11,700	9
1977								
Board of Higher Education Records 7%	27,000	4	19,700	5	15,700	7	12,500	9
General Assembly 4.5%	26,300	5	19,200	6	15,400	8	12,200	9
Governer's Action 2.5%	25,800	6.5	18,900	8	15,100	10	12,000	9

Note: The University of Illinois is granting the smallest salary increase in the Big 10 for FY 1977. The range is from 2.5 percent to 8 percent, with the University of Illinois being 2.5 percent. The next lowest salary increase given in the Big 10 was 4.3 percent.

Source: University of Illinois at Urbana-Champaign, Office of Planning (1976).

**Table 24. Increases in Faculty Salaries in Thirteen State University
Systems**

State University Systems	Percentage Increases		
	FY 1976 Over FY 1975	FY 1977 Over FY 1976	Cumulative Two Years
Texas	14.3	6.8	21.1
Mississippi	9.0	7.0	16.0
Louisiana	10.0	4.3	14.3
West Virginia	7.0	6.3[a]	13.3
Maryland	9.0	3.5	12.5
Virginia	5.4	6.0	11.4
Tennessee	2.1	9.0	11.1
Alabama	7.0	4.0	11.0
Kentucky	5.4	5.0	10.4
South Carolina	6.0	4.0	10.0
North Carolina	1.0	5.6[b]	6.6
Florida	-0-	5.0[c]	5.0
Georgia	5.0	-0-	5.0

[a]$1,000 across the board.
[b]4 percent plus $300.
[c]Union negotiations still in progress; increase will probably be approximately 5
percent.
Source: University System of Georgia, 1976.

consistency over four years, be taken with little reservation as guiding principles" (National Association . . . , 1960, p. 7). This finding
was substantiated by the Jenny and Wynn study (1970) of forty-
eight private liberal arts colleges over the 1960–1968 period: "The
basic principles which guide the allocation of resources do not seem
to have undergone any significant changes during the period
studied" (p. 3). College administrators finding serious variations
from these norms in their own situations would be well advised to
study carefully the cause, as well as the effect, of such variations to
ensure that the operational policies reflected by the variations are
sources of unique strength rather than weaknesses in their
academic enterprise.

The second conclusion drawn from the two NACUBO
studies was that they did not support the hope that increases in
contributions, endowment earnings, or tuition fees would go
primarily to raising faculty salaries. The allocation of funds to the

instructional program averaged 50.2 percent in 1953–54 and 49.8 in 1957–58; these consistent figures indicate that only about half of any new income filtered through to the function of instruction. And the portion of that allocation which went to faculty salaries declined from 40.7 to 40.6 percent (1960, pp. 7, 35).

The Meeth study (1974), referred to earlier, included sixty-six reputable independent colleges ranging in enrollment from 151 to 2,183 students, with forty institutions having between 500 and 1,000 students and only one having more than 1,500. Table 25 shows cost and other data for the 1970–71 academic year. The items listed in this table are the basic ones needed for any cost analysis of the academic program. Meeth concludes: "The fact that these institutions substantiate the findings of the 1962 study of quality and cost of liberal arts programs (Hungate and Meeth, 1964) adds evidence that colleges in these studies are typical of most other liberal arts colleges. Hence, these data are significant for all of private higher education" (p. 33).

An imaginative and controversial study of the "financial health" of higher education was published by *Change* magazine (Lupton, Augenblick, and Heyison, 1976). The authors asserted that past studies provided (1) an inadequate data base for making national conclusions about institutions' financial health, (2) particularized data that were not comparable on a national basis, and (3) no national measurements that could serve as yardsticks. Their study used data supplied by each college and university to the U.S. government through the Higher Education General Information Survey (HEGIS). The analysis included 2,163 institutions on which adequate data were available and excluded 1,024 institutions with inadequate data. Using the discriminant analysis statistical procedure, the authors determined the sixteen variables that were most significant in determining financial health (Table 26a). *Change* magazine, in cooperation with the researchers, has made available diagnostic worksheets and instructions that will enable administrators to arrive at a score (as shown in Table 26b) indicating their institution's state of health. The authors contend that comparisons with all other institutions are thus possible.

What are some results of the *Change* study? It rated 25.1 percent of all the 2,163 institutions in the A or healthiest category;

Table 25. Comparison of Averages in Sixty-six Colleges—1970-71

Item	Under 500 Students		500-1000		Over 1000		All Colleges	
	Mean	Range	Mean	Range	Mean	Range	Mean	Range
FTE faculty	27.1	12.4-44.5	46	22.3-71	82	58.1-107.5	42.7	12.4-107.5
Average class size	17.7	9.9-28.6	21	12.2-34.7	22.1	17.5-26	20.1	9.9-34.7
Average teaching load	12	9.1-14.5	10.8	6.8-14.3	11.6	10.8-13	11.2	6.8-14.5
Average faculty productivity (in student credit hours)	408.6	224.9-535.3	494.2	348.3-770	542.4	439.9-749.9	470.8	224.9-770
Average student credit-hour load (1st sem.)	14.6	9.3-16.8	14.6	9.1-19.2	14.8	13.3-15.9	14.6	9.1-19.2
Faculty-student ratio (1st sem.)	13.3	10.5-17.4	16.4	11.3-24.4	17.3	14.2-19.1	15.5	10.5-24.4
Average FTE faculty cash salary	$9267	$7265-11,633	$9503	$7094-13,416	$8715	$7369-10,343	$9369	$7094-13,416
Average FTE faculty benefits	$576	$80-1052	$812	$199-1551	$854	$692-1161	$746	$80-1551
Average FTE total faculty compensation	$9843	$7686-12,101	$10,315	$7713-13,911	$9569	$8061-11,505	$10,115	$7686-13,911
Overhead ratio	1.8	.7-3.5	1.9	.89-2.9	1.82	1.3-2.5	1.85	.7-3.5
Average cost per student	$1944	$1360-2,930	$1848	$1169-2534	$1564	$1249-1979	$1857	$1169-2930
Average income per student	$1185	$691-1679	$1409	$457-2052	$1324	$1061-1541	$1330	$457-2052
Total educational expense	$692,480	$397,375 to 1,040,974	$1,363,386	$743,594 to 2,447,108	$2,209,789	$1,535,253 to 2,725,763	$1,211,740	$397,375 to 2,725,763
Total educational income	$435,791	$161,821 to 717,630	$999,370	$266,317 to 1,730,954	$1,871,804	$1,476,671 to 2,315,903	$884,401	$161,821 to 2,315,903
Percent of expenditure borne by tuition and fee[a]	57.2	38.7-85	70.4	33.9-97.8	79.3	66.7-89.1	66.8	33-97.8

[a]Excludes unfunded scholarships.

Source: Meeth, 1974, p. 34.

Table 26a. Sixteen Indicators of the Financial Health of Colleges and Universities

Private Control	A categorical variable distinguishing privately controlled institutions from others.
Two-Year College	A categorical variable distinguishing two-year institutions from others.
Trend in Undergraduate FTE Enrollment	Undergraduate full-time-equivalent enrollments.
Trend in Graduate FTE Enrollment	Graduate level full-time-equivalent enrollments.
Trend in Educational and General Expenditures	Educational and general (E and G) expenditures.
Trend in Plant Addition Expenditures	Plant additions: the increase or decrease in reported book value for a given year. A 10-percent increase in this item indicates that total expenditures for plant and equipment in 1974 were 10 percent above those made in 1972, not that total plant in 1974 was 10 percent greater than in 1972.
Current Funds Revenue-Expenditure Ratio	The current funds revenue-expenditure ratio summarizes whether the institution's operating funds cover its operating expenses.
Current Funds Revenues: Fixed Operating Costs Ratio	This ratio was intended to measure the institution's ability to cover its fixed costs. Since, because of tenure policies, we regarded most labor costs as fixed, this ratio is not strictly comparable to its business counterpart.
Gift, Grant, and Contract Revenue: Current Funds Revenue Ratio	This ratio measures the importance of gifts and outside nonresearch support (excluding direct governmental subsidies for instruction) among the institution's revenue resources.

Categorical Variables

Trend Variables

Financial Ratios

Academic Mission Expenditures: Educational and General Expenditure Ratio	Academic mission expenditures include all educational and general expenditures except maintenance, plant operation, and administrative costs. The ratio indicates how much of the institution's resources are devoted to academic uses.
Tuition and Fees: Student Aid Revenues	Student aid revenues include all monies received for or restricted to student aid. As mentioned in the text, this ratio may serve as a proxy for student aid effort.
Current Funds Revenues: Plant Assets Ratio	Plant assets are measured at book value. This ratio measures the revenue productivity of the institution's assets.
Plant Assets: FTE Enrollment Ratio	This ratio indicates the amount of plant assets "used" in educating one student and is a rough indicator of how intensively the plant is utilized.
Graduate FTE: Undergraduate FTE Ratio	The ratio of graduate FTE to undergraduate FTE, as is explained in the text, serves as a proxy for major research institutions.
Educational and General Expenditures: Degrees Conferred Ratio	This is an estimate of the cost of producing one degree graduate. Graduate and undergraduate costs are averaged.
Freshman FTE: Undergraduate FTE Ratio	This ratio reflects persistence patterns among the undergraduate population within the institution. It is affected by attrition and by the mix (if any) between students in two- and four-year degree programs.

Note: Educational and general expenditures are defined in accordance with 1975 USOE HEGIS instructions. They include most current operating costs of institutions, such as instruction, student aid, research, and maintenance expenses, but do not include the costs of hospitals and other "major service programs" or those of auxiliary enterprises such as bookstores, dormitories, and dining halls.

The first two indicators are categorical variables which take on a value of one for private institutions and two-year colleges respectively, and zero for all others. The four trend variables cover the period of 1972 to 1974 and were input as logarithmic transformations. The remaining 10 variables are FY 1974 financial ratios.

Table 26b. Five Scores of Financial Condition

-3.0	-2.5	-2.0	-1.5	-1.0	-0.5	0	.05	1.0	1.5	2.0	2.5	3.0

| | Unhealthy (E) | | Relatively Unhealthy (D) | Mean Score (C) | Relatively Healthy (B) | | Healthy (A) | |

Source: Lupton, Augenblick, and Heyison, 1976.

18.8 percent in the B or relatively healthy category; 6.9 percent in the C or mean category; 34.8 percent in the D or relatively unhealthy category; and 14.4 percent in the E or unhealthy category. The authors concluded that this distribution depicts financial stress in higher education, because one would expect a more normal distribution, given the statistical method used (p. 23).

They also concluded that the "states that perform well on a broad number of indices are not necessarily the states with the most healthy institutions. The correlation between higher education appropriations as a percentage of total state budget and institutional health is minimal, as is the correlation between institutional health and appropriations for higher education as a percentage of personal income" (pp. 28–29).

The authors did, however, find some relationships between institutional expenditures and financial health. Using the changes in educational and general expenditures between 1972 and 1974 and the changes in expenditures for plant additions over the same period, they discovered that "among the most healthy institutions, expenditures grew at one-half the rate exhibited by the most unhealthy institutions. While all schools reduced plant addition expenditures over the two-year period, the healthiest institutions reduced such expenditures three times as much as did the least healthy institutions. . . . Healthy institutions were also characterized by an emphasis on academic-mission expenditures. While the weighting of this factor is relatively small, institutions that emphasized instruction rather than public service or research . . . prove to be healthier. This finding supports the thesis that institutions that spread themselves too thin in response to perceived societal pressures will be adversely affected in a time of slowed growth, and that institutions with a clear focus on purpose are more efficient" (p. 31).

The study has stimulated much discussion and controversy, including the careful comments made by C. Van Alstyne (1976), chief economist for the American Council on Education. She favors "the basic idea of combining the opinions of a panel of economic and financial analysts about what constitutes college and university financial health, with statistical procedures to identify indicators and group institutions by apparent financial condition," calling this "a genuinely new approach which is worth pursuing." But the Van Alstyne comments on the whole are quite critical of the statistical procedures and some conclusions of the authors: "the authors and the publisher of *Change* magazine simply went too far, too fast, in drawing conclusions intended to influence management decisions and public choices affecting the financing of higher education" (p. 2).

Another major criticism relates to how the study might be used—or misused. Members of governing boards usually are successful businessmen and are accustomed to making the "bottom line" the principle criterion for judging success. But it is a mistake to equate financial health with academic excellence. The importance of sound management has been stressed at several points in this book, and in the years ahead administrators will give it further emphasis, but a well-managed and efficient college is not necessarily a place where excellence in learning and teaching is evident also. A financially healthy institution may provide a dynamic learning environment for students and faculty members alike, or it may be dullsville. We must appraise teaching and program excellence primarily by other criteria.

Change editor Bonham wrote in his introduction to the report: "The time is again ripe when one can talk about both dollars and philosophy in the same breath" (Lupton, Augenblick, and Heyison, 1976, p. 20). It has been customary to discuss aims without giving much consideration to the economic side. But few institutions can divorce the two, and somewhere there is a meeting ground where the starting point—philosophy/mission—is tempered by economic realities.

To sum up, the institutional evaluator will want to ask at least these questions: Are comparisons with selected, similar institutions made regularly? Do these analyses use comparable data? Are the results of these comparisons used effectively?

33. Is the investment portfolio managed well?

The proper management of endowment funds is a significant factor in the financial status of most private colleges and universities, and of many public institutions also. Bristol (1970, chap.
8, p. 447) writes, "McGeorge Bundy and a host of others have
eloquently pointed out that more money has been lost by educational institutions through poor investment of their endowment
portfolios than from all other factors combined. . . . The fault lies
in the absence of a sound organizational structure and the failure
to recognize the need for professional management."

The investment objective of most colleges and universities
has been to preserve the principal and the production of dividends
and interest. More recently, a broadened concept of return on investments has developed, according to which changes in the market
values of portfolio securities also affect the return on assets. In this
approach, the "total return" is the sum of (1) the net realized and
unrealized appreciation or shrinkage in the portfolio value and (2)
the yield on dividend and interest income.

Most institutional investment policies are based on three
premises: operating expenses have risen substantially and continue
to rise faster than the general price level and endowment income
can be expected to do; the endowment income's importance to the
overall budget is being diluted; and attempts to maximize endowment income most likely will be shortsighted, as they entail a high
risk of a loss in purchasing power. It follows, therefore, that
portfolio management policies should seek to increase the corpus
of the endowment fund and the annual income that it provides.

A report by Cary and Bright (1969) to the Ford Foundation
was critical of the investment policies of the 1960s: "In a decade
when the average price of common stocks has risen seven times as
fast as the cost of living, and dividends on common stocks have
risen three and a half times as fast, many endowments have been
exceedingly hard pressed even to keep abreast. To some extent this
has been the result of conscious choice on the part of endowment
fund managers. As a group they are conservative, and some of
them have insisted that their only duty is to safeguard the original
dollar value of the funds entrusted to their care."

Subsequently, the Advisory Committee on Endowment
Management (1969) of the Ford Foundation issued a report which

contained a number of recommendations, including these: (1) endowment funds should be managed to maximize a long-term total return, considering a dollar of capital gain as equal to a dollar of income; (2) there should be a specific plan for endowment support of operations, under which each year an amount equal to 5 percent of the three-year moving average of the market value of the fund is transferred from endowment to operating funds; (3) a careful legal review should be undertaken of all endowment funds that in the past have been classified as restricted as to principal, in order to reduce this total to the minimum legally required; (4) all funds that may have to be converted into cash within perhaps five years should be removed from the endowment portfolio and invested separately in prime short-term obligations, but any decision to spend endowment should be made by the trustees only after considering the opinion of the investment committee about the timeliness of the necessary security sales; and (5) trustees should not themselves attempt to manage their endowment portfolios but should delegate that responsibility clearly and fully to an able professional portfolio manager who is selected for his past record and whose performance is regularly evaluated on the basis of comparisons with the investment performance of the endowment funds of other colleges and of mutual funds.

These general principles of endowment management have been generally accepted, although now they are occasionally criticized because some endowment funds would have fared better in this period of falling stock market prices if they had had a larger proportion of bonds. But such criticism is inconsistent with the principle of maximizing the long-term total return, which is supported not only by the Ford Foundation but by the Carnegie Commission. It recommended that colleges and universities should (1) aim to maximize long-term total return in the investment of endowment funds, (2) delegate responsibility for portfolio management to an able professional, and (3) generally follow modern principles of endowment management (1972, p. 148).

Selecting and recommending an outside investment firm may be the most important action taken by the investment committee of the governing board. An important criterion for this choice should be the firm's performance record over several years and particularly the record of those staff members who will manage the endowment account. A publication of the National Association of College and University Business Officers (1974, p. 152) gives seven criteria that might be useful in selecting an investment firm.

1. Workload: the number and type of accounts and the degree to which the firm's time is spent in nonportfolio activities, such as administration and marketing.
2. Organization: the depth, experience, and retention of key persons; for example, the number of persons, their backgrounds, and length of service.
3. Investment philosophy and style: the procedures used in making portfolio decisions, the criteria for selecting investments, the degree of concentration or diversification in a typical portfolio, the types of companies and industries favored, the degree of risk taking, the expected performance during market rises and declines, and the changes in key strategies and method of operation during recent periods.
4. Research: the quality and quantity of research and the ability to relate research to portfolio management.
5. Trading: the ability to execute purchase and sale orders and the use of commissions.
6. Control: the supervision of portfolio managers and their results, and adherence to stated objectives and company policy on strategy.
7. Communication: the frequency and manner of reporting and the past success at retaining accounts.

Another useful source of information is the NACUBO Comparative Performance Study of 161 endowment pools representing 144 widely varying types of institutions, which provides benchmarks for analyzing the performance of one's own investments (National Association . . . , 1975b).

The answer to the question "Is the portfolio managed effectively?" rests with each institution. The investment committee, working with the institution's chief financial officer and the chief administrative officer, should continually review the performance of the investment manager, seeking to develop a diversified and sound yet successful program. The institution's future endowment should be protected even in times of austerity. Using the endowment principal, which is particularly tempting to private colleges with enrollment declines, should be done only under extraordinary circumstances and then only once.

In addition to the foregoing suggestions, the evaluator might consider the following questions. (1) Has the management of the portfolio been reviewed recently? Such a review should be done in detail and by a neutral third party, perhaps an acknowledged expert on another campus. (2) Does the nature and use of the portfolio reinforce the goals and objectives of the institution? And (3) do the investment policies and procedures follow sound financial practices?

34. **Does the institution have an effective system for demonstrating its accountability?**

To be truly accountable to its constituents, public or private, an institution must show that it uses its human and material resources effectively to achieve accepted goals and objectives. To that end, it may engage in program budgeting, cost-benefit analyses, systems analysis, or management by objectives; use computerized systems for long-range projections; or adopt other kinds of systems for making better use of its resources.

Several factors have brought about a more precise approach to demonstrating accountability. One is the increasing use of management information systems (MIS), which have been applied in business and industry for a number of years and, more slowly, in higher education. Bogard's survey (1972) of 1,873 institutions found that only 13 percent had a management information system, although in schools with more than six thousand students, the figure was 32 percent.

A MIS should serve three basic needs. It should provide administrators with information about day-to-day operations, provide the information and analytical techniques needed to do both long- and short-term planning, and make possible the reports required by the societal and economic pressures for accountability. According to Balderston (1974, p. 227), such a system should also have (1) the capacity to analyze the costs, interactions, and goal contributions of programs, and access to comparative data to buttress the findings of such analysis, (2) a way of joining credible and expert academic judgments with financial information, (3) an institutional process that meets conditions of fairness, and (4) a quality and range of academic and administrative leadership that can reach and enforce decisions without losing the ability to function in the future.

Before I take up more specific approaches to accountability, a cautionary note about planning is in order. Advocates of planning might want to pause a moment to consider its negative aspects, and its zealots may achieve some slight degree of humility through this exercise. Massy (1975, p. 1) points out three objections to planning and the application of analytical tools to academic administration. "Centralized planning is dangerous because it takes the initiative away from those best able to exercise it—the faculty, department chairmen, and the deans of individual schools. . . . Detailed and scientific modeling schemes that often are associated with centralized planning will make it difficult for profound but qualitative judgments to make themselves felt. . . . [And] 'planning doesn't work anyway. We've been planning for five years and look at the mess we're in now!' " A fourth criticism is that planning can dampen or inhibit the creativity and spontaneity that are essential for keeping ideas and programs dynamic and strong.

In recent years a substantial majority of the major universities have developed MIS, although their effectiveness is mixed if they are judged by their ability to provide useful data for establishing priorities for programs. A good number of regional colleges and universities have also established such systems, but here the record is even more spotty. And only a minority of smaller colleges and universities have moved in this direction owing to inadequate data about the advantages, a lack of technical expertise, and insufficient money. But any college or university can adopt a more systematic approach to the collection and utilization of data on a scale that it can afford and manage, and every institution with a continuing management information system should periodically examine its efficiency (in terms of time and money) and effectiveness (in terms of assisting decision making).

A number of exemplary models for MIS and for achieving accountability can be found. For example, the "Meeth System"

(Meeth, 1974) has been used extensively by small colleges, and it has been modified and incorporated in two major projects by the Council for the Advancement of Small Colleges: the 1973–1976 project on Institutional Research and Planning, provided with more than $1 million under Title III by the United States Office of Education; and the new Institutional Development Project (1976–1980), funded for $4.5 million under Title III.

NACUBO (National Association . . . , 1975) has published a "practical guide"—*College Planning Cycle: People, Resources, Process* —to assist institutions with their planning and budgeting. This revised guide has benefited from the widespread exposure and use of the original manual (published in 1969). The guide provides detailed and concrete steps and checklists for implementation. Adequate planning and accountability, according to the NACUBO model, requires at one time or another these data: "staffing tables (including projected sabbatical leaves); cost of instruction by department; total cost of instruction per student; student aid (by type) per student; faculty and departmental course load; student enrollment by department and by class; faculty compensation by rank; a line-item budget (including historical cost data); balance sheet assets, including current funds, student loan funds, endowment funds, and plant funds; and various projections of enrollment, cash flow, and capital expenditures" (p. 6). This system, like the one developed by Meeth, does not require a computer.

The models used by Stanford University were developed by Massy (1975). The years of decentralization and incremental budgeting at Stanford were effective in developing quality programs, but it became apparent in about 1970 that these methods would not be satisfactory in the years ahead. So planning processes and models were developed to approach the future quite differently. Massy writes about what the Stanford models were designed and not designed to do: "They do not say what programs should be strengthened, retained, or reduced in scope. They do not indicate where to find 'slack' in administration or elsewhere. They do not even indicate what tuition to charge, how many students to admit, what the right payout from endowment ought to be, how large the budget should be, or how large a deficit or surplus ought to be run in a given year. They *do* provide some practical guidance on the latter set of issues. And by so doing, they make possible greater participation in the planning process by members of the institution and provide a useful input to the more detailed and qualitative aspects of faculty and staff planning" (p. 2).

A critical concept in the Stanford models is *long-run financial equilibrium*. When a budget is in equilibrium, income equals expense in the current base year, and the overall growth rates of income and expense are equal. Making estimates of long-range growth rates and bringing them into the planning process avoids the temptation to deal with budget imbalance by making short-term "fixes" that may obscure real problems or create more serious problems in the long run. Massy writes that "a number of key trade-offs are highlighted if long-run financial equilibrium is thought of as a constraint on the planning process. These include the tuition growth rate, the amount of budget reallocation (reductions in program to make funds available for new ventures), endowment payout, and possible changes in the institution's size and structure. The notion of a trade-off is critical; when an item is 'pushed in' somewhere in the system, the requirement for balance of budget levels and growth rates causes something to be 'pushed out' somewhere else. Quantification of such relations is a major objective of modeling" (1975, p. 3).

Massy gives some reasons why the models have had a substantial impact at Stanford (pp. 5–7):

> 1. Long-run financial equilibrium is a useful construct that is understandable and has considerable appeal to common sense. From a technical standpoint, it provides a set of terminal conditions for what otherwise would be an infinite-horizon decision problem.
> 2. It is possible to establish a local and explainable relation between the highly disaggregative bottom-up, five-year forecast and the gap-closing target that would bring about equilibrium. Without this link it would have been much more difficult to agree on a realistic target.
> 3. The model brings the funded improvement factor (set at 1 percent), the tuition growth rate, endowment payout, and other variables all together in the same conceptual package where the effect of trade-offs could more easily be seen. For example, the effect of changes in tuition or

funded improvement policies could easily be represented in terms of the "gap."

4. It is possible to do sensitivity analysis of key parameters. . . . It rather conclusively demonstrates that the recovery in the stock market hoped for by many would not make the problem go away. Thus it eliminates from contention the argument that a strategy of "watching and waiting" might be better than a painful budget-balancing program.

5. Since it is easy to rerun the model when data change (currently a run costs about twenty-two cents), it is possible to track variations in forecasts, assumptions, and choices on the budget-balancing target. Since October 1974 the gap has migrated from $10.2 million up to more than $12 million and back down to between $9 and $10 million. Thus the budget-balancing program can be dynamic in the sense of being responsive to changing conditions and assumptions.

6. The model deals with a multiyear time horizon. Since the achieving of equilibrium is set at several years in the future, extreme short-term fluctuations should be damped out. This property will become particularly important as the model is run and rerun over a succession of years, with differing assumptions.

Another systematic approach to planning and resource reallocation, aimed partly at demonstrating accountability, was initiated by President Frank Newman at the University of Rhode Island shortly after taking office. A Budget Task Force was established to review all university income and expenditures, to recommend a budget in accordance with proposed state appropriations and projected income from all other sources for that period, and to formulate recommendations for longer-range financial planning. Specifically, the Task Force was (1) to develop and present the university budget for the 1975–76 fiscal year, (2) to recommend ways and means of generating additional and new income for the university, (3) to recommend measures that would effect economies of operation and reduce expenditures, (4) to recommend procedures, programs, policies, and so on which would result in a creative and judicious use of university resources, (5) to recommend policies, programs, plans, and procedures that would stimulate the growth and development of the university, and (6) to recommend a procedure that could be followed in future years for building the university budget.

As the Task Force moved ahead in its work, two types of matters received its attention: *topics* (such as telephones, course duplication, fund raising, travel, building utilization, and personnel procedures, such as retirement policies) and defined *units* within the university structure (academic departments and colleges, special service units, such as the Counseling Center, administrative units like the Office of the Coordinator of Research, auxiliary enterprises, such as Housing and Health Services, and other units, including Custodial Services and Central Mailing).

Extensive reviews and recommendations by the Budget Task Force have continued, and the work of budget and program review has taken on a more or less permanent nature. Many of the more than two hundred recommendations have called for reductions in programs and personnel. In speaking about the aims of this extensive endeavor, President Newman stated: "One goal of this effort is to reduce or eliminate those programs that are weak or are of low priority. The importance of doing this in an intelligent and open way has increased as the state's (and consequently the university's) financial constraints have become more stringent. A second and more important goal is to develop and strengthen proposals which help encourage the latent capacity for imagination and improvement that is inherent in every operation of the university. A third goal is to free the resources to allow us to develop the occasional new program without which, or the potential for which, institutions become moribund."

Princeton University was able to eliminate within two years an annual $1 million deficit through developing a new budgeting and accountability process. Under the leadership of Provost Bowen (now president) and a group of systems analysts, Princeton altered its budget cycle to permit simultaneous consideration of all major claims on university resources. Previously, decisions on faculty salary increases, new positions, financial aid, and tuition were made throughout the year without sufficient consideration of related factors and on the basis of income projections made during the preceding summer. The new system enabled the university to develop a more precise set of priorities and to understand and act upon knowledge about the growing gap between income and expenditures.

Princeton also developed a multiyear planning system which projected future income and expenditures, and it devised a system for relating faculty staffing to teaching requirements. A university priorities committee of faculty members, students, and administrators (chaired by the provost) was established to broaden participation in the budgeting process and to explain to the university community the need for selective cutbacks.

Oklahoma State University had a Planning Council for some ten years before it adopted its planning and reallocation model. These early planning efforts were far from extensive, and the vast majority of the university community was unaware that the council existed and hence obviously was not involved in planning.

In 1974 a new and extensive planning and evaluation system was initiated by the president and coordinated by the Office of the Vice President for Academic Affairs. The system consisted of three separate yet closely related phases: program identification, the establishment of program priorities, and resource allocations. In phases one and two units reported and discussed what was in existence; phase III required more sophisticated and difficult decisions because each unit was asked to explore the future carefully and to set goals and objectives for itself. Each unit was asked to identify its highest priorities. In addition, the university administration selected certain programs that would be pushed to levels of excellence and national reputation. To provide money for the high-priority programs designated by the unit and by the administration, an "Excellence Fund" was created in the 1975 fiscal year. The Fund, essentially a self-tax, assessed units an amount equal to 2 percent of their 1975 budget, 4 percent of the 1978 budget, and 6 percent of the 1979 budget. (The 1972 Carnegie Commission report on *The More Effective Use of Resources* recommended "that colleges and universities develop a 'self-renewal' fund of 1 to 3 percent each year taken from existing allocations.")

In turning from these brief case studies of accountability systems, several questions are helpful for an institution seeking to make some judgments about its own accountability system: (1) Does the institution have both means for doing institutional research and a management information system? (2) Do administrators use the data produced by the IR office and the MIS in short- and long-range planning and for making operational decisions? Bogard's survey found that administrators did not make adequate use of these capacities in decision making. (3) Is there general consensus about what accountability is and is not? (4) Does the accountability system require a reasonable amount of paperwork? Some systems can create a paper blizzard and require inordinate amounts of professional time to develop statistics. More than a few systems have fallen under their own bureaucratic weight. (5) Has the management system been given a fair time trial? Generally speaking, the system should be given two or three years to prove itself, depending on the complexity of the system and the size of the institution and system.

Conclusion

Financial problems for higher education are the bad news; but there is some good news also—as Cheit (1973) points out:

> The financial problems of higher education have done more than stimulate cost-consciousness. They have led to significant new policies and practices on the campuses. In addition, the question of how to finance higher education has engaged the interest of a growing number of economists. It has produced a major management movement, complete with new techniques and a new vocabulary, and it has stimulated policy reviews by important organizations like the Committee for Economic Development. It has produced influential state studies in Washington, New York, and many states between. It has stimulated the invention of new devices for increasing income—the Common Fund (for cooperation in managing endowments) is one example; the income-contingent loan (deferred tuition) is another. It has brought action in about one-third of the states to increase public support of the private sector.

Good management is a means to other ends: better education for students, more effective public service, and greater research opportunities. This chapter is related to the previous one on administrative leadership because the overall quality of the money management will reflect the effectiveness of the chief administrative officer—if only in employing competent professionals to whom he or she can relate. The top campus executive does need to be quite involved in financial matters at many points, as in making policy decisions about the budget, about resource allocations, about investments, and about the institution's general financial health. The next five to ten years will produce little relief from the imperatives for this involvement.

And a final note on accountability and systems: A grain, or several grains, of common sense and perspective are in order. Adams (1974, p. 124) points out that "it would be ludicrous to improve the efficiency of a symphony orchestra by pruning the oboe players (who for long periods are doing nothing), or streamlining the violins (many of whom are playing the same notes and are thus guilty of duplication), or eliminating some of the musical passages (many of which are repetitious and hence seem redundant)." And Bowen (1976, p. 10) speaks to the same issue in this manner: "A family is a place where people live. When we speak of efficiency for a family, we do not talk of brownie points (credits) earned, cost per person, ratio of parents to children, or index of space utilization. . . . From a narrow pecuniary point of view, the typical American family is grossly inefficient. It wastes housing space. It provides specialized rooms for sleeping, eating, work, and recreation which are unused most of each day. . . . Indeed we applaud these inefficiencies by calling them a high standard of living." Demonstrating accountability is important, and management systems can be useful tools for providing more efficient operations and more effective learning, but systems and efficiency are not ends in themselves. They provide analytical assistance that can facilitate decisions being generally right, rather than precisely wrong if too much weight is given to the techniques.

9

Reviewing the Operation of the Governing Board

"Not many years ago, if you received a letter asking you to become a college trustee, you would probably have accepted without much concern. You might have asked if the duties were onerous and would have been assured the contrary. . . . If you receive the same invitation today, you would do well to consider before replying. First of all, you had better be prepared to work. Monthly or periodic meetings are only the beginning—there will be committees and luncheon conferences and telephone calls. Second, you may have to decide on some sticky issues on student protest and faculty discipline and to respond to the pressures of concerned alumni, public officials, and citizen groups. Third, the honor of your position will be recognized only in serving it to the best of your conscience and ability and not in any public acclaim or approval" (Heilbron, 1973, pp. 24–25).

With the founding of William and Mary College in Virginia in the late seventeenth century, there was introduced in America the Scottish university tradition of placing collegiate governance in the hands of prominent lay community members. The power of the trusteeship increased with the establishment of colleges by religious denominations and continued to grow throughout most of the eighteenth and nineteenth centuries. By the latter part of the nineteenth century, however, increasing secularism and strong presidential leadership in some notable universities were slowly eroding this power. The Carnegie Commission (1973a) pointed out that the board of the University of California first delegated authority to the president in 1891, when the president was permitted to hire a janitor, provided he reported his action promptly to the board (p. 31).

Much has happened since. The actions of students, faculty members, states, and the federal government have diminished some roles and powers of boards; and some observers, studying these historical trends, are predicting the complete demise of the board. Paltridge and his coauthors (1973) found that the number of boards dropped significantly during the decade of rapid college expansion in the 1960s because of multicampus and statewide systems. In 1960 there were 380 public four-year institutions governed by 218 boards; by mid 1972 the number of public four-year institutions had increased to 430 but the number of boards had dwindled to 164 (p. *iv*). Several states (including Wisconsin, Montana, Rhode Island, North Carolina, Nebraska, Tennessee, and Georgia) have abolished institutional boards in favor of ones at the state level.

This pattern has not resulted in an appreciable diminution of board power but, rather, in a greater concentration of it in fewer boards. The strength of the trustees has been diminished in one way, however. Because board members for systems or states cannot know in detail the issues and problems of each institution, the board staffs, with their primary knowledge, have become more important and powerful. But the trustees in private colleges still play a vigorous role and will undoubtedly continue to do so. In general, then, the board can be expected to remain a crucial element in institutional or system governance because it is needed. The Carnegie Commission (1973a, pp. 32–33) concluded that the board, at its best, serves these functions:

> • It holds and interprets the "trust"—the responsibility for the long-run welfare of the total institution; it defines the purposes to be followed and the standards to be met; it is the guardian of the mission of the campus; it evaluates overall performance.
>
> • It acts as a "buffer" between society and the campus, resisting improper external interference and introducing a necessary contact with the changing realities of the surrounding society; it is the principal gatekeeper for the campus, and its judgment about what is improper interference on the one hand, and what is constructive adjustment on the other, is of the utmost importance to the conduct of the institution.
>
> • It is the final arbiter of internal disputes involving the administration, the faculty, and the students—the court of last resort for most disagreements.
>
> • It is an "agent of change" in what is historically a conservative institution, deciding what changes should be permitted and what changes should be encouraged and when. The great period of modernization a century ago took place under the supervision and with the concurrence of the then existing boards; so have other major changes since that time.
>
> • It has the basic responsibility for the financial welfare of the campus.
>
> • Above all, it provides for the governance of the institution—even if it no longer actively governs in detail; it appoints and removes the president and other chief officers, and it arranges for the administrative structure.

What kinds of matters currently come before boards of trustees and what can be expected in the future? Table 27, from the Paltridge study of nineteen colleges and universities, indicates what aspects of institutional life were dealt with by the boards. There were noticeable shifts in this eight year period away from actions concerned with physical plant and toward educational programs, and slightly more attention was given to personnel items. Paltridge also found a small but perhaps significant shift toward greater

Table 27. Board Actions by Major Subject Areas

Subject Area	1972 (14 Boards) N = 3,203	1972 (5 Boards) N = 730	1964 (14 Boards) N = 3,273	+/−[a]
Personnel	21%	23%	19%	+
Student Affairs	2	3	3	−
Business and Finance	24	23	24	
Physical Plant	21	19	28	−
External Affairs	2	2	2	
Internal Affairs	4	3	3	+
Administrative Organization	3	4	3	
Ceremonial Actions	2	2	2	
Educational Programs	17	16	12	+
Other	4	5	3	+

[a]Increase/decrease is for fourteen boards.
Source: Paltridge and others, 1973, p. 31.

interest in matters related to tenure, and boards generally became more interested in appointments. Student newspapers and codes of student conduct likewise received greater attention, but interest waned in scholarships and athletic programs. The decreased interest in legal affairs is a bit surprising. But one expected and found increased attention to the operating budget and to gifts and endowments. In the category of educational programs, fewer actions were taken regarding research grants and contracts, probably because the amount of federal and state money for these activities shrank. The number of actions related to long-range plans grew substantially, and trustees also became more interested in degree programs.

In the future, trustees can be expected to give greater attention to academic programs, according to the findings of an Association of Governing Boards (AGB) survey by Zwingle and Mayville (1974). This study of 599 board chairmen focused on the dominant concerns of trustees. In reacting to the statement "Trustees and regents necessarily must be more responsible for helping to assess program needs of students than was probably true in preceding decades," 83 percent agreed and 14 percent disagreed. The respondents also agreed (70 percent to 18 percent) that their "education" or "academic" policies committee has become more important in recent years (pp. 44–45). Similar attitudes were expressed by Bean (1975), a private college trustee with twenty-five years' experience, who spoke of the past reluctance of board members to venture into the "education" part of the collegiate enterprise: "The barbed wire and electric fences which existed then have been neither lowered nor deactivated. I suggest that it is time for faculties and administrations to reevaluate this situation in the light of the fact that they are dealing with a new breed of trustees. These trustees are almost all college-educated. . . .They are alive to varied organizational styles. . . .They are continually subjected to the educative process in their own businesses or professions. . . . I suggest the time has come not merely for the trustee to interest himself in the guts of the educational process but also for faculties to welcome that interest and advice. The gradual erosion of the defensive position which faculties have taken will be beneficial to the world of education in the broadest sense" (p. 42).

As we have seen, reviewing the institution's financial operation is an increasingly prominent trustee function, especially of the board's financial or budget committee. These three questions may help the evaluator sharpen his focus on this function: Are monetary affairs managed efficiently and effectively? Do budget decisions reflect the aims of the institution? What changes in management might improve the institution's fiscal health?

Board members are also likely to become more concerned with the related functions of institutional planning and management. Freeman (1976, p. 35) believes that "board members are becoming increasingly involved and better informed about the overall management of their institutions. Many trustees appear determined to play a stronger role, influencing not only fiscal policies but also more substantive issues related to basic programs of instruction, research, and service. Such 'trustee-activism' seems to be essential if our nation's colleges and universities are to remain viable in serving the educational needs of a society gripped by the forces of rapid social, political, and technological change."

We turn now to the four criterion questions that deal with evaluating the functioning and performance of the board.

35. **Are the policies and procedures developed for conducting board affairs satisfactory?**

Zwingle and Mayville's general impression was "that neither presidents nor boards have deliberated seriously about the question of role and scope for the board. It is not a general question but a specific issue for each board. Bylaws are intended to specify the procedures to be followed by a board; but bylaws are subject to neglect and are frequently out of date. Something more is needed as a current declaration of board-administration procedures" (1974, p. 9). The board's effectiveness is closely related to the structure of its organization and the conduct of its meetings. The board's rules, formulated gradually and frequently based on habit or tradition, determine these matters. An effective board periodically takes time to sort out its duties, critically review its organizational structure and rules of procedure, and update its policy or operations documents.

A starting point for this "something more" might be to assess the current policy manual of the institutional or system governing board using the following checklist:

A. Legal Provisions

    1. Quotes or states the source authorizing board power.
    2. Distinguishes between statutory law and board policies.
    3. Quotes or states the statutes where they relate to board policies.

B. The Board: Membership, Duties, Powers, and Organization

    4. States the method of selection and the term of office of board members.
    5. States the compensation of board members.
    6. States the method of orientation of new board members to their duties and powers.
    7. States the duties, powers, and functions of the board.
    8. Delineates the organization of the board.
    9. States the duties and powers of the board officers.
    10. States the composition, duties, and powers of board committees.

11. States the governmental and administrative lines of authority or includes an organization chart.
12. States the time and place of regular board meetings.
13. States the meeting procedures of the board.
14. States the policies dealing with public attendance at board meetings.
15. States the availability of the board policy manual as a public document.
16. States the policies for amending the policy manual.
17. States the policies for awarding honorary degrees.

C. The University President and Staff

18. Explains the relationship of the university president to the board.
19. States the policies or laws pertaining to the appointment of the university president.
20. States the duties and powers of the university president.
21. States the policies pertaining to the appointment of the university president's administrative staff.

D. The Board's Chief Executive Officer and Staff. (This section applies only to state boards having more than one institution under their control and to boards having an executive officer other than the president.)

22. Explains the relationship of the board's chief executive officer to the board itself.
23. Explains the relationship of the board's chief executive officer to the university president(s).
24. States the policies or laws pertaining to the appointment of the board's chief executive officer.
25. States the duties and powers of the board's chief executive officer.
26. States the policies pertaining to the appointment of the chief executive officer's staff.

E. The Institution's Professional Staff

27. States the appointment policies.
28. States the duties and responsibilities.

29. States the policies dealing with the participation of the professional staff in board policy formulation.
30. States the policies for settling faculty-administration disputes.
31. States the rank, promotion, and salary policies for the professional staff.
32. States the absence, leave, and vacation policies.
33. States the tenure, retirement, and discharge policies.
34. States the policies on academic freedom.
35. States the policies on consulting practices and outside employment.
36. States the policies on patents and copyrights for the professional staff.
37. States the policies regarding political activities on the part of the professional staff.
38. States the policies regarding the employment of persons who advocate the unlawful overthrow of the Government of the United States.
39. States the employment policies regarding persons who knowingly have become associated either as members or as sympathizers with one or more subversive or unlawful organizations or movements as defined by state law.

F. The Institution's Nonprofessional Personnel

40. States the appointment policies.
41. States the absence, leave, and vacation policies.
42. States the termination and retirement policies.
43. States the policies regarding political activities on the part of the nonprofessional staff.

G. Students

44. States the admission, enrollment, retention, and attendance policies.
45. States the fees and tuition policies.
46. States the policies on students' participation in board policy formulation.

H. Educational Organization and the Research Program

    47. Clarifies the institution's educational purposes, objectives, and functions.

    48. Delineates the institution's educational organization.

    49. States the institution's policies dealing with research.

I. Business Management

    50. States the institution's budget policies.

    51. States the institution's auditing and accounting policies.

    52. States the institution's purchasing policies.

    53. States the institution's policies concerned with insurance.

    54. States the institution's policies dealing with the acceptance and management of gifts, grants, endowments, and donations.

    55. States the institution's development and long-range planning policies.

    56. States the institution's policies dealing with the use of physical facilities.

    57. States the institution's construction and maintenance policies.

J. Public Relations

    58. States the policies for dealing with citizen complaints.

    59. States the policies concerned with solicitations and advertising.

    60. States the policies for dealing with national, state, or local community organizations or agencies.

    61. States the policies concerned with extramural athletics.

    62. States the policies dealing with alumni affairs.

    63. States the policies concerning articulation with other universities, colleges, or schools.

    64. States policies regarding the sponsored appearance of nonuniversity persons on campus.

    65. States the institution's policies dealing with publication and information service.

K. Physical Characteristics of the Manual

66. Is separately bound.
67. Provides for the addition of new policies and for the orderly revision of old ones.
68. Contains an adequate table of contents and/or index.
69. Has an attractive format and employs a readable type.
70. Utilizes effective captions and is logically organized.

The following more general questions, based on AGB surveys, may be helpful in evaluating the institution's guidelines for conducting board affairs. (1) Within the past two or three years, has the board formally reviewed its procedures and policies? (2) With respect to the board's agenda, does it focus on issues of policy that the board needs to consider? Is it accompanied by appropriate supporting information in the right amount? Does it reach board members sufficiently in advance of the meeting? And does it allow the board ample time to consider key issues? (3) Do board policies provide for rotating leadership in key board offices?

36. **Do the trustees understand the differences between policy formulation and policy implementation and do they apply this knowledge?**
    The Paltridge study (1973) referred to above considered not only the subjects of board decisions but also their level of importance: level I, decisions of prime importance to institutional goals; level II, control decisions having to do with direction, arbitration, special appointments, or contract awards; and level III, routine decisions on rules and procedures, appointments, or personnel, or awards made on the basis of prescribed procedures. Most board policy decisions (about 42 percent) were level III decisions—and 90 percent of these dealt with appointments. About 37 percent were level II decisions, and about 7 percent were level I actions (the remaining 14 percent were uncoded). Of the first-level decisions, the largest number were concerned with educational matters and the next largest with money matters. The *number* (not percentage) of decisions on tuition and fees more than doubled from 1964 to 1972. One might conclude that these data

confirm the rubber-stamp characterization of most board actions, yet level I decisions, being the most complicated, entail more prolonged discussion and debate, and therefore fewer of them should be expected.

The total number as well as the percentage of policy decisions made by institutions in the Paltridge sample is given in Table 28. A total of 3,303 decisions were made in 1972 as compared with 2,731 in 1964, or a 17 percent increase. In the categories of decisions, personnel actions increased 33 percent, business-finance increased 14 percent, all educational programs increased 39 percent, and physical plant actions decreased 12 percent.

Paltridge and his associates studied what decisions were made as well as the processes of decision making in more than one hundred meetings by nineteen governing boards of public four-year institutions, concluding: "The most significant finding of this research is that boards undertake a tremendous volume of decision actions in the course of a year's meetings, and much of this volume is in the form of pro-forma actions on long lists of detailed operational matters. [Their] responsibility for legislative policy formation, long-range planning, administrative guidance, review of performance, and support of the institution as it faces hostile critics from within and without the campus is frequently given minor attention or left to the initiative of administrators or governmental agencies" (1973, pp. *iv-v*).

The line between policy and procedure can be thin indeed, and considerations of politics or sensitivity can elevate procedure above policy. Procedure, for example, is all-important where due process is at issue, and the fact that process is at least as important as product in academe can place much importance on procedure. Yet policy should be separated from procedure as carefully as possible, and the chief campus officer, working closely with the board chairperson, should develop the agenda. The chief administrative officer also has a major responsibility for educating board members so that they become more sensitive to their obligations as policy makers.

The following questions may be useful in appraising whether the differences between policy and procedure are being understood. (1) Do board rules and procedures provide some gen-

Table 28. Major Areas of Governing Board Decisions, by Level

	1972 (14 boards)				1964 (14 boards)			
	I	II	III	N=	I	II	III	N=
All Personnel Actions	2.6%	14.5%	78.8%	925	2.3%	17.4%	78.3%	624
Appointments	2.7	1.9	90.6	651	2.6	3.9	92.7	385
Academic salaries	3.9	31.6	61.8	76	-	23.9	70.4	71
Employment conditions	-	56.0	42.4	66	1.4	58.5	40.0	70
Staff benefits	-	87.7	15.3	46	-	82.0	15.3	39
All Business-Finance Actions	7.0	36.7	51.0	926	5.6	36.0	53.6	800
Gifts, endowments	-	4.0	96.0	205	-	7.3	92.6	164
Legal matters	-	68.6	31.4	150	-	57.6	42.4	189
Tuitions, fees	9.9	46.6	42.8	131	8.0	46.7	43.5	62
Budget transfers	-	17.1	82.9	111	-	32.7	66.3	92
Physical Plant Actions	5.2	53.6	38.3	796	7.7	46.7	40.3	904
Stages, conditions	-	68.8	31.1	180	-	54.2	45.7	214
Fund appropriations	13.4	79.1	7.3	149	21.5	70.5	7.9	153
Contract awards	-	26.1	73.0	126	-	34.3	63.6	181
Lease easements	-	10.0	90.0	90	-	7.7	91.3	91
All Educational Programs	14.6	62.6	17.6	656	8.5	64.5	19.5	403
Grants, contracts	.4	97.7	-	222	-	97.2	-	185
Intrainstitutional programs	20.5	52.6	9.0	78	33.9	33.9	9.4	53
Cooperative programs	-	54.1	41.0	61	-	38.2	55.9	34

Source: Paltridge, 1973, p. 40.

eral guidance for developing agendas that focus on policy issues?
(2) Does the board chairperson pay close attention to the policy and
procedural aspects of agenda items? (3) Does the board periodically
assess how well it is doing in keeping the primary focus on policy
issues? Are adjustments made after such an evaluation reveals the
focus is incorrect?

37. **Does the governing board work effectively with external con-
    stituencies?**
    An important role of trustees is to represent the institution
to the public. This role calls for listening and learning from members of the community and sometimes explaining the institution to
them. This function is an important reason why chief campus administrators need to keep trustees regularly informed about the
institution and its activities.

Trustees normally understand the complexities and sensitivities of their role as spokesmen for the institution. Unless authorized by the chairperson, individual trustees should not take public positions on issues related to the institution, leaving this to the
chairman or the chief campus administrator.

Trustees must be staunch defenders of academic freedom—the right of professors and others to speak and to publish
without fear of censure, reprisal, or dismissal. Henderson (1972)
contended: "A prime responsibility of the board is to protect the
institution from the wrath of groups that would destroy the function [academic freedom]. The board must guard zealously the
privilege of objective search and responsible advocacy regarding
change in our society" (p. 15). And Babbidge (1975, p. 40) spoke in
these terms: "Trustees will have to develop the conviction and
courage to face their business and professional associates—and
their neighbors—and their political leaders—and argue for the
obvious truth: that in a free society, ideologically tyranny is more
dangerous than 'fuzzy-headed thinking'; that mediocrity and con-
formity cost more in the long run than do duplication and inefficiency; that eccentric, even jagged patterns of organization contribute more to human advancement than do any of the symbols of
symmetry—the pyramid that crumbles or the perfect billiard ball
that will roll in whatever direction it is pushed."

Fund raising is a third dimension of external relations. Trustee participation in fund raising varies greatly; members of system boards have no responsibility, whereas trustees of many private institutions play a very significant role. Radock (1976, p. 23) tells of one president who suggested that trustees must "Give, get, or get off." Another advised that trustees must furnish "Work, Wealth, Wisdom." This was revised by a president who said, "Let the trustees furnish the Work and Wealth. I will furnish the Wisdom." (Presumably these suggestions were made by presidents to researchers or colleagues rather than to board members!)

The following checklist (Radock, 1976, p. 27) can be useful to trustees as fund raisers:

1. Do you have a written statement defining your personal role in the fund-raising effort?

2. Are you convinced that the institution does indeed need private dollars?

3. Do you give your support to providing the necessary budget for a good fund-raising program?

4. Are you on the lookout for possible sources of private support?

5. If the institution has a major campaign, are you willing to give leadership in the effort?

6. Are you willing to make a gift commensurate with your ability to pay?

7. Are you positive in your own mind that the cause merits your support and the support of others?

8. Are you willing to use your influence to establish priorities for the institution?

9. Are you willing to support the president and executive officers when certain policies are needed to ensure a smooth fund-raising operation (such as guidelines for fund raising and capital campaigns)?

10. Are you prepared to authorize or assist in the conduct of feasibility and planning studies?

11. Are you willing to discuss openly with institutional leaders points of difference or misunderstanding?

12. Do you assist in enlisting top volunteer leadership for your institution's development program?

Presidents believe that the fund-raising abilities of trustees should be a more prominent factor in their selection, according to the findings of Davis and Batchelor (1974). One hundred eighty-six presidents said "fund-raising capability" *is* the eighth most important influence in appointing trustees, but they listed the same item as the fourth most important factor that *should be* considered in these appointments (p. 45).

In assessing the quality of the board's relationships with external constituencies, the evaluator might consider the following questions.

1. To what extent does the board keep itself well informed about the educational and manpower needs of its primary community constituency?

2. To what extent has the board established channels of access and exchange between the board and the community?

3. Has the board been willing to take strong stands against unwarranted attacks on academic freedom and other intrusions into the institution's internal affairs?

4. Are the board's fund-raising activities effective, and is about the right amount of board-member time devoted to them?

38. Does the board contribute positively to improving the institution?

The board, given its ultimate responsibility for the institution, can have a decisive influence on the directions and quality of the institution. Its usefulness is directly related to vigorous and periodic self-evaluation. In the AGB survey by Zwingle and Mayville (1974), cited above, the 599 board chairmen responded to a number of questions beginning with the phrase "Within the past two years, has your board . . ." Their responses are shown in Table 29. The institutional evaluator might rate his or her own board on these items.

Another type of self-rating by board members is presented in Davis and Batchelor (1974), who asked the 186 presidents and 1,495 board members in their sample to rate the general effectiveness of the current board in these four categories: clearly in the highest category for institutions of this type; not of the highest order, but satisfactory; less than completely satisfactory—at least in some respects—but adequate; in need of major change toward improvement of persistent problems. (Table 30 indicates the ratings for the highest category.) The respondees were quite pleased

Table 29. Board Chairmen's Evaluations of Board Performance in Percentages

	Summary		Public Two-Year		Private Two-Year		Public Four-Year		Private Four-Year	
	% Yes	% No	% Yes	% No	% Yes	% No	% Yes	% No	% Yes	% No
Within the past two years, has your board . . . taken measures to increase the effectiveness and contribution of the educational policies or academic affairs committee?	71	24	59	32	83	15	64	27	77	21
conducted, with the chief executive officer, any sort of a "retreat" to discuss in depth key issues bearing on the future of the institution?	46	52	44	51	46	54	51	48	47	53
revised substantially its policy with regard to faculty tenure?	25	72	26	72	22	54	26	71	25	73
attempted to evaluate its performance?	56	42	61	36	58	39	44	51	57	42
attempted to evaluate the performance of the chief executive officer?	63	33	74	26	49	49	60	35	61	35
adopted a formal policy concerning what has been termed "social responsibilities" regarding the institution's portfolio?	21	71	27	62	24	66	15	77	21	74

Source: Zwingle and Mayville, 1974, p. 47.

Table 30. Percentages of Trustees and Presidents Giving Selected Dimensions of Board Effectiveness the Highest Rating

	Institutional Group															
	Public Two-Year		State College		Public University		Private Two-Year		Private Lib. Arts		Private University		Institution Black		Total	
Dimension	T	P	T	P	T	P	T	P	T	P	T	P	T	P	T	P
Overall effectiveness	51%	54%	40%	35%	50%	52%	50%	40%	51%	44%	54%	48%	43%	36%	48%	46%
Board-president relationship	62	76	55	62	60	57	56	80	70	79	65	67	61	43	63	68
Rapport among members	55	57	60	43	60	47	54	53	64	72	56	67	58	36	59	56
Direction by chairman	38	40	38	29	53	34	51	50	52	62	46	74	49	57	48	49
Sense of accomplishment	50	62	38	38	50	40	34	27	44	56	42	42	39	29	43	46
Board member diversity	45	27	45	33	48	20	36	27	41	23	45	38	32	29	42	27
Board strength	37	35	38	29	41	37	38	33	43	49	47	52	31	43	41	40
Member involvement	38	43	30	19	49	47	28	20	40	30	34	33	28	21	36	33
Sense of priorities	27	27	25	24	31	13	29	33	39	42	33	38	34	21	33	29
Sensitivity to different views	27	32	32	38	40	30	24	33	31	35	28	33	32	36	30	34

	Board structure	Financial support	Knowledge of institution and higher education
	30	13	22
	30	23	22
	16	9	18
	19	5	10
	40	15	22
	33	7	13
	22	14	14
	33	0	20
	33	34	24
	30	33	20
	37	44	18
	33	29	29
	25	15	23
	38	14	21
	30	25	20
	31	19	20

Source: Davis and Batchelor, 1974, p. 39.

with the board's performance, since only 3 percent of the presidents and 4 percent of the trustees rated the board in the bottom category.

A question arises about the effectiveness of these kinds of self-evaluation. The exercise itself can stimulate analysis, but the sensitive, important, and sometimes political nature of trustees' responsibilities may deter careful self-analysis, especially if the results might find their way into the newspapers. Nevertheless, board members may profitably go through a self-analysis and evaluation, and an impartial outsider (consultant or outside trustee) might be helpful in the process.

In addition to those already presented, the AGB "Survey Form Used for Study of Effectiveness of Governing Boards" can be used as a checklist by the board itself or perhaps by an impartial outsider also. Since this survey form has been used for several trustee studies, the data it has produced could be the basis of comparison studies. Another helpful resource is a set of self-study guidelines and criteria published by the AGB in 1976 (available from the AGB, One Dupont Circle, Washington, D. C.). Developed by James Paltridge and others at the Center for Research and Development in Higher Education, University of California, Berkeley, the self-study guidelines are the same for public and private two-year colleges, four-year colleges, and universities, but there are some small differences among the excellent and simplified criteria for the three sectors.

The following five questions, based on these AGB guidelines, can assist in evaluating the board's contribution to improving the institution.

1. Does the board periodically review its statement of purpose and educational goals and examine the policies that implement them?

2. Does the board help to determine basic educational policies?

3. Does the board require, participate in, review, and approve comprehensive institutional planning regarding enrollments, staffing, physical facilities, the availability of resources, and educational programs?

4. Does the board fully accept its responsibility for prudent financial management?

5. How do board activities influence the quality of the institution? How could these activities contribute more to that quality?

Conclusion

Comprehensive institutional evaluations or more particular assessments of areas such as goals and objectives, personnel policies and procedures, planning, financial resources, and governance should not be undertaken without the involvement of the board. And the quality of these efforts will be significantly related to the quality of the board. The board's quality is related to the extent the board evaluates itself. As Zwingle and Mayville (1974, pp. 25–26) point out:

"It is noteworthy that one aspect alone in all the educational structure is exempt from scrutiny—the governing board. . . . Until governing boards themselves decide on their own initiative to maintain a program of evaluation and improvement, advice offered from outside will continue to float about but will continue to be gratuitous. . . . Members of a board may privately concede the need for change, but seldom will one or more of them take the initiative. . . . A board that will adopt a standing regulation calling for periodic outside appraisal, with the result made a part of the record, can set a new pace."

A study by Hartnett (1970, pp. 41–42) found "that on a campus where the trustees have liberal views regarding academic freedom, the faculty members tend to perceive the institution as being a 'free' place. Conversely, on campuses where trustees are more guarded in their views, the faculty perceive a climate that places more restraints on the academic and personal lives of faculty and students. Trustees' attitudes about 'democratic governance'— the extent to which members of the college community other than trustees and administrators are involved in making decisions—are similarly related to faculty members' views of how democratically their institution is governed." A weak or divisive or arrogant board can noticeably affect the performance of the institution's most crucial functions. It is essential, therefore, that any comprehensive institutional evaluation include an appraisal of the governing board.

10

Studying the Varieties and Impacts of External Relations

External relations vary considerably among different colleges and universities. Still, every institution has some, and in many cases one or more of these relations are critical to the institution's well being or survival. Professors can, and some should, live in ivory towers, but administrators cannot. Spending about one third or less of their time on curriculum and instruction and about two fifths of it off campus, chief campus administrators know well the importance of external relations.

Colleges and universities have many constituencies. Those identified by Kotler (1975, p. 18) are administrators and staff members, alumni, the business community, competitors, current

236

students, faculty members, foundations, the general public, government agencies (local, state, federal), high schools, the local community, the mass media, parents of students, prospective students, suppliers, and trustees. The extent of a school's involvement with these many external constituents remains a sensitive issue on many campuses. The primary question is, At what point is academic quality diminished by external activities?

The issue is far from new, and the two basic positions can be traced to Ancient Greece. Barzun (1968, p. 285) spoke of them in these terms: "the university must make up its mind and choose between two attitudes which go with two messages incessantly heard. One is: 'Behold our eminence—it deserves your support and affectionate regard after you have attended and shared our greatness.' The other is: 'We are a public utility like any other—drop in any time.' Both messages are spoken by the same voice and both, perhaps, should remain unspoken, but the first should secretly inspire the 'university conceived.' Let it be clear: The choice is not between being high-hat and being just folks. It is not a question of hospitableness—a university should be hospitable; it is a question of style, reflecting the fundamental choice as to what the university thinks it is. It can, from generous but misguided motives, yield to the assimilating effect of cooperation with the world."

Appraisal of the extent, nature, and quality of the external program can be facilitated by questions such as these:

1. Is the external program consistent with the institutional goals and objectives statement? If not, which is out of step—the statement or the external involvement?

2. Where are the institution's strengths in public service? Some colleges and programs have long and successful traditions in public service that should be continued, but in a time of tight resources it may not be realistic for some institutions to initiate new thrusts in this area.

3. What are the advantages of making a greater commitment of human and material resources to external affairs? Some private liberal arts colleges have concluded that their salvation is in external involvement, and in some cases it may be, but others are finding that this pot at the end of the rainbow is more illusory than real unless hard work and imagination are applied in generous proportions.

4. What are the disadvantages? Decisions on external involvement tend to be based more on alleged and hoped for advantages than on careful analyses. A number of issues need to be
addressed, such as, What are estimated costs of the new thrusts,
and will support for these programs require reallocation of money
from somewhere else? And how will these decisions be made? Will
increased off-campus involvement weaken some on-campus
academic programs, and if so, is this trade-off consistent with
where the institution wants to go?

39. **To what extent do the institution's activities contribute to
the quality of life in its primary service area?**
    The introduction to this chapter refers to two different posi-
tions on community relations. One group of institutions that established their position a long time ago are the land-grant universities,
which have made significant contributions to social welfare in many
areas. In agriculture, for example, they have revolutionized our
farming techniques, and a more recent thrust has been toward
greater urban involvement. Institutions that choose the latter
might evaluate their efforts in light of the work of Nash and his
coauthors (1973), who present four ways to become involved with
urban, community, and minority-group problems.

> First and foremost, the college should become in-
> volved as an educator. There are five different ways in
> which it can do this:
> 1. It can become an educator of different types of
> people—primarily those who in the past have not met the
> "normal standards" for admission. . . .
> 2. It can provide a different and more relevant type
> of education to prepare people to life in cities and to deal
> with urban problems. This type of education may include
> student volunteer work in the community, programs that
> send students out into the community for part of their edu-
> cational experience, and black studies programs.
> 3. It can provide education for public officials and
> technologists who will work in cities. Fels Institute at the
> University of Pennsylvania and the New School's Institute
> in New York City are in the forefront here.
> 4. It can provide continuing or extension education.
> The University of Wisconsin is a leader here.

>   5. It can play a role in educating paraprofessionals,
> new careerists, and the hard-core unemployed. . . .
>   The second major area for involvement of colleges
> and universities in their communities is in their role as
> neighbor and citizen. Some colleges have attempted to re-
> build and revitalize their neighborhoods. The third and
> most traditional role of colleges and universities in dealing
> with the urban crisis is to provide services. Traditionally this
> has meant to do research. The fourth way in which the
> university can deal with the urban crisis is by serving as a
> model or example for the rest of society [pp. 2–3].

An interesting model of an institution that is designed to be "committed to the improvement of all aspects of community life" is the
"community renewal college" (Gollattscheck and others, 1976,
p. *xi*).

    An important element in that community life, and hence in
the institution's external relations, is private enterprise. People in
academe and the business world usually emphasize their differences rather than their similarities, but one industrial leader,
Morgens (1973, pp. 3–10), has identified these similarities: "Both
the business community and the academic community are great
forces for change in our society. . . . Each is a force for *continuity* in
our lives. . . . If sweeping changes were the only factor, our society
would lose its balance. We need a sense of continuity in all that we
do. Both are large and diverse and the people in them fall into the
familiar human categories—good, bad, and indifferent. Both are
in some trouble. Both have lost a great deal of public confidence. . . . Both reached a low point in public esteem about three
years ago [1970]. Since then, I think both have turned a corner and
are gradually moving upward. Both are great forces for change in
our society."

    Effective and amicable university-industry relationships may
not be easy, and representatives of both groups need to accept
problems as challenges rather than as obstacles. The criteria for
cooperation should be developed jointly as a prelude to mutual
activity so each group can better understand the other as well as the
process itself.

    Another aspect of external relations concerns other post-
secondary institutions. General rapport and effective working

relationships with other colleges and universities in the region are desirable and in many cases necessary even considering the enlightened self-interest that leads every institution to place itself first.

Consortia and interinstitutional cooperation must serve bona fide needs and interests, and each partner must be willing to give a little in the interests of others. And systematic and periodic evaluation of the cooperative arrangement should be undertaken. Though such evaluations can be complicated, they can be done fairly well. More research and study of evaluative methods for consortia are needed, however.

These questions might be helpful in appraising interinstitutional relationships:

1. Are general feelings toward other postsecondary institutions in the region friendly and cooperative, and vice versa?

2. Have media stories been favorably inclined toward the institution in terms of its relations with other colleges and universities in the region? If not, what concrete steps can be taken to ameliorate the situation?

3. Have formal and informal programs for sharing human and material resources been explored and tried? What evaluations of these efforts have been made, and with what results?

4. Has the institution taken sufficient initiatives toward cooperative endeavors?

The influence of a college on its community can be measured. Chief administrative officers, particularly in private institutions, know the importance of reminding community leaders of the economic, educational, social, and cultural benefits of having the institution located in the community. One systematic approach to assessing this impact has been developed by the National Center for Higher Education Management Systems (NCHEMS) of the Western Interstate Commission for Higher Education (1975). This technique measures the institution's focus on the local community, which is defined to include "the geographical area in which the majority of an institution's students, faculty, and staff reside; the community in which an institution's major business transactions (purchases of goods and services) take place; and the community in which an institution's direct public service activities . . . are arranged to meet the needs of the particular groups." The NCHEMS surveys and questions use these categories of impact: (1) *Education*—enrollment of nondegree/diploma/certificate students; community participation in community education programs offered by the institution; community participation in extension services; and educational goals achieved by community participants. (2) *Service*—the institution's participation in community affairs; community participation in an institution's social, cultural, and recreational programs; and community use of institutional facilities. (3) *Economic Impact*—the institution's payment of local taxes, state taxes, and tax compensation; the institution's purchase of locally provided utilities; the institution's purchase of locally delivered goods and services; the institution's capital equipment expenditure relevant to the local community; the institution's capital construction expenditure relevant to the local community; local expenditures by faculty and staff members; local expenditures by students; and local expenditures by visitors (National Center..., 1975, p. 167).

One of the NCHEMS surveys (p. 227), for appraising the economic impact on the local community of faculty and staff members, is shown below (I have omitted the answer spaces that are provided in the original).

1. What is your primary employment status at [name of institution]?
   Full-time faculty
   Part-time faculty
   Full-time staff
   Part-time staff
2. Approximately how many miles do you live from campus?
3. In what type of housing do you reside?
   Rent
   Own home
4. Please estimate your average monthly expenditures in the following categories. (Note: These estimates will be strictly confidential.)
   Rent or house payment
   Utilities (water, gas, electric, telephone, disposal)
   Food and beverages

Real estate and other local taxes
Automobile (payment, repairs, gas, insurance)
Charitable donations
Cleaning and laundry
Clothing
Entertainment
Furniture
Health (include dental and insurance)
Insurance (except auto and health)
Local public transportation
Magazines and newpapers
Personal items
Miscellaneous

5. What is your yearly expenditure for books and educational supplies?

Two additional models for measuring the impact of a college or university on the local economy may be helpful. The best known was developed for the American Council on Education by Caffrey and Isaacs (1971). A lesser-known but effective model (shown in Figure 3) was developed initially in 1970 by the State University of New York and used annually except for two years. What results does an application of this model produce? An example is the analysis of the 1975–1976 fiscal year at S. U. N. Y. Brockport, a campus with close to ten thousand students, which revealed that its economic impact on Monroe County exceeded $34 million. Included were the expenditures by professional staff members who would not be area residents if they had not been attracted to positions on the campus. They spent $9 million. Dormitory students who came to Brockport from homes outside Monroe County spent $6.4 million. And the campus purchased $2.6 million in local goods and services. Of all the income generated as the result of the campus' presence, it was estimated that $18.5 million was spent within the county itself. Local vendors and businessmen, in turn, recirculated a significant amount of this income in area transactions, increasing the true economic impact of the Brockport campus by an additional $15.8 million and bringing the total to $34.3 million for the year.

Figure 3. Model of the Economic Impact of an Institution on the Local Community

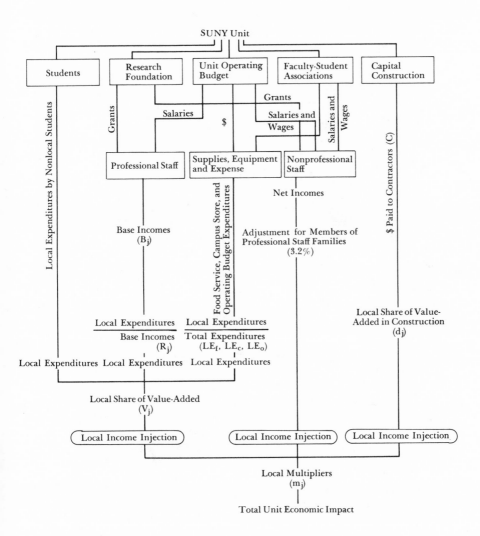

Source: State University of New York, 1978.

The study also highlighted another significant effect of expenditures by professional staff members, dormitory students, and the campus itself. This was an expansion of support services throughout Monroe County which created sixteen hundred new jobs. Not included in the impact figures was the more than $3.3 million in take-home pay received by the nonprofessional staff, who, for purposes of the survey, were considered to be members of the local community.

Dormitory students also brought increased state aid to Monroe County, the town of Sweden, and the village of Brockport. Since college students are counted as residents of their institution in the computation of per-capita state aid, the county, town, and village shared a combined total of $100,793 as the result of the college's enrollment.

40. **Are the institution's relationships with the state higher education (coordinating or governing) office effective?**

The questions today do not swirl around whether there should be statewide coordination or governance; the questions are, By whom, how, and to what ends? For those who wish state boards would go away, the outlook is not very promising. Millard (1976, pp. 12–13) sees these trends:

> None of the states that have established coordinating or consolidated governing agencies have abandoned them for a return to no coordinating or voluntary coordination. While bills to abolish boards have from time to time been introduced in state legislatures, the end result usually has been to strengthen these rather than do away with them. *If there is a trend, it has been in the direction of increasing the role or power of such boards and in some cases substituting for a coordinating structure a consolidated governing board structure.* The last state to move from voluntary coordination to a statutory coordinating board was Indiana in 1971. During the late 1960s and early 1970s, three states that began with coordinating boards replaced these with consolidated governing boards (Utah, 1969, North Carolina 1972, and Wisconsin, 1973). In the case of Rhode Island, a single governing board for all of education was established, and the law was further clarified and strengthened in 1973. The tendency to move from coordinating to governing struc-

tures may not be over; discussions of the possibility of such moves are going on in other states at the present time.

Since 1970, apart from the changes from coordinating to governing board structures, twenty states have taken legislative or constitutional action to modify their existing coordinating or governing structures, and . . . with one exception (South Carolina), the section has strengthened rather than weakened the respective boards.

The following criteria are offered to assist in evaluating the effectiveness of institutional liaison with state-level boards.

1. Appropriate institutional representatives have fairly regular contact with their counterparts in the state (or system) educational office.

2. Appropriate state-level officers visit the campus occasionally, and they have first-hand knowledge of the institution and its programs.

3. Amicable relationships exist between appropriate institutional administrators and state education officials.

4. The institution receives an equitable share of state funds for its operation. (Determining this equitable share is complicated but it can be, and usually is, done by someone.)

5. If some relational deficiencies have been revealed, the institution has given careful thought to specific ways of improving the situation.

41. **Is the institution's relationship with the federal government effective?**

The federal government has been involved in higher education for well over a century, beginning in a substantial way with the Morrill Act of 1862. Since 1944 the federal government has taken a steadily increasing role, as is indicated by the following major actions and events.

- 1944 Servicemen's Readjustment Act, "The G. I. Bill of Rights."
- 1948 Public Law 550 extended the G. I. Bill of Rights to Korean War veterans.
- 1954 *Brown* v. *Board of Education of Topeka* (347 U. S. 483) made school desegregation mandatory.

- 1957 National Defense Education Act.
- 1963 Higher Education Facilities Act provided financial support for public and private colleges and universities in construction of dormitories and other buildings.
- 1963 Vocational Education Act provided for technical education, state plans, area vocational schools.
- 1965 Higher Education Act, omnibus bill of financial aid to students and to institutions.
- 1970 National Labor Relations Board claimed jurisdiction over private nonprofit colleges and universities with respect to collective bargaining.
- 1972 The Education Amendments to the Higher Education Act of 1965 established the 1202 Commissions for Postsecondary Education.

The federal government has received increasing criticism in recent years for establishing and enforcing so many guidelines on civil rights, sex discrimination, and equal employment opportunities. Institutions are finding that considerable time and money are required to comply with the data requirements of the various forms. Ostar (1976, p. 31) mentions an American Council on Education study which reported that the financial exigencies experienced by some institutions "are attributable in large part to the added costs of implementing a larger and larger number of federally mandated social programs. The study found that at six schools in 1974–75, the cost of implementing the federally mandated social programs was between $9 and $10 million, representing between 1 and 4 percent of the operating budgets of the respective institutions. These are funds which will not be reimbursed through increased state appropriations or aid from the federal government. If the handrails in your institution happen to be forty-three inches high instead of forty-two inches, the cost of replacing all those handrails, which you must do, must come from somewhere." A number of institutions have initiated legal actions to test the government's authority to bring about compliance. The problem of compliance has caused much controversy, and it likely will remain a stormy issue for some years to come.

How, then, does one assess the effectiveness of an institution's relations with the federal government? Meaningful appraisal is based on a statement of these relationships and their objectives, a statement that should already have been prepared by the administration. Then the evaluator can use it to compare performance with expectations. The following questions point to areas where evaluation might take place:

1. Have the uses of federal support contributed positively to the institution's goals and objectives?

2. Has the process of securing and using federal funds contributed to the advancement of knowledge, public service, and classroom teaching and graduate study?

3. Are institutional managers able to cope with federal requirements in an orderly and effective manner?

4. Are the federal benefits gained commensurate with institutional efforts?

5. How does this institution, in terms of the procurement and use of federal funds, compare with benchmark institutions?

42. Is the institution able to secure acceptable levels of funds from private sources and foundations?

Philanthropy is big business in the United States. Education received $4.66 billion in 1977, or slightly more than 13 percent of the total figure of $35.2 billion. Drawing on his experience at the University of Michigan, Radock (1976, p. 26) sees these trends in college fund raising:

> 1. A period of intense competition for private dollars. Among the competitors will be private and public colleges and universities, junior and community colleges, museums, performing arts centers, minority groups, consumers, environmental, public affairs, and veterans' groups, women's groups, historical centers, youth and health organizations.
>
> 2. A time of increasing sophistication in fund-raising techniques involving complex data-processing systems, improved graphic arts, electronic message devices, improved direct mail.
>
> 3. A greater demand for accountability and increased scrutiny of financial resources by faculty, staff, and students, as well as foundations, corporations, consumer groups, and governmental agencies.

4. More frequent, more numerous, and larger capital campaigns as colleges seek funds for facilities, urgent needs, endowment, and student financial aid.

5. More designated giving by corporations with emphasis on program and project grants.

6. Inclusion in capital campaigns of sizeable amounts for student aid and minority programs and endowment for maintenance.

7. Continuation of foundations as a major source of support for large prestigious universities which have special potential and resources to respond to the needs of society.

8. Periodic proposals for tax reform which will affect private giving and worry major donors and foundations.

9. Far less distinction between public and private institutions, more private support for public institutions and more tax support for private institutions.

10. Greater reliance on thorough prospect research and market research by institutions, matching the prospective donor's interests with the institution's needs and educational programs.

11. A substantial increase in fund-raising goals for colleges as they seek to maintain their reputation for excellence, compete for new students, establish innovative programs, and provide those educational facilities and programs not financed either by state or federal appropriations or by tuition and fees.

12. Increased giving to higher education as more colleges establish comprehensive fund-raising programs including annual giving, deferred giving, major donor programs, parent's organizations, foundation and corporation programs, and special opportunity-type projects.

Several of these trends suggest aspects of the private-solicitation program that should be evaluated.

Also useful in this respect is Nelson's "checklist" for corporate giving (1970, p. 191). Nelson examines three parts of the fund-raising project: the case, the prospect, and the solicitation itself. With respect to the *case*, he suggests four questions. (1) Have we related our case to the following motives that influence corporate support—the *quid pro quo* benefit, the public relations benefit to the corporation, the effect on the firm's ability to attract needed personnel, the identification of our institution with free enterprise, the benefits to society, and the known personal convictions and objectives of corporation officers? (2) Have we matched the prospect with the appropriate type of support program? (3) Have we clearly identified the purposes for which funds are requested? And (4), have we shown the qualifications of our institution for carrying out these purposes?

Regarding the *prospect,* these questions are appropriate: (1) Have we established a list of corporations to which the institution has logical avenues of approach? (2) Have we given special attention to past donors, trustee-related companies, companies employing alumni, companies utilizing placement services, and companies with employees enrolled in programs of the institution? (3) Is continuing research conducted to keep prospect files up to date on corporate earnings and activities and changes among executives and directors? And (4), is a continuing program of public relations carried on to inform and cultivate the corporate constituency?

Regarding *solicitation,* Nelson recommends that the evaluator ask these questions: (1) Do members of the board of trustees assume leadership responsibility in corporate solicitation? (2) Does the president of the institution participate in presenting the institutional case to major corporate prospects? And (3), is there an organized program for corporate solicitation in which volunteers are helped to succeed in their assignments through adequate servicing by development staff members?

Corporations, though certainly important, are not as significant a private source as foundations, which rank second only to individual donors in voluntary support for American higher education. In 1976 foundations gave an estimated $550 million to colleges and universities, an increase of about $100 million or 22 percent over the previous year (Council for Financial Aid to Education, 1976). This was the largest increase in twenty years. Yet the methods of obtaining foundation assistance—aside from a few professional entrepreneurs and university and association development officers—are the least understood of the various kinds of fund raising.

The following questions may be helpful in evaluating the effectiveness of foundation solicitation by colleges and universities:

1. Does the development office maintain an active file of foundations that have contributed to the institution, and have the performances of these foundations been followed over the past five years?

2. Is the development officer assigned to foundations given adequate time and resources to pursue foundations effectively? Franz (1970, p. 163) has pointed out a self-evident truth that is sometimes overlooked: "It is important to understand that one of the essential characteristics of philanthropy is that effort is required to obtain it."

3. Does the institution have effective ways and means of soliciting ideas and projects from faculty members? Good ideas and programs are what count with foundations—along with the person doing the study and the abilities of the institution.

4. Does the institution have an established format for foundation proposals? Broce (1970) writes that the proposal should answer these questions: What will the grant accomplish (what need will be met)? Why is it important or unique? What period of time will be required to accomplish the program or complete the project? Will the project be continued after the grant expires? If so, how will it be financed? Who is responsible for the project, and what are his or her qualifications? (If more than one person will participate directly, a curriculum vitae on each is helpful.) Have similar projects been undertaken previously? How much money is required for the project? (An accurate and well-considered budget, including matching funds from the institution itself or other outside agencies, is essential.)

5. Does the institution have a strategy for approaching each foundation? Is adequate homework done?

6. Does the institution practice simple amenities, whether successful or not in receiving funds? These include prompt "thank you's" in either case.

7. Does the institution have an effective procedure for processing grant money—one that is so judged by professors who may be grant directors and by the foundations that awarded the grants?

8. How does the institution's success in securing foundation support compare with that of selected, similar institutions?

9. Has the institution assessed the impact of foundation support on the quality and direction of its academic program?

Conclusion

Donne's observation that "no man is an island" certainly applies to colleges and universities also. Every collegiate institution has at least one of the four kinds of external relations described in this chapter, and the institution's quality is tied to how well it handles these relations. One key element concerns the compatibility of the college's goals and objectives. What are the practical manifestations of the two different positions on external relations outlined at the beginning of this chapter?

The notion of trade-offs is also important. The comment of Massy (1975, p. 3), mentioned in an earlier chapter, bears repeating: "When an item is 'pushed in' somewhere in the system, the requirement for balance of budget levels and growth rates causes something to be 'pushed out' somewhere else." Where, then, are the funds for new or expanded programs of external relations? With standstill budgets the rule of the day in many institutions, additional funds for anything must come from somewhere else.

11

Developing a Commitment to Institutional Self-Improvement

Hope and risk taking are the essence of institutional improvement, as they are at the heart of the human urge to improve through innovation. Gabor (1970, p. 1) has observed: "When *Homo sapiens* appeared on the Earth, more or less in his present shape, innovation began. Early Man was equipped with the same sort of brain that later could write the *Principia Philosophiae Naturalis* and the *Principia Mathematica,* but the brain was almost empty. First had to come the greatest of all inventions: language; then tools, weapons, and a primitive social organization suitable for agriculture and the domestication of animals. Then, much later, came writing, and what we now call history. What is now called innovation still has an element in it of the instinct that drove primitive man to produce such wonderful inventions as the bow and arrow, or to devise such complicated social arrangements as totemism."

Self-improvement is a crucial element in all social and industrial organizations, and "adapt or die" applies to all types of collective human enterprises. Although some colleges and universities have forgotten or have not learned this simple truth or delude themselves by thinking that words about change will substitute for action, many others are taking self-study and improvement more seriously than ever before.

One can conclude, however, as did Martorana and Kuhns (1975, pp. 8–9), that "the art of stimulating and directing effective innovation in colleges and universities is not yet adequate for the tumultuous times ahead in higher education. Change is being pursued mainly as a reactive response to immediate problems; most of the energy for change is concentrating on the initiation of the process rather than on its assessment and evaluation; there is a dearth of information about effective change processes; and there is little effort to apply the information that does exist from such basic social sciences as sociology and psychology."

What do we know at present about the pressures for academic reform and the barriers against it? Hefferlin (1969, pp. 140–142) in his study of administrators' and faculty members' views of innovation, found the following factors important in stimulating change.

> One basic factor is simply the possibility of benefit or reward. Program change within any organization or institution is unlikely unless the change appears to lead to greater reward than does the present program. . . . A second factor is individual influence. It seems clear that to bring about change in colleges and universities, as in other organizations, advocacy is imperative to overcome innate institutional inertia. Call it inspiration, leadership, persuasion, or politicking; without it change is unlikely. . . . Third, the structure of the institution has an effect on the process of change through its openness to influence.
>
> Perhaps the most important conclusion of all, however, about the factors that are influential in academic reform concerns their origin. . . . The sources of academic

reform—as well as the constraints on reform—are primarily external to the system.

There seem also to be certain internal precursors of successful change efforts, according to Astin (1976), who names these five: receptivity to participation, depth of understanding, willingness to change, and constructive suggestions—all on the part of faculty members and administrators—and the presence of data that are related to the proposed change (pp. 38–40).

With respect to the external forces that are most influential, both in maintaining stability and in stimulating innovation, Hefferlin obtained the results shown in Table 31. The respondents said

Table 31. **External Groups Most Influential in Higher Education, and Direction of Influence**[a]

Most Influential External Group (listed in order of frequency)	For Stability	Varies	For Change	Total
	Direction of Influence (%)			
State government (29 cases)	55.2	10.3	34.5	100.0
Accrediting agencies (27)	44.5	22.2	33.3	100.0
Other colleges and universities (19)	10.5	10.5	79.0	100.0
Employers (18)	33.3	16.7	50.0	100.0
Churches (16)	62.4	18.8	18.8	100.0
Local interests (16)	18.8	25.0	56.2	100.0
Federal government (14)	0.0	21.4	78.6	100.0
Professional or scholarly associations (14)	21.4	7.1	71.5	100.0
Alumni (13)	61.5	7.7	30.8	100.0
Foundations (7)	0.0	0.0	100.0	100.0
Graduate schools (6)	60.0	20.0	20.0	100.0
Social trends (4)	0.0	0.0	100.0	100.0
Donors (3)	0.0	0.0	100.0	100.0
Average (193 cases)	33.7	14.5	51.8	100.0

[a]This table indicates, as an illustration, that of the 29 respondents who mentioned state governments as the outside force having the most influence on the academic program, 55.2 percent, or 16, consider state government as a force for stability, while 10.3 percent see it as a variable force and 34.5 percent view it as a force for change.

Source: Hefferlin, 1969, p. 98.

that the external groups supported change more often than did groups within the institution. And of these external forces, the respondents cited state governments and accrediting agencies as the most influential and graduate schools and churches as the most conservative (favoring stability).

Further confirmation of the idea that innovation derives from external sources is provided by Taylor (1971, p. 56), who observed: "Changes inside the educational system come primarily from the outside. The society and the goals it has set for itself exert the pressures, assert the demands, and supply the funds for what the society wants done."

What are the internal obstacles to academic reform? Table 32 gives more results of the Hefferlin study. Perhaps the most interesting finding here is that the faculty or departments were cited as the biggest barrier by administrators *and* faculty members themselves, whereas only about 13 percent of the faculty named the administration as the chief obstacle.

With this information as a background, the institutional evaluator can proceed to consider the last three of my forty-five criterion questions.

43. **Does the institution seek improvement through innovation and experimentation?**

Martorana and Kuhns (1975) developed a conceptual framework and a unique system which can be used to plan, project, implement, and assess change. Their "interactive forces theory" can be used to "evaluate the progress of any particular change, monitor how well particular tactics and strategies are working, predict the likely outcome of these tactics and strategies in light of the multitude of forces impinging on the innovation, judge when the innovation is in danger, and take remedial action to assure its implementation."

Innovation and experimentation need to be both planned and spontaneous, both encouraged and controlled. Unless some planning and coordination are done, new ideas and approaches can spring up without pattern and consume inordinate amounts of time and energy without producing compensatory success. Yet spontaneity is a crucial element in any campuswide effort, because one can never predict the derivation of useful ideas and ap-

Table 32. Obstacles to Academic Change

Respondents	Obstacles to Change (Percentage of Respondents Citing Each as Chief Obstacle)									
	Faculty or Depart-ments	General Inertia or Conserv-atism	Lack of Funds or Resources	Adminis-tration	Lack of an Adequate Staff	Confusion over or Problem with Goals	Trustees	External Influence	Miscel-laneous[a]	Total
Administrators	45.9	22.9	12.0	3.6	6.0	2.4	2.4	0.0	4.8	100.0
Department chairman	36.4	14.5	18.8	13.1	4.3	4.3	1.4	0.0	7.2	100.0
Professors	38.1	14.9	17.0	12.8	2.3	8.5	0.0	0.0	6.4	100.0
All respondents	40.8	18.1	15.6	9.0	4.5	4.5	1.5	0.0	6.0	100.0

[a] Among the miscellaneous obstacles are these: too rapid growth of the institution and subsequent loss of communication; small size of the college; lack of mutual understanding among departments; the institution's system of committees; the need to convince department chairman of the need for change; too little time and too many other commitments.

Source: Hefferlin, 1969, p. 100.

proaches. Innovating and experimenting should be encouraged and also controlled because not all innovations and experiments are promising. A backlog of experience can provide a shield against new ideas that have little chance of success or that require additional thought and planning.

There is no clear answer to the question "How much innovation and experimentation is enough?" The essential element in improvement (as compared with change) in the classroom is the individual teacher trying new ways on his or her own. At the departmental, college, or institutional level, innovations and experimentation need to be carefully designed, operationally monitored, coordinated, systematically evaluated, and selectively disseminated. Errors usually are made on the side of informality, a paucity of communication or coordination, little or casual evaluation, and dissemination as an afterthought. Spontaneity and trial and error as aspects of innovation are particularly important in the classroom, and they can be evident at other levels also, but more planning and coordination are needed at the departmental or institutional levels.

Every college or university needs someone who serves as a vice president for innovation—but without such a presumptuous title—and who is directly responsible to the chief administrative officer or at least to a person next to the chief. This individual should have significant responsibility for five crucial elements of this endeavor: stimulation, implementation, operation, evaluation, and dissemination. And, finally, the chief administrative officer's vigorous and sustained support of innovation and experimentation will go a long way toward setting the tone and style for the campus.

By way of summary, then, the following questions may assist in appraising whether the institution is indeed seeking improvement by these means. (1) Does the chief campus administrator actively encourage and support innovation and experimentation? (2) Is someone at the institution clearly in charge of innovation and experimentation? (3) Are faculty members involved significantly in innovative and experimental processes? For the campus as a whole, is the extent of faculty involvement consistent with providing quality teaching and learning?

The next three questions were developed by Katz and

Epperson (in Astin, 1976, p. 69): (4) Is the institution aware of its significant problems? (5) Are institutional politics intractable? That is, are various departments so checkmated that change in any one is resisted to preserve the status quo? (6) Is it possible to detect any institutional idealism? That is, are there key people who believe that the institution can and will improve and who can stimulate constructive thinking about policy changes?

44. Do campus groups have positive attitudes toward self-improvement?

"A visitor intent upon discovering the character of an institution will easily sense the educational tone of the place. It appears in the attitudes and practices of leadership—the president, or dean, or registrar, or business manager; it reveals itself in the habits and conversations of instructors; it is apparent in the conduct of students in the classroom, in the library, and on the grounds. One soon becomes aware of the existence or absence of a spirit of earnestness, or unity and mutual respect, of loyalty and energy, of intelligence and economy in the use of resources, of emphasis upon things that are vital, of conditions that make for high morale" (Haggerty, 1937).

The considerably greater complexities of contemporary institutions do not allow us to "easily sense the educational tone of the place," as suggested in the preceding passage from North Central's volume on the faculty, but perceptive observers with sufficient student-faculty-administrative experience and numerous campus consultations can discover something about the dynamism and morale of the campus if that is their objective.

A number of writers have stressed the role of leadership in creating and maintaining a positive attitude. Mayhew (1976) refers to Levine and Weingart's argument (1973) that if an institution had a well-developed philosophy of education, then capable administrators having power, resources, and the ability to use techniques of personnel management could produce changes. Mayhew also cites Greeley's finding (1968) that whether the Catholic colleges composing his sample improved or remained static depended chiefly on the professional (managerial) competence of the administrative leadership. Hefferlin (1969), also giving administrative leadership a significant role, noted that leadership would be more likely to succeed if it were avuncular in style rather than authoritarian or laissez-faire. Watson (Baskin and others, 1967) observed that changes affecting the entire institution were usually initiated and carried out by top administrators. Mayhew contends, however, that effective leadership cannot compensate for a lack of technical competence within an institution (1976, pp. 5–6).

Another significant source of a positive tone is the unrelenting pursuit of excellence. It is a key concept in institutional improvement—excellence in terms of specific aims that mesh idealism with realism. A policy statement by the American Association of State Colleges and Universities (1971, p. 2) declares: "Excellence or quality ought to be the goal toward which every institution strives," and a Carnegie Commission report (1972, p. 23) contends: "Quality is of the essence in academic life and it is hard to measure; but among carefully selected institutions and within the same institution it may be assumed to be sufficiently equal so that comparisons can be made—it is easier to compare quality than it is to measure it."

The problem of excellence and equality is age-old, and each generation must come to terms with it in the context of the pressing societal forces and needs at that time. Gardner's book on *Excellence* (1961) is subtitled *Can We Be Equal and Excellent Too,* which expresses the predicament of democratic forms of government (and organizations) in an age in which political viability requires equality and technological advancement requires excellence.

Thus, excellence can become a political concept when applied to considerations of equal educational opportunity. For example, compliance with affirmative action guidelines need not conflict with the pursuit of excellence; many institutions have been able to maintain quality and also satisfy the law's provisions concerning equal educational opportunity, but more intensive and specific search procedures are needed to achieve compliance.

The question "Whose standard of excellence?" sometimes arises. Mayhew and Ford (1971, pp. 53–54) contended that institutions can aspire to excellence, "but solid questions can be raised if every institution aspires to the same sort of excellence—an excellence characterized by increased selectivity and increased academic vigor in verbal and quantitative styles of reasoning. It should be possible for an institution to aim at the education of second-or-third-chance students, and to do so as excellently as does the institution which concentrates on highly talented potential academicians. It should be possible for a junior college to strive for excellence in the training of technicians without feeling inferior to the medical school, which strives for similar levels of achievement in a different domain."

The pursuit of excellence is not without its critics, however. Sanford (1968, p. 13) wrote that "the recent celebration of excellence . . . has left me with two major complaints. The first is with the conception of excellence that is too vague and general: excellence without reference to any particular action or quality, or simply excellence in all things. When the word is breathed, or shouted, we feel excited or guilty or anxious—the more so because we are not clear about what we are supposed to do. The accent on excellence without definition not only cuts off the search for genuine purposes but often serves as a screen behind which people conceal their real values and intentions. My other complaint is about a conception of excellence that is too narrow. Predominant in our schools and colleges today, this conception of academic and vocational excellence is endangering some of our highest values."

The pursuit of excellence clearly requires judgments about quality. If programs and units cannot maintain acceptable levels of excellence as defined by institutional goals and objectives, then their continuation should be questioned. Standards of excellence also relate in the same way to personnel decisions on promotion and tenure.

If taken seriously, the pursuit of excellence will not be the most comfortable guideline to live with. It requires, first of all, persistent advocacy by the chief administrative officer, with actions to fit the words. The following questions may be helpful in assessing the pursuit of excellence, and therefore also in appraising the campus attitudes toward improvement.

1. Has the institution addressed conflicts that can arise between the pursuit of excellence and compliance with laws requiring equality of educational opportunities?

2. Do the institution's goals and objectives statements clearly declare its aims with respect to the pursuit of excellence or quality?
3. Has the chief campus administrator made clear his vigorous support of the pursuit of excellence? Do his actions support the words?
4. Is the chief executive officer's position also evident in the words and actions of other key administrators?
5. Is the pursuit of excellence a functional guideline at the college and departmental levels?
6. Is the pursuit of excellence a functional consideration in making the difficult decisions about personnel and programs?

45. Does the institution have adequate established procedures for self-evaluation?

Evaluating one's own effectiveness should be done in the context of specific and circumstantial considerations and also in terms of general problems confronting contemporary organizations. For the latter dimension, Bennis and Stater (1968, pp. 57, 71) identified five human problems confronting contemporary organizations as well as what they believed to be essential elements of revitalization. These five are (1) integration, or the problem of how to integrate individual needs and management goals; (2) social influence, or the problem of the distribution of power and the sources of power and authority; (3) collaboration, or the problem of managing and resolving conflicts; (4) adaptation, or the problem of responding appropriately to changes induced by the environment of the organization; and (5) revitalization, or the problem of growth and decay. And the essential elements of revitalization, according to these authors, are "an ability to learn from experience and to codify, store, and retrieve the relevant knowledge; an ability to learn how to learn, that is, to develop methods for improving the learning process; an ability to acquire and use feedback mechanisms on performance, in short, to be self-analytical; [and] an ability to direct one's own destiny."

In regard to campus, rather than contextual, considerations, institutional evaluation should begin with the chief administrative officer. If this person is effective, then his or her support is critical to its success. If the chief is weak and ineffectual, then others may

need to initiate the process delicately. One might suppose that
every president is interested in evaluating the efficiency and effectiveness of the institution, yet in practice this information is not
eagerly sought by some academic administrators. In fact, a few
actively seek to avoid it, perhaps believing that the conclusions
might be embarrassing or that the institution does not have the
competence to undertake such studies.

But assuming that the president does actively support
evaluative efforts, someone at the vice-presidential level should be
clearly designated as the one in charge of these activities, and this
individual should report directly to the president. Though one
person should have the major responsibility, many others must be
intimately involved in the enterprise or it will go nowhere.

In addition to someone being in charge, there must be procedures for accomplishing the evaluation, and some materials that
have already been developed can be useful. For example, an institution might want to test its health or vitality against these ten
criteria developed by Miles (1964, pp. 14–17) for this purpose:

> *Goal focus:* The goals of the organization should be
> reasonably clear to those in the system.
>
> *Communication adequacy:* There should be relatively
> little distortion of communication—vertically or
> horizontally—and information should travel reasonably
> well.
>
> *Optimal power equalization:* Subordinates should be
> able to influence upward, and even more important, they
> should perceive that their boss can do likewise with his boss.
> Intergroup struggles for power should not be bitter al-
> though conflict would be present.
>
> *Resource utilization:* The system's inputs, especially
> human resources, should be used cohesively.
>
> *Cohesiveness:* The organization should know "who it
> is"; its members should feel attracted to the organization.
>
> *Morale:* Individuals should take satisfaction from
> their work, and a sense of general well-being should prevail.
>
> *Innovativeness:* A healthy system should tend to in-
> vent new procedures, move toward new goals, produce new
> kinds of products, diversify itself, and become more rather
> than less differentiated over a period of time.
>
> *Autonomy:* The organization should attain that de-

gree of independence from the environment which allows interaction with the environment but not control by it.

Adaptation: The system should be able to bring about corrective change in itself faster than the change cycle in the surrounding environment.

Problem-solving adequacy: Problems should be solved with minimal energy; they should stay solved; and the problem-solving mechanisms used should not be weakened, but maintained or strengthened.

Some institutional evaluation procedures might also be derived from research programs concerned with the college as an "environment" or with its "climate." Astin (1968a), Chickering and others (1969), Pace (1963, 1969), Pace and Stern (1958), Pervin (1967a, 1967b, 1968), and Stern (1962) have conducted studies on this aspect. And Feldman (1971) reviewed the literature, as do Miller and Prince (1977). The College and University Environment Scale (CUES) developed by Pace and the College Characteristics Index (CCI) developed by Stern describe the climate of a college in terms of "the aggregated perceptions of individuals in the college of the events, conditions, practices, opportunities and pressures of the total environment" (Feldman, 1971, p. 52). The Transactional Analysis of Personality and Environment (TAPE) of Pervin measures "the college environment by focusing on the way students as individuals and as groups perceive the environment. It is Pervin's contention that typical analyses using instruments such as the College Characteristics Index or the College and University Environment Scale fail to place sufficient attention on the interactions or transactions among parts of the university system (students, faculty, and administration)" (Falk, 1975, pp. 31–32).

A more comprehensive but related instrument is the "Institutional Functioning Inventory" (IFI), developed by the Educational Testing Service to help an institution "take stock of itself by systematically evaluating its strengths and weaknesses, the concerns of people at the college regarding programs and priorities, its readiness or climate for change. . . . The IFI helps to show how faculty, students, and administrators, and other constituent groups perceive the college—its teaching practices, governance arrangements, administrative policies, types of programs, the characteristic attitudes of groups of people, and other important aspects of campus life." Specifically, the IFI analyzes the college or university in terms of 132 items in these eleven categories (Educational Testing Services, 1972, pp. 5-6):

1. *Intellectual-Aesthetic Extracurriculum* (IAE): the extent to which activities and opportunities for intellectual and aesthetic stimulation are available outside the classroom.
2. *Freedom* (F): the extent of academic freedom for faculty and students as well as freedom in their personal lives for all individuals in the campus community.
3. *Human Diversity* (HD): the degree to which the faculty and student body are heterogeneous in their backgrounds and present attitudes.
4. *Concern for Improvement of Society* (IS): the desire among people at the institution to apply their knowledge and skills in solving social problems and prompting social change in America.
5. *Concern for Undergraduate Learning* (UL): the degree to which the college—in its structure, function, and professional commitment of faculty—emphasizes undergraduate teaching and learning.
6. *Democratic Governance* (DG): the extent to which individuals in the campus community who are directly affected by a decision have the opportunity to participate in making the decision.
7. *Meeting Local Needs* (MLN): institutional emphasis on providing educational and cultural opportunities for all adults in the surrounding communities.
8. *Self-study and Planning* (SP): the importance college leaders attach to continuous long-range planning for the total institution, and to institutional research needed in formulating and revising plans.
9. *Concern for Advancing Knowledge* (AK): the degree to which the institution—in its structure, function, and professional commitment of faculty—emphasizes research and scholarship aimed at extending the scope of human knowledge.
10. *Concern for Innovation* (CI): the strength of institutional commitment to experimentation with new ideas for educational practice.

11. *Institutional Esprit* (IE): the level of morale and sense of shared purposes among faculty and administrators.

Norms have been developed for the IFI, based on a carefully selected sample of thirty-seven colleges and universities that followed the national distribution. Figure 4 indicates how the IFI can reveal differences among institutions.

Evaluating one's own effectiveness requires time and resources, including technical competence and money. A survey by Hodgkinson and others (1975) asked what percentage of the total operating budget of an institution was devoted to evaluation. Seventy-one percent of the institutions responding indicated that

Figure 4. Faculty Members' Perceptions as Judged by the Institutional Functioning Inventory (Mean Score Profile)

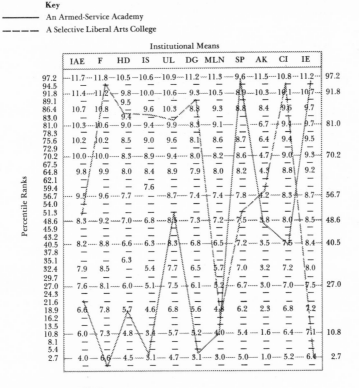

Key
———— An Armed-Service Academy
– – – – A Selective Liberal Arts College

Source: Peterson (1973).

they could not answer this query. The authors concluded: "This suggests (1) the amounts spent on evaluation were too small to mention, or (2) most institutions cannot break out expenses for evaluation as requested. We suspect that (2) is most common. We wanted to know whether or not an institution-wide committee on evaluation was part of the campus committee structure. Thirty-one percent of the institutions surveyed had such a committee (p. 234). Evidently some institutions are saying they do more evaluation than their allocations of time and money would substantiate.

How does the institution verify its own evaluations? Can the institution accept judgments rendered through its own policies and procedures as final and accurate, or is another step sometimes desirable, namely, some other verification process? This may involve another committee, another individual, or an outside reviewer or committee. Financial limitations may preclude more elaborate procedures, but some verifications are desirable if for no other reason than as a check on the functioning of the established evaluation policies and procedures.

The following questions may be helpful in appraising the institution's ability to evaluate itself.

1. Is the president sensitive to and persistent in having evaluations done?
2. Has the president assigned someone to take the major responsibility for evaluating programs, units, and the institution as a whole?
3. Does the institution have some policies and procedures for accomplishing the evaluation?
4. Do these policies and procedures allow for significant faculty involvement? And is there significant faculty involvement?
5. Does the institution commit sufficient time and resources to make these efforts effective?
6. What verification procedures does the institution use to check on its own evaluations?

Conclusion

The institutional environment has interested educators for some time, at least since the early Greek period, and persistent, systematic efforts toward self-improvement constitute a key element in a positive academic environment. Such self-improvement is also the best deterrent to excessive influence from external forces and the best catalyst for charting one's own destiny. Thus the majority of institutions, which do not have the ability to "ride out" the bottoms as a few major universities do and which are rather directly and after quite quickly affected by outside influences, should be especially concerned with improving themselves.

Finally, I would like to return to "hope" and "risk taking," which were mentioned in the first line of this chapter as being at the heart of the human instinct to improve through innovation. The late Loren Eiseley (1972) placed these values on them: "I have said man's entire career has been a crisis and he has survived by mother wit. . . . But [humans] did more than seek survival. They risked. They risked the mounting of the first wild stallion, they risked their lives on water. They eyed for long centuries the air and mastered it. . . . This touches upon hope, the hope of a crisis animal who risks and gives himself to good; to good causes and to bad, but who risks, risks always against the future. . . . Hope and risk, are they too great to expect of man? I do not believe it. They constitute his shadow. They have followed him for a million years."

12

Implementing Comprehensive Institutional Evaluation

The fact that evaluation does take place more often than we realize—and often for the wrong reasons and by those unfamiliar with its intricacies—deserves to be repeated here. The basic assumptions in Chapter One form a useful backdrop for contemplating an institutional evaluation. But before any plan is considered, there is a prior question: *Should an institutional evaluation be undertaken at all?* "Is this trip necessary?" This automobile bumper sticker seen during gas rationing in the Second World War poses the question that should be answered

affirmatively before we make the considerable investment of resources required for institutional appraisal. Dressel (1976, pp.
412–414) has raised the following further questions that can guide
the answer to the initial query:

> 1. Is the problem one requiring restudy of goals or
> operating policies, or is it primarily a failure in supervision,
> management, or administrative performance? . . . A self-
> study usually avoids pinpointing individual weaknesses
> and is not likely to correct problems created by poor admin-
> istration. . . .
> 2. Is the problem one which should be consid-
> ered and resolved through existing committees or other
> agencies? . . .
> 3. Is the problem of sufficient significance that re-
> sources can be allocated to support in-depth study over a
> period of weeks or months? . . .
> 4. Are the incentives or pressures which appear to
> require the . . . study of sufficient gravity to cause general
> acceptance of the need for the study, willingness to contri-
> bute to it, and readiness to attend to the results? . . .
> 5. Are administrative officers willing to make avail-
> able to a . . . study group all the information required to
> fully understand a problem and the implications of various
> solutions?

Other questions may be raised also, such as, Is the campus political
climate receptive to such a study? Is the *timing* of the study right?
(The answer lies in previous and current campus activities and in
the campus climate.) And does the campus have sufficient expertise to conduct the study, if that alternative is chosen, or can money
be found if outside expertise is preferred?

Before moving seriously into all that an institutional evaluation entails, the chief administrative officer and whomever he assigns the responsibility for appraisal should answer *in the affirmative* these questions as well as others that may be raised locally.

Once the decision is made to proceed, the next question is:
What kind of evaluation can be most useful? What Kipling once
wrote—"There are nine and sixty ways of constructing tribal lays,
and-every-single-one-of-them-is-right"—points up the importance
of developing an approach to evaluation that is tailored to the

specific institution. Not all the available techniques will be "right" in terms of conceptual design, institutional climate, and the personnel involved; so the particularizing process must be given careful attention in the earliest deliberations. But this process of course does not rule out making use of information from national surveys and comparative data.

Two general types of evaluation can be identified. One cluster consists of all those that are less than institution-wide in scope—the assessments of programs, faculty, students, and so on that have been dealt with in earlier chapters. Of these, ratings of the quality of graduate programs have probably been used most often to support judgments about the whole institution. (See Appendix A for a more extended discussion of these ratings.) The second type of appraisal, that of the entire college or university, has received considerably less attention, although interest in overall quality is increasing significantly. The next section of this chapter discusses five approaches to institutional evaluation that are currently being used: educational auditing, assessments by external consultants, self-studies for accreditation, self-studies for other purposes, and state and federal reviews.

Educational Auditing

The concept and practice of auditing is far from new. The establishment of the Securities and Exchange Commission in 1934 was in response to serious questions about the conduct and disclosure of business operations. Earlier, in 1917, the American Institute of Accountants published a list of standards for the preparation of audits. And more recently, the American Accounting Association (Mautz and Sharaf, 1961, p. 42), developed the following eight postulates. "(1) Financial statements and financial data are verifiable. (2) There is no necessary conflict of interest between the auditor and the management of the enterprise under audit. (3) The financial statements and other information submitted for verification are free from collusive and other unusual irregularities. (4) The existence of a satisfactory system of internal control eliminates the probability of irregularities. (5) Consistent application of generally accepted principles of accounting results in the fair presentation of financial position and the results of operations. (6) In the absence of clear evidence to the contrary, what has held true in the past for the enterprise under examination will hold true in the future. (7) When examining financial data for the purpose thereon, the auditor acts exclusively in the capacity of an auditor. And (8) the professional status of the independent auditor imposes commensurate professional obligations." As Harcleroad and Dickey (1975, p. 15) pointed out, "With some slight modification and changes in terminology, these same postulates might very well be applied to the process of institutional auditing and accrediting. The verifiability of data, determination of adequate sampling, and probability theory would be characteristic of both business and educational institutions."

Of the various differences between business and educational audits, perhaps the most important one relates to scope. The financial audit is only a part of the educational audit, whereas it is the significant aspect of evaluation in business. Some individuals, particularly those with business backgrounds, may equate institutional health almost exclusively with financial health. But, as I pointed out in Chapter Eight, such an equation should be avoided by institutions of higher education because of their purposes and funding procedures through government and private sources, a pattern fundamentally different from that of business.

Harcleroad (1976, p. 18) writes that educational accreditation (and, by extension, institutional evaluation) can profit in a number of ways from some of the experiences of the auditing profession:

> (1) There might be improvement in the total process if more of the work were to be carried on by full-time professionals, without losing the value of having many of the participants serving on a part-time basis as at present. (2) There is a need for a research staff, similar to that of the Financial Accounting Standard Board, to be working on basic principles of assessment and procedures to be followed. (3) Some form of continuity is needed for the institution involved and the main members of the team which will work with it as a representative of the accreditation body. (4) The standards of the regional associations and the specialized associations, and their respective commissions, should be similar enough to discount claims that great dif-

ferences invalidate the entire process. The business auditing system, even with all its current problems and its many
auditing firms, has sufficient comparability in its standards
and their application to be quite credible, most of the time.

Private managerial firms are becoming interested in the
audit approach to higher education; and the first Newman report
(1971, p. 70) spoke of the creation of new regional examining
universities. In considering the evaluation of higher education,
Bowen (1974, pp. 1–21) wrote that one of the needs is to find a
means of appraisal that is genuinely disinterested and yet takes
account of the many intangible elements. Perhaps a new profession
of independent judges of productivity and performance should be
created to evaluate institutions as well as higher education as a
whole.

Assessments by External Consultants

A number of colleges and universities as well as state systems
have chosen to use external consultants for departmental and
institutional studies. The New York Board of Regents' study of
doctoral-program quality, the Illinois Board of Higher Education's
Commission of Scholars, and the Louisiana Board of Regent's
doctoral-program study all relied on such consultants. The University of Chicago, as a specific institutional example, makes extensive
use of recognized scholars from similar universities in analyzing its
various programs. Their reports are printed in an official publication called The University of Chicago *Record.*

The use of external reviewers/consultants carries the primary advantages of selected expertise and impartiality. The selection committee can comb the nation for the individuals or consultant firms who will be most likely to provide the expertise needed in
a specific circumstance. And outside reviewers can be expected to
provide an impartiality that may be very difficult for internal personnel to achieve. The use of external reviewers also has two possible disadvantages. One advantage is characterized in a "Report of
the Visiting Committee to Evaluate the University of Chicago's Department of Anatomy" (1975, p. 109): "None of us is confident that
a single experience, however concentrated, can reveal all the details

of a complete system, nor that our responses are the most appropriate ones possible." The use of the phrase "the most appropriate ones" implies another possible disadvantage, namely, the repercussions of ill-advised remarks, statements, or conclusions. The reviewers leave on the afternoon airplane, but those remaining must live with the report. If the report opens old wounds, makes strong recommendations on extremely sensitive matters that are not subject to solution at the time, or discusses the wrong problems and issues, the reviewers can create more problems than they solve.

O'Connell and Meeth (1978, p. 41) cite the following advantages and disadvantages of internal and external evaluators. The *external* reviewer is competent in program evaluation techniques, has no vested interest in the program, and removes the evaluation burden from the existing staff. But this person may take longer to understand the program and the evaluation requirements, lacks working relationships with program staff and institutional personnel, and may be regarded with suspicion by program staff. The *internal evaluator* is familiar with the program and staff, understands channels of communication within the institution and its larger community, is familiar with the details of the program, and may be able to integrate the evaluation into the life of the program. On the disadvantage side, this individual may not have the skills required for the evaluation, may have a vested interest in the program, and may be overburdened with other duties.

The following questions, taken from a report by Pottinger (1975, pp. 2–4), might assist in choosing and using consultants.

1. How do you decide that a reviewer/consultant is needed?
   A. What is the nature of help needed?
   B. Is the circumstance specific enough to articulate clearly what is needed in the way of outside assistance? Some possible motivations include sorting out ambiguous problems, instilling motivation, gaining fresh perspectives, and recommending decisions that internal personnel prefer not to make.
2. How do you choose the proper consultant?
   A. Does the consultant have expertise in your specific area of need?
   B. Several questions might be asked of others who have used the consultant: (1) Did the consultant help you

further articulate your circumstance without prematurely anticipating a solution? (2) Did the consultant help identify resources and approaches within your situation which assisted after departure? (3) Did you feel more capable of dealing with the problem after the consultant left? (4) Knowing what you know now, would you hire the same consultant if you had it to do over again?

3. How do you most effectively use consultation?
   A. Make one person clearly responsible and accountable for the consultant's work.
   B. Take ample time to define clearly the problem.
   C. Explore expectations again about what can and cannot be done. Have a written record.
   D. Use consultant's time effectively. This requires carefully developed visitation schedules.
   E. Have a clear understanding of what evaluations and reports are expected or required from the consultant and within what time frame.

Self-Studies for Accreditation

Self-study in order to gain regional accreditation has been in existence throughout the twentieth century. (See Annotated Bibliography for further discussion of this topic.) The Council on Postsecondary Accreditation gives these historical and current goals of accreditation (1976a, p. 3): "foster excellence in postsecondary education through the development of criteria and guidelines for assessing educational effectiveness; encourage improvement through continuous self-study and planning; assure the educational community, the general public, and other agencies or organizations that an institution or program has both clearly defined and appropriate objectives, maintains conditions under which their achievement can reasonably be expected, appears in fact to be accomplishing them substantially, and can be expected to continue to do so; provide counsel and assistance to established and developing institutions and programs; encourage the diversity of American postsecondary education, and allow institutions to achieve their particular objectives and goals; and endeavor to protect institutions against encroachments which might jeopardize their educational effectiveness or academic freedom."

The New England Association of Schools and College's Commission on Institutions of Higher Education (1973, p. 1) wrote that the purpose of evaluation is twofold: "First, the institution is encouraged to analyze and appraise its own functions, its educational effectiveness, its strengths and weaknesses, in order to improve the quality of its performance. Second, the results of this analysis, together with the report of an evaluation committee, will be considered by the Commission in deciding whether or not to recommend an institution's application for membership." And the 1977 statement by the Commission of Higher Education of the Middle States Association of Schools and Colleges contends that "Middle States accreditation involves a long-range process designed to help an institution analyze its functions, appraise its educational effectiveness, and discover means by which its work can be strengthened. Institutional improvement is the objective, and the accrediting process should facilitate the attainment of that goal rather than make accreditation an end in itself" (p. 3).

One example of an accrediting association's approach to self-study is shown in Figure 5. And the Northwest Association of Schools and Colleges (1975, pp. 9–10) makes the following recommendations: "(1) Use a small steering committee with an active, interested coordinator to plan the work, hold it in balance, suggest new approaches, and edit the final report. (2) Use a process of involvement because an evaluation is an analytical project, requiring the combined forces of faculty, administration, governing board, and students. (3) Organize the study committee so that their work represents the entire institution. (4) Adopt a definite timetable; make it realistic and insist on maintaining it. (5) Carry the results of the study through to action."

The regional accrediting associations perform an active and useful function in higher education, and their methods for self-evaluation should be reviewed by any college or university that plans such an enterprise. Again, the approach should be to "adapt, not adopt" their procedures.

Self-Studies for Other Purposes

Hundreds of institutional self-studies have been initiated in recent years, and dozens are under way at any one time. The na-

Figure 5. Self-Study Sequence Recommended by Accrediting Association

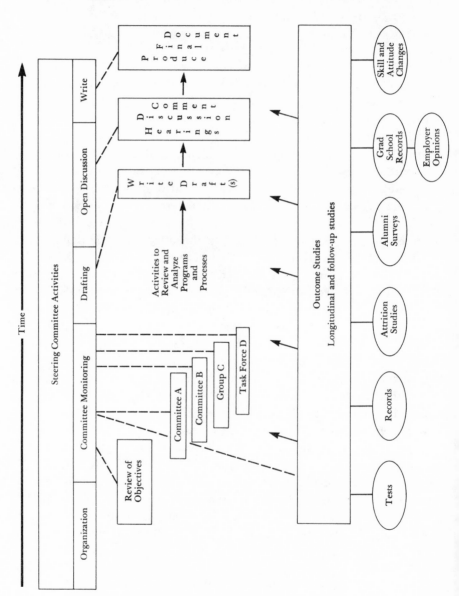

Source: Middle States Association of Colleges and Universities, 1974, p. 25.

tional trend is toward more rigorous and frequent assessments. Such self-analyses can be an important means of self-improvement. The regeneration of the University of Kentucky in the mid sixties, sparked by a dynamic and experienced new president, came from an intensive and extensive self-study, which then became the basis for an equally comprehensive master plan. Mayhew and Ford (1971, p. 125) mention that "Stanford University shifted its character from that of a strong regional university appealing to bright, wealthy, underachieving students to a university of international stature primarily as a result of the findings of a self-study. Stephens College undertook a self-study when its administration believed that the time had come to minimize the traditions of an earlier era. That self-study was used to loosen the soil of academia so that a new president could have a reasonable chance of exercising academic leadership."

The results of self-studies, however, have not been appraised to any noticeable extent. One evaluative effort, undertaken by Ladd (1970, see Appendix B), included self-studies done at the University of California at Berkeley, the University of New Hampshire, the University of Toronto, Swarthmore College, Wesleyan University, Michigan State University, Duke University, Brown University, and Stanford University; he also examined, in less detail, the self-studies of Columbia College and the University of California at Los Angeles. The author reached several conclusions after analyzing these and other self-studies:

> Unhappily, the results of these studies seem to lend support—at least in a negative way—to the efficacy of pressure politics as a way of bringing about change. There is little indication in any of the experiences to support the idea that the study-and-report technique is an effective way of gaining acceptance of the *need* for change or creating enthusiasm for involvement in developing new policies. Where the study-and-report processes were intended primarily to challenge the status quo, they largely failed to do so. When the essential objective was to develop the details of a change in the status quo after the community had already accepted the need for some change or where pressures for change from outside the faculties were much in evidence, the study-and-report processes were much more effective [pp. 197–198, 200].

The cases indicate in both positive and negative ways that strong, skillful leadership is virtually mandatory for the success of any serious effort at educational reform. . . . A primary task of academic leadership is to try to counter the pressures favoring the status quo by creating or maintaining an atmosphere of receptivity to change [pp. 205–206].

On the whole the educational policy changes proposed vary considerably in their venturesomeness, and they often seem to speak indirectly—if at all—to the deep malaise which presently affects so much of American higher education. Nevertheless, if the proposals were to be adopted by the institutions concerned, truly consequential changes would be made in the educational policies of those institutions. Generally speaking, the cases demonstrate that the proposals developed in the studies became less venturesome or simply disappeared as they passed through the various centers of decision making except where some form of countervailing power was present [p. 9].

The self-studies examined by Ladd were undertaken between 1966 and 1969, during the period of student unrest. One suspects that some of them were done to alleviate the tense and politicized campus climate at the time. A comment by Dressel (1976, p. 409) is pertinent: "When the only goal of self-study is the alleviation of pressure, the preservation of accreditation, or the attainment of a foundation grant, success or failure in attaining the goal often ends the self-study. Therefore, one would expect quite modest success or less the results of self-studies conducted under these circumstances yet the conclusions reached by Ladd bear careful study.

Self-assessment procedures for institutions of higher education also have been developed outside academe. The American College Testing Program (1970) initiated the Institutional Self-Study Service (ISS) to help an institution to see itself through the eyes of its students; aid in the quantitative appraisal of college student development; and enable the institution to observe and explore longitudinal trends in student development and opinions on campus. The aspects of student services covered in the ISS survey are faculty advising, counseling, financial aid, extracurricular advising, orientation, housing selection, housing advising, health care, and remedial instruction. The survey asks students to indicate the degree of importance they attach to academic, vocational, social, and nonconventional goals. Instruction, college policies, and physical facilities also receive students' evaluation.

The ISS obviously makes the student the primary evaluator, and few will disagree with the idea that students' views should be a significant part of an institutional self-study, provided the students answer questions that are within the scope of their knowledge and experience. But there are some essential components in any comprehensive self-analysis—the quality of the faculty, academic and institutional leadership, financial management—that cannot be evaluated effectively by students. Although their opinions on these subjects may be useful, data also need to be gathered from other constituencies.

Manning (1976), working with the Research and Development Center for Teacher Education at the University of Texas, developed a "Trouble Shooting" Checklist (TSC) for Higher Educational Settings. This instrument was created to help people concerned with change to assess these organizational variables that can predict an institution's potential for successfully adopting innovations. The TSC consists of 100 Likert-type items which are grouped in five categories: organizational change, organizational staff, communications, innovative experience, and student characteristics. The diagnostic and predictive instrument is designed to aid users in estimating the effects of particular variables on the adoption/diffusion process. That is, the TSC provides users with a means of systematically organizing descriptive information in a predictive way. The validity of the TSC remains to be determined, although the data on its reliability are positive.

State and Federal Reviews

Earlier I discussed the general expansion of governmental influence in higher education, but its more specific role in institutional evaluation has not been treated.

State educational agencies have moved aggressively into the area of program evaluation since about 1972, largely in an effort to stem the tide of new graduate programs that were being developed without careful consideration of their monetary requirements or of long-range institutional goals. Perhaps the most extensive of these efforts has been the doctoral program review undertaken by the New York Board of Regents and paid for by outside sources (federal grant funding). Initiated in 1975, this program utilizes carefully selected out-of-state scholars selected jointly by the Board's staff members and the institution being reviewed. The program has reviewed all doctoral English and chemistry programs in the state of New York. Another example of state review is the "Commission of Scholars" established by the Illinois Board of Higher Education to examine selected doctoral programs and make their recommendations to the Board's academic staff. This commission consists of five distinguished educators and scholars. A third example is the evaluation of all doctoral programs in Louisiana, initiated in 1975 by the Board of Regents. This study used out-of-state consultants who were considered to be nationally eminent and who represented both public and private schools from various geographic areas. Their recommendations, made in late 1976, called for the elimination of several programs and the consolidation of others.

State agencies for higher education have also undertaken evaluations of educational quality and self-study. For instance, the Performance Funding Project launched by the Tennessee Higher Education Commission is exploring the feasibility of allocating some portion of state money on a performance criterion. Each of eleven campuses has contracted to produce a set of institution-wide instructional goals, a set of corresponding performance indicators, and a report on how these goals and indicators were developed. A major assumption of the project is that state allocations will continue to be based primarily on enrollment but that a complementary feature might be built into the formula to promote effective instruction. Supported by national foundations, the project comprises two doctoral universities, six regional universities, and three community colleges. The plans call for the construction of a model framework or composite of the quality indicators developed by the eleven campuses. The framework will take into account the types of institutions and programs, the types of students served, and the types of institutional goals. This model, it is hoped, will highlight the importance of the indicators of instructional effectiveness being developed locally and will provide background data for figuring out how to allocate money on the basis of performance.

Another enterprise of the New York Board of Regents is a series of projects on the self-assessment of colleges and universities, assisted by a federal grant. The intent is that the participating institutions will recognize the need for self-assessment, develop assessment techniques, train faculty and staff members as evaluators, and use the findings for decision making and action. The nine projects, which are under way in private as well as public institutions, focus on "career preparation," "curricular ingredients for success," "faculty evaluation," "curricular design for industrial careers," "professional preparation," "student achievement," "contract learning for graduate students," "program effectiveness," "quality of achievement," "evaluation for quality," "the part-time student," "planning," "faculty as evaluators," "review of staff evaluating systems," and "assessment of administration." The expertise in self-assessment developed through this project will, it is hoped, both encourage more frequent self-analyses and promote more effective self-evaluations and follow-ups.

State-level auditing of higher education activities is also becoming more prevalent, as I pointed out earlier. In order to forestall auditing controlled by state workers who are not educators, the State University System of Florida has developed an office of internal management auditing whose director reports to the chancellor of the system. The office has a full-time auditor on each campus who reports to the director. The auditing thus far is confined to financial affairs. This approach is preferable—at least to educators—to the increasing attempts by regular state auditors to broaden their responsibility to include performance reviews of institutions.

The goals of state auditing are exemplified by the "audit guide" issued by the Auditor General of Illinois (1976) for all state agencies, which include the colleges and universities. These guidelines specify a program audit that "seeks to determine— according to established or designated program objectives, responsibilities, or duties, including statutes and regulations, program performance criteria, or program evaluation standards—(1)

whether the objectives and intended benefits are being achieved, and whether efficiently and effectively; (2) whether the program is being performed or administered as authorized or required by law; and (3) whether the program duplicates, overlaps, or conflicts with another state program" (p. 6).

The auditors approach higher education as any other service, and in one respect this is proper, since education should be able to stand systematic and thorough financial scrutiny. But institutions of higher education also are different from those related to other state agencies, and it is these differences that allow colleges and universities to make their vital contributions to society—some of which are experimental, trial and error enterprises, and not particularly cost-effective. A balance needs to be maintained between systematic costing and individualistic learning.

The federal government too has taken an increasingly active role in appraising, or asking others to appraise, the quality of institutions of higher education. A 1976 report of the Council on Postsecondary Accreditation points out that since 1968 the U. S. Office of Education (USOE) has "aggressively answered" in its own ways the question "Should accreditation be used for determining eligibility for federal funds? If so, what procedural pattern should be employed?" The accrediting associations, with some reluctance and occasional misgivings, have generally gone along with the government's approach.

How did this situation develop? Congress decided to make use of accrediting associations in establishing eligibility for federal funds. The USOE then created an Accreditation and Institutional Eligibility Staff and an Advisory Committee to assist the Commissioner of Education in "recognizing" accrediting associations for this purpose. The USOE pressed the accrediting associations to change or modify certain practices in order to better accommodate the eligibility-determination process. The associations have been urged to take on a role beyond their traditional functions; specifically, the USOE has proposed that they serve as a "reliable authority as to the quality of education or training and the *probity of institutions and programs.*" This latter function would put accrediting associations much more in the monitoring business than has been the case (Council. . . , 1976b, pp. 7–8).

The federal government has been active in a number of other ways that can influence the quality of institutions of higher education. Three examples are the use of federal funds and various grant and loan programs, civil rights legislation, and affirmative action procedures and mandates. As the federal government continues or expands its activities in higher education, it will continue to be concerned about institutional quality. Since the federal government appropriates billions of dollars of public money for higher education, this concern is proper and should be expected. Concern, however, is different from control or excessive influence. Institutional and state education officials are willing to work with the federal government in achieving the mutually desirable goal of better quality control through cooperation and coordination.

General Guidelines for
Institutional Evaluation

Assuming that "this trip is necessary," the ten general categories and the more specific criteria in this book can be starting points in an institutional evaluation. It would be difficult to conceive of an institution-wide appraisal that did not include most of these ten areas as well as many of the forty-five criteria, yet each institution should particularize the criteria to ensure that they are timely and appropriate to its traditions and styles. In any case a relatively short list of criteria should be developed. A large number of criteria may provide some short-term gains in initial campus acceptance, but the impact of the final report likely will be inversely proportional to the number of criteria used and the number of recommendations made.

The following six guidelines may be helpful in tailoring an evaluation plan to a specific institution or system.

1. **Vigorous and sensitive administrative leadership is crucial to effective institutional appraisal.**

    Research by Hodgkinson and others (1975) indicates that effective, action-oriented institutional evaluation cannot take place without vigorous and sensitive administrative leadership, nor should it. This role includes providing the initial impetus for the appraisal, taking the lead in the group directing the efforts, and moving recommendations into action.

This administrative position need not be confused with the man-on-the-horse style or the Machiavellian approach, although there may be a grain of each in effective administrative leadership. Good administration includes developing broad support, working hard, having a proper perspective, and the capacity for empathy; and it includes a healthy respect and understanding of the two primary campus constituencies—students and faculty members.

2. **An overall evaluation plan should be developed and communicated.**

The plan should not be frozen in concrete, yet those on campus should know that an evaluative effort is being made, that certain individuals have some designated responsibilities, that mandates and charges exist for the effort, and that some reporting dates are scheduled, open hearings planned, and recommendations anticipated. A number of organizations have prepared recommendations about self-study plans. For example, the Northwest Association of Schools and Colleges' Commission on Colleges (1975, p. 6) states that the ideal evaluation process "is flexible and permits different approaches; is attuned to current institutional priorities; utilizes recent institutional research or studies; involves as many people as possible; has enough breadth and depth to review accountability; focuses study on results of the educational program; uses information and results to improve the document; yields a concise, readable, useful document; and fosters ongoing self-study and planning."

Another list of suggestions has been developed by the New York Board of Regents (1977) project on Self-Assessment for Colleges and Universities, which I described earlier:

> 1. A clear definition of the goals of the assessment, as distinct from the goals of the specific area being assessed, should be made. The main focus of assessment should be on evaluation of educational quality as measured by the outcomes which are meant to reach those goals.
> 2. All persons who are affected and interested in the programs under review should be continually made aware

of and often involved in the assessment process. Responsibility for setting priorities, designing the assessment, collecting and analyzing data, and evaluating and using them should be assigned to appropriately skilled persons.

3. A determination of how well the goals of the specific area assessed are being met should be made. The appropriate instruments and techniques must be selected and administered to the constituencies who are involved (such as administrators, faculty, students, graduates, employers, and outside groups).

4. The process of collecting data should be established in such a way that it can continue beyond the first self-assessment as a routine function of the master-planning and decision-making process.

5. Analysis of data, reporting of findings, and recommendations for action should be carefully monitored by the person(s) responsible for the self-assessment. Periodic follow-up of recommendations is essential to determine if any *actual* results have occurred.

6. Essential to effective self-assessment is the periodic evaluation of the system itself. The system should be cost-effective in both dollars and human time spent to provide vital information for decision-making.

Those developing a plan for institutional evaluation are advised also to read Balderston's "checklist for academic quality assessment and program evaluation" (1974, pp. 283–286) and Dressel's outline for a comprehensive self-study (1976, pp. 419–422).

The successful completion of an institutional evaluation with action recommendations is a difficult, complicated, sensitive, and usually somewhat political task. Those charged with the responsibility for guiding the study may encounter a variety of defensive tactics employed by committee members and others who wish to avoid coming to grips with the study or to sabotage it. On the basis of a study of thirteen committees at thirteen institutions, Astin (1976, pp. 75–85) developed this catalog of academic games that people may play:

> *Rationalization,* a familiar defense mechanism, is especially suited to the style of many academics, because it is highly verbal and depends heavily on abstract reasoning . . . . Several reports tended to rationalize under two

conditions: when data were perceived as unflattering or negative, and when the committee had not made concrete recommendations for change.

Passing the buck: A frequent method of side-tracking an issue in academe is to form a committee or a task force to study it—in short, passing the buck.

Obfuscation: One common form of obfuscation is to invoke platitudes or high-sounding generalizations that lead nowhere but that create the impression of genuine concern and interest.

Co-Optation . . . involves the open acceptance of the existence of a problem, together with the suggestion that steps have already been taken to remedy the problem or, in its extreme form, that the problem has already been solved.

Recitation: Some committees managed to avoid any serious attempt to relate the data to institutional policy by plodding methodically from one item to the next and simply converting the numbers into prose statements.

Displacement and projection: The basic function of displacement and projection is to obviate the need for serious consideration of the data or for subsequent action by citing inadequacies in the data or in the services provided by the initiator of the project or supplier of the data. . . . One form of displacement is caution. This game involves a litany of technical limitations in the data, followed by a statement indicating that it would be hazardous to attempt to formulate meaningful interpretations or generalizations concerning policy because of these imperfections.

At least three additional circumstances can cause problems. Some committees do not take the time to analyze their charge, or the charge is too general. Or the group or committee may feel that initial openness about its charge and the committee's plan may decrease its flexibility later on. These possibilities do exist, but semi-secrecy by a committee gives rise to suspicions and rumors that can be more damaging than the perils of openness. A third difficulty is an understandable desire by most committee members to avoid as many verbal tussles as possible. But this early avoidance effort can lead to greater controversy later on. Or conversely, a committee may spend an inordinate amount of time in discussion because some members consciously or unconsciously confuse words with action or confuse the design of the study with its substance. The chairperson will need to keep the study from becoming bogged down in semantics and "losing the name of action."

3. **The process of institutional appraisal is as important as the product.**

The way in which activities are conducted is very important to their eventual success or failure. Careful attention should be given to the representative character of the group that is doing the evaluation, to creating a systematic and logical study design, and to ensuring openness in the group's deliberations and adequate opportunities for discussion. It is better to touch bases than mend fences, yet not every decision should be put to a faculty or student vote. Just as excessive controls and secrecy about the project can diminish credibility and ultimate acceptance, so excessive participation and openness can make the effort grind to a halt through frustration and excessive slowness.

Some evaluation committees start with givens over which they had no control, such as the necessity to eliminate "X" number of personnel. The most sensitive and fairest procedure in such circumstances will not blunt the human problems caused by such decisions. It is to be hoped that rationality and calmness can prevail in such situations and that faculty members and others will judge the committee on its equity, systematic procedures, and openness rather than on whether they like or dislike its decisions.

4. **Institutional evaluators should use objective data where available and purposeful but make no apologies for using subjective data.**

Or, it is better to be generally right than precisely wrong. This book does cite objective data, yet considerable variation exists in the availability of such evidence (surveys, research, and so on) and also in its quality. The absence of objective data should stimulate those responsible for institutional evaluation to devise their own survey instruments, guidelines, and checklists, or to use systematically treated judgment as bases for decision making. The lack of "hard" data should not deter careful and systematic decision making about important institutional matters. A solid foundation for decision making can be developed by using whatever hard data are available along with experience, judgment, and common sense. Important institutional decisions often are made on much less.

5. **Institutional evaluation should be action oriented, with plans for moving reports to action.**

"Filed and forgotten" should not be the description of any institutional evaluation, considering the investment of thousands of hours and dollars and the importance of keeping the institution abreast or ahead of its problems. But the history of institutional studies does not provide cause for exuberance about the effective implementation of recommendations. Coming upon the scene today, however, are a number of excellent case studies of institutional evaluations that are oriented toward action, and a few are outlined in this book. The times demand more rigorous approaches to applying results.

The charge to the institutional evaluation committee should make clear that its work plan is geared toward recommendations for action. This position from the outset will remind those involved in the project, and others, that their efforts are less likely to be filed and forgotten.

6. **A plan for evaluating the evaluation should be included.**

Most evaluation reports make little or no provision for assessing their own effectiveness. Such evaluations of evaluations serve as testimony to the importance of assessment in future improvement, provide systematic checkpoints on progress, and supply a procedure for making orderly modifications based on subsequent findings.

Conclusion

Heisenberg, one of the early leaders in theoretical atomic physics, developed the principle of indeterminacy, or the "uncertainty principle," which states that the position and velocity of an electron in motion cannot be measured simultaneously with high precision. The Heisenberg Principle is accepted by scientists as honest recognition of imprecision, yet it has not deterred the relentless pursuit of precision. Something of this spirit would seem appropriate for pursuing institutional evaluation. The data and procedures have their imprecisions, uncertainties, and threatening aspects; yet there is a backlog of research, study, expert opinion, and demands for better performance.

In the final analysis, only people can make systems, programs, or organizations work. The process of developing, introducing, and managing a system of evaluation is a human problem. The sensitivities and fears of individuals are real and need always to be considered in developing and implementing any system, but a progressive and dynamic college or university is maintained by accentuating the positive and by moving ahead.

Appendix A

Comparative Studies of Graduate and Professional Schools

Cartter Ratings

The American Council on Education has taken an active role in rating graduate programs in major universities, beginning with the Hughes study in 1924. The most detailed ACE study, by the late Allan Cartter (1966), assessed the quality of nonprofessional graduate study in major universities. The Cartter opinion survey received usable answers from 900 department chairmen, 1,700 outstanding senior scholars and scientists, and 1,400 younger academicians. In all, persons in thirty disciplines at 106 major institutions were asked their views on (1) the quality of the graduate faculty, (2) the effectiveness of the doctoral program, and (3) the degree of expected change in the relative positions of departments offering doctoral study in the discipline of the rater.

Roose and Anderson

Five years later, another ACE-sponsored study, by Roose and Anderson (1970), essentially replicated the Cartter study but added seven disciplines and twenty-five institutions. The researchers' attitudes toward their results differed from those of Cartter, however. They wrote: "In updating the ratings of graduate programs, we have had serious misgivings about the apparent endorsement a study of this kind gives to the primacy of a . . . hierarchy of university prestige and influence. For this reason, we have sought to play down the actual scores and adjectival descriptions of faculty and program quality, preferring instead to emphasize the importance of identifying faculties and programs with scores at or above the 2.0 'floor' set five years ago" (p. 24).

Two Margulies and Blau Studies

The first report by Margulies and Blau (1973) used the criterion "that has been found to be most reliable," which was the judgment of experts in the field—in this case, deans. These researchers asked 1,180 deans in seventeen different fields in professional schools to name the five most outstanding schools in their profession but not to rank them. (The earlier Cartter and Roose and Anderson studies did not include professional subjects.)

Needless to say, the first Margulies and Blau study was discussed widely, and the second study one year later (Blau and Margulies, 1974–1975, p. 42) dealt with criticisms of the first report:

> The major criticism of our work focused on several points that deserve review here. One group of critics categorically oppose ranking schools. Such rankings, they think, engender invidious comparisons and hurt many good schools that may not be at the very top in their field,

particularly in a period when it is difficult to obtain much-needed financial resources. But this view sees the results of such rankings only from the standpoint of schools and their administrators and not from the perspective of their publics, especially prospective students and employees, who have a stake in knowing how schools compare in quality and reputation. A second criticism of our work was that it did not furnish information on the quality of professional schools, since the rankings were based on the judgment of deans and not on objective measures of quality. As one critic put it, "These are just the opinions of a bunch of deans." A third major criticism of our study was that the rankings of at least some types of schools were based on very few responses, those of only a small proportion of all deans in a field. This criticism is well founded.

Nevertheless, the results of the replication study were very like those produced by the earlier investigation. "The correlation in the new and the old study between reputation ratings for *all* schools, not only in the top five, in all types of professions is .94. . . . If separate correlations for each type between the new and the old reputation ratings are computed, thirteen of seventeen are larger than .90 and none is lower than .75" (Blau and Margulies, 1974–1975, p. 43).

1977 Cartter Study

This time Cartter analyzed education, law, and business schools. His respondents were both deans and faculty members, and since the universe was fifty-one Ph.D.-granting institutions, the professors could be expected to be research-oriented. The results of the Cartter study, and the Blau-Margulies rankings for comparison, are shown in Table 33. The correlations between the Blau-Margulies and Cartter studies are reasonably good for the first five or six places, although some striking differences do exist. These differences may be due primarily to the different ways in which the data were collected or in the clienteles sampled. Cartter (1977, pp. 42–43) supports his thesis in this manner: "Whose judgment does one trust: 146 deans asked to name only five schools, or 453 professors and deans drawn from all fifty-one doctoral-granting institutions? The most knowledgeable teachers/scholars in the field, in

Table 33. Comparison of Cartter and Blau-Margulies Rankings of Professional Schools

Top Schools of Education

Faculty Quality		Educational Attractiveness		Combined Scores		Blau-Margulies Rankings
1. Stanford University	1.59	1. Stanford University	1.46	1. Stanford University	3.07	1
2. University of Chicago	1.93	2. Harvard University	1.77	2. Harvard University	3.83	5
3. Harvard University	2.08	3. University of California, Los Angeles	1.80	3. University of Chicago	3.87	4
4. Teachers College, Columbia University	2.13	4. University of California, Berkeley	1.87	4. University of California, Los Angeles	3.94	12
5. University of California, Los Angeles	2.15	5. University of Wisconsin	1.91	5. University of California, Berkeley	4.04	—
5. University of Wisconsin	2.15	6. University of Michigan	1.95	6. University of Wisconsin	4.05	7
5. University of California, Berkeley	2.15	6. University of Chicago	1.95	7. Teachers College, Columbia University	4.27	2
8. Ohio State University	2.21	8. University of Illinois	2.03	8. Ohio State University	4.28	3
9. University of Illinois	2.26	9. Ohio State University	2.06	8. University of Michigan	4.28	6
10. University of Michigan	2.37	10. University of Minnesota	2.07	8. University of Illinois	4.28	8
11. University of Minnesota	2.38	11. Michigan State	2.09	11. University of Minnesota	4.46	10
		12. University of Texas, Austin	2.13	12. Michigan State University	4.60	11
		12. Teachers College, Columbia University	2.13	13. University of Texas, Austin	4.70	—
				14. University of Indiana, Bloomington	—	9

Top Law Schools

Faculty Quality		Educational Attractiveness		Combined Scores		Blau-Margulies Rankings
1. Harvard University	1.05	1. Yale University	1.19	1. Harvard University	2.30	1
2. Yale University	1.18	2. Stanford University	1.23	2. Yale University	2.37	2

Table 33. Comparison of Cartter and Blau-Margulies Rankings of Professional Schools (Continued)

Top Law Schools

Faculty Quality		Educational Attractiveness		Combined Scores		Blau-Margulies Rankings
3. Stanford University	1.45	3. Harvard University	1.25	3. Stanford University	2.68	6
3. University of Michigan	1.45	4. University of Michigan	1.35	4. University of Michigan	2.81	3
5. University of Chicago	1.46	5. University of California, Berkeley	1.42	5. University of Chicago	2.88	5
6. Columbia University	1.58	6. University of Chicago	1.44	6. University of California, Berkeley	3.16	7
7. University of California, Berkeley	1.74	7. University of Pennsylvania	1.64	7. Columbia University	3.26	4
8. University of Pennsylvania	1.99	8. Columbia University	1.68	8. University of Pennsylvania	3.63	9
9. University of Virginia	2.17	9. University of Virginia	1.72	9. University of Virginia	3.88	—
10. University of Texas, Austin	2.30	10. University of California, Los Angeles	1.86	10. University of California, Los Angeles	4.19	—
11. University of California, Los Angeles	2.32	11. Cornell University	1.90	11. Cornell University	4.29	—
12. Cornell University	2.38	12. Duke University	1.97	12. University of Texas	4.31	—
13. New York University	2.39	13. University of Texas, Austin	2.01	13. Duke University	4.46	—
14. Northwestern University	2.42	14. Northwestern University	2.06	14. Northwestern University	4.50	—
15. Duke University	2.50	15. University of Minnesota	2.08	15. New York University	4.58	8

Top Schools of Business

Faculty Quality		Educational Attractiveness		Combined Scores		Blau-Margulies Rankings
1. Stanford University	1.33	1. Stanford University	1.24	1. Stanford University	2.57	2
2. University of Chicago	1.59	2. Harvard University	1.37	2. Harvard University	3.09	1
3. Massachusetts Institute of Technology	1.64	3. Massachusetts Institute of Technology	1.50	3. Massachusetts Institute of Technology	3.14	6

Rank	University	Score	Rank	University	Score	Rank	University	Score	
4.	Harvard University	1.73	4.	University of Chicago	1.73	4.	University of Chicago	3.32	3
5.	Carnegie-Mellon University	1.97	5.	Carnegie-Mellon University	1.88	5.	Carnegie-Mellon University	3.85	5
6.	University of California, Berkeley	2.06	6.	University of Pennsylvania	1.89	6.	University of California, Berkeley	3.99	7
7.	University of Pennslyvania	2.12	6.	University of California, Los Angeles	1.89	7.	University of Pennsylvania	4.02	4
8.	University of California, Los Angeles	2.26	8.	University of California, Berkeley	1.95	8.	University of California, Los Angeles	4.14	8
9.	Northwestern University	2.40	9.	Northwestern University	1.98	9.	Northwestern University	4.39	11
10.	Columbia University	2.51	10.	Cornell University	2.07	10.	Cornell University	4.59	—
			11.	University of Washington	2.23	11.	Columbia University	4.75	10
			11.	University of Michigan	2.23				
			13.	Columbia University	2.24				
			14.	University of North Carolina, Chapel Hill	2.25				

Source: Cartter (1977).

our view, are much more in tune with the quality of scholarship and education in other institutions than are a few faculty stars and deans who may be more familiar with the administration." Blau and Margulies (1974–1975, p. 42) disagreed: "The central position of deans and their responsibility for recruitment should make them particularly well informed about the quality of the schools in their field. To be sure, the resulting ratings of school reputations are merely the opinions of these experts, but all professional reputations are no more than the opinions of fellow experts." It is interesting to note that Cartter's 1966 study used statistical procedures to examine the differences in ratings among department chairmen, senior scholars, and junior scholars. He found that "there is little to distinguish the ratings of the chairmen or of the junior scholars from those of the senior scholars" (p. 7).

The notion of bigger is better—that is, the fact that those institutions and departments with the largest number of graduates tend to receive the top ratings—has been criticized. Some critics say the raters probably favor those larger units because most of them are from larger graduate departments and because they retain some nostalgia for "those days in graduate school." Furthermore, the larger units are more visible in the literature, in writing and consulting, at conventions, and in the numbers of graduates, and therefore visibility can become equated with quality. But these high ratings may not, after all, be founded on bias; the larger departments may actually be better by virtue of the advantages of diversity, specialization, and collegiality among students and professors.

McGee (1971, pp. 154–155) speaks to the quality issue in terms of institutional size and type: "If we make an analogy to sports, the place of the liberal arts college is, in general, in the bush league and little league, although some of the best known and most prestigious (such as Swarthmore or Antioch) might be considered sufficiently important in American higher education to be accorded minor league standing by faculty raters. No *colleges* could ever be considered major league. Lacking graduate and professional faculties and students, their influence on higher education is simply too limited."

Study by Petrowski and Associates

The purpose of the study by Petrowski, Brown, and Duffy (1973) was to develop a system for selecting "national universities." To do so, they used the data from the ACE studies by Cartter and Roose and Anderson and developed a weighted-mean ranking that is considered to be more accurate than either of the earlier rankings.

Studies by Clark and Associates

Mary Jo Clark (1976) did an extensive questionnaire survey of fifty-seven graduate deans in a selected cross-section of universities. She asked them to indicate which doctoral program characteristics they considered most important and what indicators were acceptable, as shown (the numbers in parentheses indicate the order of importance):

> *Characteristic*: General academic ability of students entering the program (3.61).
> *Indicators*: Undergraduate grade point averages, scores on graduate aptitude tests, and scores on appropriate advanced tests were rated as good indicators, and most deans said this information was available at their universities. Rated unacceptable: student self-ratings.

> *Characteristic*: Achievements, knowledge, and/or skills of students at time of degree completion (3.61).
> *Indicators*: The deans thought the best measure would be the excellence of recently accepted dissertations as judged by external experts, but almost no one had access to such information. Other good indicators: percent of recent graduates doing work related to their fields of specialization, and percent of recent graduates who published prior to the degree. Poor indicators: scores on standardized tests, evaluations of internship or assistantship performance, oral and licensing examination performance.

> *Characteristic*: University financial support for the program (3.60).
> *Indicators*: None of the suggested financial indicators received very enthusiastic endorsement. Most acceptable was the amount budgeted per full-time equivalent (FTE)

student for education and general expense. Least acceptable was the median faculty salary by rank.

Characteristic: Library facilities (3.60).

Indicators: Good indicators were judgments of the adequacy of relevant holdings by faculty and visiting experts, but fewer than one-third of the deans indicated that such information was available. Measures not endorsed: circulation figures, self-reported library use by students or faculty, number of books in the collection.

Characteristic: Academic training of faculty (3.57).

Indicators: Good and available indicators: percent of faculty with Ph.D. or equivalent, percent of Ph.D.'s from "top" programs in each field. Least adequate measures: average grades in graduate school, ratings of excellence by enrolled students.

Characteristic: Purposes of the program (3.49).

Indicators: Good indicators were judgments of the clarity of program plans and purposes by recent graduates, faculty members, or visiting experts, but almost no university collected this information. Available but unacceptable: the ratio of graduates to undergraduates, the number of specializations within a program.

Characteristic: Laboratory equipment and facilities (3.47).

Indicators: Good indicators were ratings of adequacy by faculty or outside experts. Such ratings, however, were seldom available. Measures of space were judged least helpful.

Characteristic: Courses and other educational offerings (3.45).

Indicators: Acceptable measures: faculty/student satisfaction with courses and other offerings, judgments of these offerings by visiting experts. Few deans reported collecting such information. More available, but less adequate: number of new or revised courses, percent of student credit hours devoted to seminars and tutorials, faculty-rated ease of introducing new courses.

Characteristic: Admissions policies (3.43).

Indicators: Acceptable: percent of qualified applicants admitted, judgments by outside experts of whether admission standards should be higher or lower. Unacceptable: the cost of admissions recruiting and processing per FTE student.

Characteristic: Provision for welfare of faculty members (3.42).

Indicators: Most acceptable: median salary by rank, faculty satisfaction with freedom to plan courses and conduct research, provision for assistance to new and young faculty as judged by faculty members. Least adequate measures: turnover rate, percent on tenure, percent ranked full or associate professor.

Building on an earlier study, Clark and others (in Katz and Hartnett, 1976) examined twenty-five doctoral programs in disciplines from three areas: natural science (chemistry), social science (psychology), and humanities (history). The major purpose of the research project was to gain a better understanding of doctoral program quality by developing and field testing measures of important program characteristics. The study used questionnaire data from program participants—students, faculty members, and recent alumni—and information from departmental records, since these sources were endorsed by an expert panel and were also readily accessible. The study was exploratory in nature. It also considered program evaluation in the context of such differing program purposes as the preparation of scholarly researchers, college teachers, and other professional practitioners.

A major premise of the study was that judgments about quality in doctoral programs will be better if they are based on several indicators of quality rather than on one. Multiple-indicator procedures were judged to have at least four distinct advantages: they reduced the "halo effect" and were fairer, more useful, and more likely to stimulate internal thinking about and discussion of program achievements and shortcomings. Some pertinent results of this study, shown in Table 34, should be enlightening for an institutional evaluator who seeks to assess graduate programs.

The debate on whether "to compare or not to compare" goes on. The academic community generally opposes comparative ratings, for two primary reasons: only a few can be anointed, yet those

Table 34. Summary of Characteristics of Various Possible Indicators of Doctoral Program Quality

Characteristic	Comment
Faculty	
1. Percentage of faculty with doctorate	Very little variation across programs; not sufficiently discriminating to be very useful as index of quality.
2. Percentage of faculty with doctorate from highly rated programs	Also not very discriminating across programs in chemistry and history. More variations (and therefore potentially more useful) in psychology.
3. Peer ratings of quality of faculty	Very homogeneous (high agreement among raters) and stable over time; highly correlated with research emphasis, size, publications, and the like; not correlated with indicators of the quality of the environment for learning. Requires collection of ratings data from faculty in other universities.
4. Student-rated quality of teaching	Data reasonably easy to get; highly correlated with several measures of the quality of the learning environment; not highly correlated with faculty peer ratings.
5. Faculty-reported mean articles/book reviews in past three years	Wide variation across programs; fairly highly correlated with peer ratings; probably more useful index than mean lifetime publications; particularly appropriate measure in chemistry and psychology.
6. Faculty-reported books published	Not reported with sufficient frequency to be useful in chemistry and psychology but a more useful indicator in history than articles published.
7. Publication citation index	Very highly correlated with publication counts; requires great deal of time and effort to gather necessary data.
8. Salaries	Neither conceptually nor empirically defensible as genuine indicator of quality.
9. Research activity index	Possibly the single best indicator of the research performance of a department's faculty.

Students:

10. GRE scores (or, alternately, an index of selectivity)

Very difficult to obtain accurate data; seem to be fairly highly related to program research emphasis and peer ratings but data obtained in this study were too incomplete to permit confident conclusions.

11. Quality of undergraduate institutions

Difficult to get agreement regarding meaning of undergraduate institution quality; variable not examined in this study.

12. Student self-reported undergraduate grade average

Fairly highly correlated with graduate faculty appraisals of scholarly ability, commitment, and motivation.

13. Student commitment, motivation

Measured here by faculty ratings; highly correlated with ratings of scholarly ability and communication skills.

14. Quality of dissertations

Would require external panel of raters, perhaps also some information regarding norms for such ratings across many programs; variable was not included in this study.

15. Student attrition (or rate of ABDs)

Difficult information to collect; data reported by departments were frequently labelled as guesses; would seem to be important characteristic, but this study could not analyze in any detail.

Resources:

16. Actual physical resource measures (e.g., books in library, lab facilities, etc.)

Very difficult information to gather, especially across large number of programs; not used in this study.

17. Faculty self-ratings of adequacy of facilities (library, labs, etc.)

Data easy to collect and are quite reliable; positively correlated with peer ratings and program emphasis on research in all three fields; also correlated with program instructional quality in chemistry and psychology.

18. Financial and other program description data

Extremely difficult to obtain reliable information across programs; many analyses intended with these data were not possible because of concerns about the accuracy of the information.

19. Overall institutional financial stability indicator

Not examined in this study.

Table 34. Summary of Characteristics of Various Possible Indicators of Doctoral Program Quality (Continued)

Characteristic	Comment
Environment:	
20. Student reports about various aspects of program environment, such as faculty concern for students, competitiveness of students, etc.	Data easy to collect and are reliable; correlated with quality of teaching; not related to peer ratings and other traditional, research-oriented indicators of program quality.
21. Faculty reports about various aspects of environment, such as program leadership relations with other faculty in dept., etc.	Data easy to collect and are reliable; relationship with other traditional indicators of program quality (e.g., peer ratings, program emphasis on research) varies by discipline.
Program Procedures	
22. One or more efficiency indexes, such as costs per student credit hour or cost per degree awarded	Accurate data across programs extremely difficult to collect. Not treated in this study.
23. Student ratings of various program contents and procedures, such as flexibility of requirements, assistantship experiences, etc.	These data can be obtained fairly easily and, as measured in this study, are quite reliable. They provide a useful "process" indicator that can be compared across programs.
24. Average time to degree	Not included in this study.

Alumni:

25. Eventual, long-term, professional accomplishments (e.g., awards, professional society officerships, etc.)	Though eventual, long-term criteria would be desirable, obtaining follow-up data from those who earned their degree more than a few years ago would be extremely difficult. Not attempted in this study.
26. Professional performance (e.g., publications, job related to training) of recent degree recipients	Performance information of more recent graduates is easier to obtain, but the short time lapse since the degree provides little opportunity for stable record of accomplishment.
27. Ratings by recent alumni of various program characteristics	Alumni ratings data are reliable; overall program quality ratings of alumni highly correlated with self-ratings of faculty and peer ratings.

in academe know there are other outstanding individuals and units that deserve such recognition. Further, the technical procedures for making the ratings are quite elementary, and no one can be sure how credible the ratings are. For example, a study by Bess (1971, see Appendix B), stimulated by the two ACE studies in 1964 and 1969, compared academic departments using a greater number of quality indices than had been used in the earlier research. The final sample consisted of 456 faculty members in thirty departments in fifteen universities across the country. The study analyzed personal satisfactions (security, affiliation, autonomy, ego satisfaction, and self-fulfillment) in high- and low-rated departments on the same campus. The results indicated that the only significant difference between the high and low departments was in ego satisfaction. These findings caused the researcher to view "with considerable caution" the findings of the ACE studies (pp. 721–727).

Nevertheless, parents, legislators, and other public officials generally favor ratings, and such ratings are consistent with current emphases on consumerism. The use of comparative quality ratings will continue to evoke curiosity, outrage, or support, but in any case a healthy degree of skepticism should accompany whatever position one takes.

Appendix B

Institution-Wide Studies

This appendix contains additional approaches to institutional evaluation that did not fit at any particular point in the main text. For example, the self-study approach used by regional accreditation associations is the major stimulus for institution-wide assessment and merits more analysis than was possible within the text.

Self-Study for Accreditation

The accreditation approach has come under increasing criticism in recent years. Critics assert that (1) accreditation has defined the "quality of education" almost exclusively in terms of specific criteria (Ph.D.s among the faculty, the number of books in the library, and the like) and that the validity of these criteria has not been demonstrated. A commendable step toward responding to this criticism has been made by the Commission on Higher Education of the Middle States Association of Schools and Colleges (1977), whose "Characteristics of Excellence in Higher Education" defines quality in broader terms. (2) The accreditation process is not selective enough to tell us very much about the quality of an institution. Critics point out that 90 percent of all colleges and universities are accredited, and the reasons that most of the remaining 10 percent have been omitted are unrelated to quality. However, this argument overlooks the benefits an institution can derive from careful self-study and from its professional activities (reports, meetings, consultations) with the accrediting bodies. Furthermore, those who know the accreditation process realize that the reports made by the visiting teams usually are not rubber stamps of the institution's self-analysis; in fact, these reports sometimes raise substantial questions that require additional data and further discussion. (3) Accreditation has not focused on "educational outcomes," and longitudinal studies show little or no relationship between accreditation standards and the subsequent success (however defined and measured) of the graduates of accredited institutions and programs. (4) Accreditation depends on a "peer evaluation" system that is subject to considerable variation. The following analogy has been used: Just as in a murder trial the prosecutor can find an expert psychiatrist who will declare the defendant sane and the defense attorney finds one who says he is insane, so becoming accredited can consist of getting the right committee. (5) Accreditation, utilizing the norm of established institutions and programs, can discourage innovation and experimentation. However, recent accrediting association statements on nontraditional programs have indicated more flexibility than this criticism might suggest. (6) Accreditation has moved so far toward the concept of evaluating an institution or program in terms of its own statement of scope and purposes that meaningful interinstitutional comparisons are difficult if not impossible. It has been said that if a school for thieves stated its objectives clearly and accomplished them, an accreditation committee would have to evaluate the enterprise positively. (7) Accreditation may be used by special interest groups not so much for legitimate public purposes but as a mechanism for achieving or protecting private benefits. (8) Accreditation is very costly. The considerable investment of human and material resources that institutions must make to meet accreditation requirements is a source of increasing criticism. Some institutions, particularly professional schools and universities, have several accreditation teams on campus each year (Orlans and others, 1974, p. 73). The preparation needed—added to what must be done to satisfy multi-institutional systems, state coordinating or governing systems, and the federal government—can impair an institution's capacity to meet other important needs. This issue becomes even more striking when one notes that forty institutional and specialized accrediting bodies are listed by the Council on Postsecondary Accreditation. (The list of accrediting units recognized by the U. S. Office of Education is slightly different; it can be found in the April 14, 1975, issue of the *Chronicle of Higher Education,* p. 11).

And (9) accreditation is becoming so tied to the determination of eligibility for federal funds that it has lost some advantages that accrue to being a voluntary process, and this trend may diminish its ability to control its own destiny. As I pointed out in Chapter Twelve, educational officials in the USOE are using accreditation as the principle criterion for determining student-aid eligibility. But the regional accrediting associations may have considerable difficulty moving further into the regulatory role that is being recommended not only by the USOE but by some state legislators, some state governing boards, and others. And the associations will also find it hard to adopt more detailed, precise, and stringent approval procedures for their reports. One deterrent is the inherent conflict between being a voluntary organization whose members pay dues to support it and being a regulator of members. Some regulation, yes, but there is a point at which the membership may refuse to tolerate a more vigorous evaluative thrust. The modest size of accrediting agency staffs also precludes their being able to determine the "probity" of institutions and programs or their establishing much more stringent evaluation standards for institutions. These activities are more likely to be undertaken by those who distribute money and who have mandated authority.

Visitors to offices of the regional accrediting associations are impressed with the productivity achieved by much smaller professional staffs than one would expect. The smallness of the staffs does mean, however, that other professionals must be used extensively in the regions. These persons compose the visiting teams that are an integral part of the accrediting process and, as one would suspect, the quality of these teams varies considerably. But the visitations do help team members know and understand well another college or university, and this knowledge and perspective very likely improves general professional effectiveness back home.

In addition to the preceding criticisms, several other issues must be examined. Some questions raised by Pfnister in 1971 (pp. 558–573) are still timely: Can accrediting associations now return to assessing the overall quality of an institution? Will increased pressure for accountability have an impact on their criteria? Can they assist more directly in the improvement of institutions' educational programs? And can accrediting agencies move more toward general accrediting functions and away from geographical boundaries? The most important question, however, is "Do these associations perform sufficiently valuable services to warrant their continued existence?" The United States is almost unique in having a nationwide network of voluntary regional accreditation agencies. Dickey (1970) defends them in this way: "Accrediting institutions have often been instrumental for the maintenance of high educational standards; they have protected society from inadequately prepared professional and technical practitioners; they have aided licensing authorities and facilitated the transfer of students; they have been helpful to students and parents seeking to identify sound institutions; they have aided institutions in withstanding improper political or other noneducational pressures; and they have stimulated broad considerations of educational problems and issues of more than local concern."

Regional accrediting agencies can continue to play a valuable catalytic role if they do not succumb to federal pressures to accept too much power and authority. Serving the future needs and directions of higher education will require accrediting bodies to stress educational improvement through innovation, clearinghouse functions, consultative roles, interinstitutional cooperation, and more detailed procedures for institutional self-study. These are crucial tasks for the future of postsecondary education, and regional associations can continue to make significant contributions to them.

North Central Association Study

The six-volume North Central Association study (two of the six are Haggerty, 1937a, 1937b) of fifty institutions of higher education is one of the most comprehensive accreditation efforts to date. A composite criterion of institutional excellence was developed that included these eleven elements: (1) ratings by Reeves and Gregg (visiting observers) of the general educational quality of the institution, (2) a rating by Gardner of the general educational quality of the institution, (3) a rating by Haggerty of the general educational quality of the institution, (4) students' rank on the Minnesota Reading Comprehension Test, (5) students' rank on the Wesley Test in Social Terms, (6) students' rank on natural science examinations (the results from several tests were combined for this ranking) (7) the institution's rank on mathematics instruction (determined by a study conducted by North Central), (8) students' rank on French examinations, on (9) German examinations, and on (10) the Moss Medical Aptitude Tests, and (11) three rankings of institutions based on the work of their graduates in graduate schools. Significant correlations were obtained among the ratings of the visiting observers and also between the test results and the individual ratings. The best composite criterion of these data was called Criterion VIII, which became a general yardstick.

From these considerable data, the study developed eleven elements of academe that were critical for judging institutional excellence. These were faculty competence, faculty organization, the conditions of faculty services, the curriculum, instruction, the library, the induction of students, the student personnel service, the administration, finance, and plant. These elements, then, became the bases for appraising institutional excellence.

Faculty organization correlated most highly with Criterion VIII, while faculty competence had the lowest correlation. Instruction and the curriculum also had high correlations with the composite criterion. The relatively low correlation of administration and finance reflected another era when institutions were much smaller and less complex and therefore easier to manage. Yet data for the North Central study were collected during the Great Depression when many schools were encountering severe monetary difficulties. One would think that the crisis times of the thirties would have given administrators and financing greater importance.

The North Central study was at the breakwater between using external standards for judgment and using an institution's own objectives as the standards against which performance was judged. The Association moved toward institutional standards.

Hodgkinson's Study

Hodgkinson (1974) studied the effectiveness of programs provided as part of the Developing Institutions Program (Title III of the 1965 Higher Education Act). Data sources included a questionnaire yielding Title III program data and institutional characteristics from 1965 to 1971 for 325 institutions receiving Title III funds, and case studies, conducted in 1972, of 41 institutions and four agencies detailing their use of these funds. Eight "viability" variables were used in scoring the programs: leadership dynamism and efficiency, financial stability, the range of programs and activities offered students, cost effectiveness, the sense of role and long-range direction, students' demand for involvement and/or outreach efforts by the school to uninvolved students, faculty-administration relations, and community relations. In terms of the relative influence of these variables, Hodgkinson concluded: "Campus leadership potential appears the most important single characteristic in distinguishing the successful Title III programs from the less successful ones" (p. 19).

Gourman Report

The Gourman Report (1967) judged the undergraduate programs of a substantial number of the nation's colleges and universities, using ratings of academic departments and of other areas of operation. The departmental ratings included accreditation and the percentage of students receiving scholarships and fellowships. The nondepartmental ratings included these categories and criteria:

• *Administration*: commitment to excellence, community financial support, faculty relationships, foundation grants, general administrative considerations, government contracts, the image of institution, national institute in scope, and purposes/objectives.

• *Student services:* athletic-academic balance, comparative competition for national fellowships by students, counseling program, curriculum, financial aid, freshman year of studies, honors program, and scholarships available.

• *General areas*: alumni associations, computer center, library, plant efficiency, public relations department, and board of trustees.

• *Faculty*: faculty effectiveness, faculty morale, method of instruction, ratio of staff to students, research activity, and salary provisions.

The 1977 report, unlike the first edition, is arranged by academic area and administrative department, rather than by institution. The 1977 report assigns numerical performance ratings on a scale of 0 to 5 and lists the top-scoring institutions in each category by rank. The information was gathered from a questionnaire together with several supplemental reports by a selected team. A total of 644 colleges and universities were involved in the 1977 report as compared with 1,200 in the 1967 one, and the 1977 report ranks the leading American colleges and universities on the basis of Gourman's criteria, which remain elusive (Coughlin, 1978, p. 5).

The College-Rater

The *College-Rater* (1967) used quite different criteria from Gourman's, and perhaps its authors had the *Gourman Report* in mind when they described their own procedure: "*College-Rater* does not attempt to evaluate the academic excellence of a college or university, the competency of its faculty and staff, or the scope and variety of its curricula. Neither does it profess to measure the efficacy of the operation of its various departments or the size of its physical plant and endowment. Guidelines used do not take into account the quality of the academic program, the intellectual environment, educational techniques, facilities, and other considerations. If such imponderables could be measured, the ratings would change considerably."

Trow (1975) found that *The Gourman Report* and the *College-Rater* did come out with criteria that were quite alike and with roughly similar rankings. (The correlation between the two sets of scores was +.75.) The four major criteria used by the *College-Rater*, in descending order, were the SAT/ACT scores of recently enrolled freshmen, the proportion of the faculty that had doctorates, faculty salaries, and the library collection (pp. 368–369). These are relatively commonly used criteria for academic excellence.

Annotated
Bibliography

American Association of State Colleges and Universities. *Quality and Effectiveness in Undergraduate Higher Education.* A policy statement. Washington, D.C.: American Association of State Colleges and Universities, 1971.

"Virtually every collegiate-level institution gives at least tacit approval of the traditional definition of quality education. The customary measures of institutional quality are well known. They include such indices as the number of volumes in the library, student-faculty ratio, measures of the adequacy of the physical plant, the number of library volumes per student, the percent of Ph.D.s on the faculty, the examination score necessary for admission, the budget expenditures per full-time equivalent student, and the percent of graduates enrolling in graduate school. . . . With one exception, none of these criteria provides information related to the educational process itself, that is, what happens to the student between the time he enters the institution and his departure. . . . American higher education needs to develop additional criteria which will be useful in measuring institutional effectiveness. In addition, appropriate methods for measuring output variables of this type are also needed. Several output variables which might be useful in measuring institutional effectiveness . . . are grouped in five categories, including college and university environment, cognitive student development, affective student development, public service, and research."

Anderson, S. B., Ball, S., Murphy, R. T., and Associates. *Encyclopedia of Educational Evaluation: Concepts and Techniques for Evaluating Education and Training Programs.* San Francisco: Jossey-Bass, 1975.

This compendium brings together in one place a vast variety of evaluation materials. In addition, the encyclopedia makes these materials more comprehensible to program administrators, funding agents, students, social scientists, and measurement specialists. It approaches the field of evaluation through these eleven major concept areas: evaluation models, the functions and targets of evaluation, program objectives and standards, the social context of evaluation, planning and design, systems technologies, variables, measurement approaches and types, technical measurement considerations, reactive concerns, and analysis and interpretation.

Astin, A. W. "Measuring Student Outputs in Higher Education." In B. Lawrence, G. Weathersby, and V. W. Patterson (Eds.), *Outputs of Higher Education: Their Identification, Measurement, and Evaluation.* Boulder, Colo.: Western Interstate Commission for Higher Education, 1970.

The process of higher education is said to be composed of three conceptually distinct components: student outputs, student inputs, and the college environment. The matter of assessing the outputs of higher education involves the two basic problems of defining and measuring the relevant output variables and of determining the effects of environmental and student input variables. No man-

agement information system is of much use unless the causal con-
nections between environmental variables and output variables are
known. Further, in considering or measuring the outcomes, we
cannot limit ourselves to desired or intended outputs, because un-
intended "side effects," unlike those in medicine, may be desirable.
A preliminary taxonomy of student-output measures would include the following three dimensions: the type of outcome (cognitive versus affective), the type of data (psychological versus
sociological), and the temporal aspects of the measure (short-term
versus long-term).

Balderston, F. E. "Thinking About the Outputs of Higher Educa-
tion." In B. Lawrence, G. Weathersby, and V. W. Patterson (Eds.),
*Outputs of Higher Education: Their Identification, Measurement, and
Evaluation.* Boulder, Colo.: Western Interstate Commission for
Higher Education, 1970.

Several output measures are discussed: educational value-added
measures, which deal with what the student has attained in relation
to his or her capacity at the starting point; the number of degrees
produced, by program and level; the amount of attrition; and longitudinal data concerning the jobs and activities of former students.
The article concludes: "Both external accountability and the necessities for coherent internal priorities will force a rapid increase of
attention to the outputs of every institution."

Bess, J. L. "Ranking Academic Departments: Some Cautions and
Recommendations," *Journal of Higher Education*, 1971, *42*, 721–
727.

Stimulated by two American Council of Education studies in 1964
and 1966, the author undertook an examination of academic departments using more indices than the ACE had. The final sample
consisted of 456 faculty members in thirty departments in fifteen
universities across the country. The study analyzed personal satisfactions (as measured by the sense of security, affiliation, autonomy,
ego satisfaction, and self-fulfillment) in high- and low-rated departments on the same campus. The results indicated that the only
significant difference between the high and low departments was in

ego satisfaction. These findings caused the researcher to view "with considerable caution" the ACE studies.

Bidwell, C. E., and Kasarda, J. D. "School District Organization and Student Achievement." *American Sociological Review,* 1975, *40,* 55–70.

Using data from 104 Colorado school districts, this study examines the determinants of organizational effectiveness. Five environmental conditions of these districts, three components of district structure, and one of staff composition are linked in a causal model to the median reading and mathematics achievement test scores of the district's secondary school students. The environmental conditions are size, fiscal resources, percentage of nonwhites in the district's population, and the education and income levels of the students' parents. The measures of district structure are the pupil-teacher ratio, level of administrative intensity, and the ratio of supporting professional staff members to teachers. The staff composition variable is the qualification level of the professional staff. The results indicate that high pupil-teacher ratios and high administrative intensity depress median levels of achievement, whereas a better-qualified staff fosters student achievement. Of the environmental conditions, only the percentage of nonwhites has consistently significant direct effects on median achievement levels. But other environmental conditions, especially resources, have important indirect effects on achievement via their influence on school district structure and staff qualifications.

Bolman, F. deW. "University Reform and Institutional Research." *Journal of Higher Education,* 1970, *41,* 85–97.

Genuine institutional research should be the nerve center of the institution. It is an early-warning system for impending crises, it helps redefine the university, and it aligns the modes of operation to avoid pitfalls and achieve institutional goals. One task of institutional research is to discover why there is so much resistance to innovative and creative change in the student learning situation. The reasons may include a faculty reward system that is not based on improving the product. And also, universities have not understood research into and the development of better teaching and learning methods. In 1966 the electrical and communications industries spent 3.4 percent of net sales on research and development, but does any university spend as much as half of 1 percent on this function?

Borich, G. D. (Ed.). *Evaluating Educational Programs and Products.* Englewood Cliffs, N. J.: Prentice-Hall, 1974.

This book consists of sixteen chapters on establishing the perspective, planning the evaluation, and analyzing the data. The material is directed toward elementary and secondary programs and products, and the goals of the book are threefold: (1) to help the evaluator see himself in perspective, such as in relation to his or her formative and summative role and in the context of products, programs, and curricula; (2) to help the evaluator plan an evaluation by presenting models and strategies from which he can choose concepts for constructing an appropriate model in his own setting; and (3) to acquaint the evaluator with important considerations in collecting and analyzing evaluation data.

Bowen, H. R., and Douglass, G. K. *Efficiency in Liberal Education: A Study of Comparative Instructional Costs for Different Ways of Organizing Teaching-Learning in a Liberal Arts College.* New York: McGraw-Hill, 1971.

How can a small private liberal arts college with 1,200 students introduce innovation to improve the quality of its teaching and learning and, at the same time, reduce costs? In pursuing that question, the authors made detailed calculations of the measurable costs and outputs of instruction at a hypothetical small liberal arts college. Six modes of instruction were subjected to special analysis. These were conventional instruction, a mode featuring the introduction of large classes, programmed independent study, tutorials combined with independent study, independent study aided by modern educational technology, and a mode using certain features of all the others. The authors concluded that each of the instructional plans they studied is worth consideration. All are economically feasible, although the eclectic model promises to be the most efficient. The authors do stress that economies per se are not the desired objective, stating that "economies should be harvested as improvements in quality rather than as reductions in expenditures."

Brandl, J. E. "Public Service Outputs of Higher Education: An Exploratory Essay." In B. Lawrence, G. Weathersby, and V. W. Patterson (Eds.), *Outputs of Higher Education: Their Identification, Measurement, and Evaluation.* Boulder, Colo.: Western Interstate Commission for Higher Education, 1970.

In the past decade the field of higher education management has been influenced by three developments: the extension of general public finance analysis to the costs and benefits of higher education, the view that education can be considered as developing human capital or as an investment in developing people into more productive resources, and PPBS (Planning, Programming, Budgeting Systems). These developments have brought about the current output orientation in higher education administration. But the quest for the outputs is crippled by serious and imperfectly perceived methodological and technical difficulties. "Existing techniques were designed for organizations with an incentive to produce efficiently an agreed-on product. In contrast, a university is in many ways a nonorganization, where there is no agreement on its product, the independence of the individual faculty member is valued highly, and there is surely no inherent goal to maximize."

Brown, D. G. "A Scheme for Measuring the Output of Higher Education." In B. Lawrence, G. Weathersby, and V. W. Patterson (Eds.). *Outputs of Higher Education: Their Identification, Measurement, and Evaluation.* Boulder, Colo.: Western Interstate Commission for Higher Education, 1970.

This scheme consists of objectives, measurement devices, and a quantitative model for judging success in attaining desired goals. The growth that occurs in the collegiate environment is represented in five categories: whole-man growth, specialized-man growth, growth in knowledge, growth in society at large, and the joy of growing and of being in an educational environment. "Output choice and measurement choice relate closely. Unfortunately, broad consensus goals are immeasurable, and measurable goals lack general endorsement. The dilemma is arrogance versus imprecision. . . . The real choice is between 'no measures' (subjective judgments) and 'imperfect proxies.' " The author contends that an operational measure has these characteristics: quantifiability, additivity, divisibility, transferability, consensus acceptability, and flexibility. And he proposes forty goals, as elaborations of the five categories mentioned earlier, which are weighted on the basis of how he thinks faculty members, students, public officials, and private citizens would rate each goal. Measurement devices for each goal are suggested, as well. The scheme has flexibility in that any one or more measures can be used by any one group.

Burgoyne, J. G. "Towards an Evaluation of a Business School Graduate Programme." *Omega: the International Journal of Management Science*, 1975, *3*, 475–482.

Forty-eight graduates of the Manchester (England) Business School Graduate Course were interviewed through a carefully designed procedure. The respondents listed, in order of importance, these consequences: access to, and progress in, a successful career; flexibility and mobility in the career; overall view of problems; personal confidence; awareness of their own aspirations and career fit; frustration owing to unsatisfied expectations and unused skills; and salary increases. The study has served as a basis for more informed discussions of management education.

Council on Postsecondary Accreditation. *Evaluation of Institutions of Postsecondary Education: An Annotated List of Instruments.* Washington, D. C.: Council on Postsecondary Education, 1975.

This useful reference book describes a considerable number of evaluative instruments related to institutional self-study, students' personality characteristics, students' general academic ability and aptitude, special fields of student achievement, general academic guidance and counseling, and occupational guidance and counseling. Another part includes information on publishers and testing boards, references on evaluation in higher education, and machine scoring services.

Deferran, R. J. (Ed.). *Self-Evaluation and Accreditation in Higher Education*. Washington, D. C.: Catholic University of America Press, 1959.

This book reports the proceedings of a workshop on administration in higher education in relation to self-evaluation and accreditation, conducted in 1958. The various sections have historical interest with respect to the accrediting movement as well as to self-evaluation. Special lectures include "The Supervision of Evaluation in the United States," "The Use of Accreditation for Self-Improvement," "Background of Accrediting and the National Commission on Accrediting," and "General Procedure for Self-Evaluation."

Edel, W. "Taking a New Look at College Administration." *Educational Record*, 1974, *55*, 136–139.

In discussing the highly complex issue of evaluating academic administration, the author offers these principles: (1) Faculty members generally have little competence in administration, and most of them want no connection with it except by way of payroll; however, every faculty member feels the effects of administrative decisions and therefore he is interested when these affect him. (2) Most students have little or no competence or interest in administration except when it affects them. (3) Input from faculty members and students into the administrative evaluation process should be welcomed on matters that affect them. (4) Administrators, like faculty members and students, in most institutions range from superb to incompetent, with the majority falling somewhere in between. (5) Administrators must operate within mandates and policies laid out by trustees and others. And (6) administrative effectiveness can be measured only in terms of institutional goals and the extent to which these are met to the satisfaction of various constituencies.

Educational Testing Service. *Institutional Functioning Inventory*. Princeton, N. J.: Educational Testing Service, n.d.

The IFI grew out of a study of institutional vitality. Although designed chiefly for use with faculties, the IFI may also be completed by administrators, in part by students, and possibly by trustees and other groups in the college community. In the most general sense, the purpose of the IFI is institutional self-study, carried out on behalf of institutional reform. Consisting of 132 multiple-choice items, the IFI yields scores on eleven dimensions or scales, each comprising twelve items. The *intellectual-aesthetic extracurriculum* refers to the availability of activities and opportunities for intellectual and aesthetic stimulation outside the classroom. *Freedom* has to do with academic freedom for the faculty and students as well as freedom in the personal lives of all individuals in the campus community. *Human diversity* has to do with the degree to which the faculty and student body are heterogeneous in their backgrounds and present attitudes. *Concern for improvement of society* refers to a desire among people at the institution to apply their knowledge and skills in solving social problems and prompting social change. *Concern for undergraduate learning* describes the degree to which the college, in its structure and function and in the professional commitment of the faculty, emphasizes undergraduate teaching and learning. *Democratic governance* reflects the extent to which individuals in the campus community who are directly affected by a decision have the opportunity to participate in making the decision. *Meeting local needs* refers to an institutional emphasis on providing educational and cultural opportunities for adults in surrounding areas. *Self-study and planning* has to do with the importance college leaders attach to continuous long-range planning for the total institution. *Concern for advancing knowledge* reflects the degree to which the institution emphasizes research and scholarship. *Concern for innovation* refers to an institutionalized commitment to experimentation with new ideas for educational practice. *Institutional esprit* refers to a sense of shared purposes and high morale among faculty members and administrators.

Enthoven, A. E. "Measures of the Outputs of Higher Education: Some Practical Suggestions for Their Development and Use." In B. Lawrence, G. Weathersby, and V. W. Patterson (Eds.), *Outputs of Higher Education: Their Identification, Measurement, and Evaluation.* Boulder, Colo.: Western Interstate Commission for Higher Education, 1970.

This paper offers suggestions on developing and using output measures for higher education based on the author's experience in the development and use of Planning, Programming, Budgeting Systems (PPBS) in the Department of Defense. The development of output measures for public programs is said to be an inductive process, not a deductive one. It is a matter of cut and try, of successive approximations. One should not expect to be able to develop a hierarchy of criteria that will logically order the university program. It may never be possible to do a satisfactory job of relating alternative instructional programs to such broad measures of social welfare as increases in state or national wealth or in personal happiness. One should start with simple, crude criteria and refine them. "It is better to be roughly right than exactly wrong."

Herold, D. M. "Long-Range Planning and Organization Performance: A Cross-Valuation Study." *Academy of Management Journal*, 1972, *15*, 91–102.

Three pairs of chemical firms and two pairs of drug firms (each pair composed of a planner and a nonplanner) were studied over a seven-year period. All had participated in an earlier study by Thune and House (described later in this Bibliography). These findings clearly indicate that companies actively engaged in formal long-range planning in the drug and chemical industries significantly outperformed those that are not. The results also indicated that other factors, such as R and D expenditures, also are correlated with superior performance.

Hough, R. R. "The Outputs of Undergraduate Education." In B. Lawrence, G. Weathersby, and V.W. Patterson (Eds.), *Outputs of Higher Education: Their Identification, Measurement, and Evaluation*. Boulder, Colo.: Western Interstate Commission for Higher Education, 1970.

A primary problem in the study of undergraduate education is the lack of consistent and reliable qualitative output measures for institutions of higher education. In creating models of output analysis, the author considers an analogy between the form of micro-economic theory and institutions of higher learning. He suggests that degree output and projected degree output are useful and important measures of institutional size. The use of enrollment figures alone for estimating size may generate misleading conclusions. Further, he recommends a close examination of the experience of students who remain in a baccalaureate program for a number of years to determine the nature of student productivity. The "slippage" in quality that appears in response to increasing student-faculty ratios may have little to do with the content of the program. A change causing a decrease—a kind of reverse "Hawthorne effect"—may be responsible for declining productivity, and therefore significant increases in the student-faculty ratio would only serve to increase campus tensions. There are few, if any, institutions with average entering-freshman SAT scores *and* low student-faculty ratios.

Karger, D. W., and Malik, Z. A. "Long-Range Planning and Organizational Performance." *Long-Range Planning*, 1975, *8*.

This study sought to measure the effects of formal, integrated long-range planning (FILRAP) on commonly accepted financial performance measures in industrial concerns. Ninety U. S. companies, representing five generic groupings (clothing; chemicals, drugs, and cosmetics; electronics; food; and machinery), took part in the survey. The analyses indicate strongly that the planners outperformed the nonplanners by a wide margin except on those measures involving capital spending, stock price, and distribution of earnings as dividends. The planners were more aggressive and better sellers of goods, they controlled margins so as to reap great profits, and they earned higher returns on capital.

Klitgaard, R. E., and Hall, G. R. "Are There Unusually Effective Schools?" *The Journal of Human Resources*, 1975, *10*, 90–106.

The research dealt with the basic reason why some secondary schools consistently produce outstanding students even after sophisticated statistical procedures have made allowances for different initial circumstances and abilities of their students. Data from Michigan, New York, and Project Talent were used. Comparability of data was achieved through various regression equations. Histograms of residual data showed no evidence of extreme overachievers, but comparisons, over different years and grades, of the performance of consistently overachieving schools with the performance expected by chance showed some evidence of unusually effective high schools. Outstanding Michigan schools had smaller classes, better-paid teachers, and more teachers with more than five years' experience.

Ladd, D. R. *Change in Educational Policy: Self-Studies in Selected Colleges and Universities*. New York: McGraw-Hill, 1970.

Eleven case studies of self-evaluation are described and analyzed, and a commentary by Katherine McBride is included. The eleven case studies are Education at Berkeley, by the Select Committee on Education, Academic Senate, University of California, Berkeley, 1966; Toward Unity from Diversity, by the University-wide Educational Policies Committee, University of New Hampshire, 1967; Undergraduate Instruction in Arts and Sciences, by the Presidential Advisory Committee on Undergraduate Instruction, Faculty of Arts and Sciences, University of Toronto, 1967; Critique of a College, by the Commission of Education Policy, Swarthmore College, 1967; the Study of Educational Policies and Programs at Wesleyan University, 1968; Improving Undergraduate Education, by the Committee on Undergraduate Education, Michigan State University, 1967; Varities of Learning Experience, by the Subcommittee on Curriculum, Undergraduate Faculty Council, Duke University, 1968; Interim Report and Recommendations, by the Special Committee on Educational Principles, Brown University, 1969; Study of Education at Stanford, Stanford University, 1969; the Reforming of General Education: The Columbia College Experience in Its National Setting, by Daniel Bell, 1966; and Report, by the Committee on Academic Innovation and Development, Academic Senate, University of California, Los Angeles, 1967. The author concludes: "On the whole the educational policy changes proposed vary considerably in their venturesomeness, and they often seem to speak indirectly—if at all—to the deep malaise which presently affects so much of higher education. Nevertheless, if the proposals were to be adopted by the institutions concerned, truly consequential changes would be made in the educational policies of those institutions. Generally speaking, the cases demonstrate that the proposals developed in the studies became less venturesome or simply disappeared as they passed through the various centers of decision making, except where some form of countervailing power was present."

Lawrence, B., Weathersby, G., and Patterson, V. W. (Eds.). *Outputs of Higher Education: Their Identification, Measurement, and Evaluation.* Boulder, Colo.: Western Interstate Commission for Higher Education, 1970.

The seminar from which this book is derived was convened in the belief that resource inputs, activities in the educational setting, and the outputs of higher education need to be considered as related parts of a whole. The report includes these authors and papers: F. E. Balderston, "Thinking About the Outputs of Higher Education"; John Vaizey, "The Outputs of Higher Education: Their Proxies, Measurement, and Evaluation"; David G. Brown, "A Scheme for Measuring the Output of Higher Education"; C. West Churchman, "R^2 on E: Some Suggestions for Research on the Role of Research in Higher Education"; Alain C. Enthoven, "Measures of the Outputs of Higher Education: Some Practical Suggestions for Their Development and Use"; Kenneth S. Tollett, "Higher Education and the Public Sector"; Alexander W. Astin, "Measuring Student Outputs in Higher Education"; John E. Brandl, "Public Service Outputs of Higher Education: An Exploratory Essay"; Robbin R. Hough, "The Outputs of Undergraduate Education"; and John P. Miller, "Outputs of Higher Education: Graduate Education." All but the papers by Churchman and Tollett are described elsewhere in this Annotated Bibliography.

Leister, D. V., and Maclachlan, D. L. "Organizational Self-Perception and Environmental Image Measurement." *Academy of Management Journal,* 1975, *18*, 205–223.

How higher education institutions in western Washington State perceive themselves as organizations and what image the people in their environment have of them were the subjects of this study. The authors indicate that self-perception and image can be measured through the techniques generally known as multidimensional scaling and multidimensional unfolding. They also found that some of the dimensions of organizational image may be identified and measured relative to each other in terms of influence on the assessor. It is important for any complex organization to know its perception-of-self as well as its image among other groups. This information can be useful to management strategy and planning.

McCloskey, J. "Innovation in Private Colleges and Universities in California." In A. M. Mood and others, *Papers on Efficiency in the Management of Higher Education,* Berkeley, Calif.: Carnegie Commission on Higher Education, 1972.

A study of fifty-seven California institutions (consisting of face-to-face and telephone interviews) produced these conclusions: (1) Private institutions seem to be run no more efficiently than public institutions. Since they are largely dependent on tuition for their financial support, they find it difficult to engage in long-range budget planning or in even rudimentary cost-benefit analyses because they do not know how many students they will have until the day of enrollment. (2) The very smallness of their student bodies, while an advantage from one point of view, limits opportunity for innovation. There simply are not sufficient funds to invest in innovation. (3) Private institutions are under much the same pressures from parents to avoid radical innovations as public institutions are from governmental agencies. (4) The innovations being considered by private institutions are much like what public institutions are thinking about.

Miller, J. P. "Outputs of Higher Education: Graduate Education." In B. Lawrence, G. Weathersby, and V. W. Patterson (Eds.), *Outputs of Higher Education: Their Identification, Measurement, and Evaluation.* Boulder, Colo.: Western Interstate Commission for Higher Education, 1970.

The variety of questions concerning the use of resources in higher education emphasizes the need for a pluralistic definition of outputs and a complex system of measurements. The value-added concept is useful for judging the overall effectiveness of the total system of graduate education. It has the advantage of being expressed in the common denominator of money, and therefore benefits can be balanced against costs. Other obvious output measures are the number of person-years of study and the number receiving different degrees. The comparison of those matriculating who complete their degrees and those who do not is another useful output measure. An analysis of the employment experience of alumni may also produce useful output information. Each of these various quantitative measures of performance has serious limitations, and not one of them provides a single-value measure of output. But from them can be constructed a view of trends, and the resulting view can be related to differences in level or type of output.

National Center for Higher Education Management Systems. *Outcome Measures and Procedures Manual: Field Review Edition.* Technical Report No. 70. Boulder, Colo.: Western Interstate Commission for Higher Education, 1975.

This manual defines a range of measures of outcomes (results or impacts). These are student growth and development, including knowledge and skills development, educational career development, educational satisfaction, occupational career development, personal development, and social/cultural development; new knowledge and development of art forms; and community impact, including education, service, and economic effects. The suggested methods for collecting data on each outcome measure are not all-inclusive but are intended only as a possible starting point. The procedures rely on questionnaires and searches of institutional records. "The manual is designed to serve as a flexible and practical guide for acquiring the data necessary to obtain a wide range of outcome information. It does this by presenting an array of alternative procedures that can be used by institutional researchers and planners to obtain local data for a select number of outcome measures (indicators)."

North Central Association of Colleges and Secondary Schools. *The Evaluation of Higher Institutions.* Six vols. Chicago: University of Chicago Press, 1936–1937.

This study was done as a basis for examining accreditation policies and procedures. The six volumes have the following titles: I. *Principles of Accrediting Higher Institutions*, by G. F. Zook and M. E. Haggerty; II. *The Faculty*, by M. E. Haggerty; III. *The Educational Program*, by M. E. Haggerty; IV. *The Library*, by D. Waples; V. *Student Personnel Service*, by D. H. Gardner; and VI. *Administration*, by J. D. Russel and F. W. Reeves. A composite criterion of institutional excellence was developed comprising eleven elements: ratings by Reeves and Gregg, by Gardner, and by Haggerty (three elements) of the general educational quality of fifty-six of the sixty North Central Association institutions, based on personal visits; rankings based on students' scores on the Minnesota Reading Comprehension Test, on the Wesley Test in Social Terms, on the natural science examinations, on French and German examinations, and on the Moss Medical Aptitude Tests (six elements); and on a ranking derived from a study of mathematics instruction in each institution; and three rankings based on the work of their graduates in graduate schools. The corelation of each of the three personal-visit ratings by the experts with a composite of three ratings was: Gage, .97; Reeves, .93; and Zook, .97. And the coefficients of correlation between the test results and the individual ratings were: Gardner, .39; Haggerty, .45; and Reeves-Gregg, .31. The study rated these institutional aspects: faculty competence; faculty organization (includes faculty-student ratio, distribution of competence, training and instruction, pattern versus function, faculty meetings, and committee meetings); conditions of faculty services; curriculum; instruction; library; student personnel services; administration; finance; plant; institutional study; and athletics. The correlations between these items and the composite criterion of institutional excellence are given in the final chapter.

Pace, C. R., and associates. *Higher Education Measurement and Evaluation Kit*. Los Angeles: Laboratory for Research on Higher Education, Graduate School of Education, University of California, 1975.

The purpose of the kit is to measure and evaluate the effectiveness of a program or a college through obtaining (1) information about the development, progress, and attainment of students; (2) information about the educational experiences, processes, and contexts

that affect students' development, progress, and attainment, and
(3) a reasonable baseline against which students' performance and
characteristics may be compared. The first section includes measures of students' activities and their interest in general culture by
means of very short tests in nine areas, such as art, national and
state politics, and religion; measures of students' attitudes about
major social issues; and measures of their progress toward attaining broad objectives and benefits. The second section focuses on
students' characteristics, their style of effort, their experiences, and
the campus environment. The third section offers measures of the
student body from the viewpoints of academic orientation, cos-
mopolitanism, personality dispositions, and values and priorities.

Palola, E. G., Lehmann, T., and Blischke, W. R. "The Reluctant
    Planner: Faculty in Institutional Planning." *Journal of Higher
    Education*, 1971, *42*, 587–602.

The data gathered by these authors came from a study conducted
by the Center for Research and Development in Higher Education
in Berkeley. The authors concluded that two steps need to be taken
if faculty members are to have a key role in institutional planning.
Adequate resources must be provided, including released time for
faculty members, secretarial assistance, research personnel, and office space. And the criteria for faculty promotions must fully recognize participation in institutional planning as a legitimate part of
the faculty member's performance. In general, planning is not so
recognized at present.

Perlman, D. H. "New Tools and Techniques in University Ad-
    ministration." *Educational Record*, 1974, *55*, 34–42.

The term *management information systems* (MIS) refers to the processes and procedures by which raw data are organized into information useful for administrative decision making. These systems are
usually computer based. Another tool, program budgeting, estab-
lishes the program rather than the department as the important
budgetary unit. It is primarily for planning and resource allocation; it does not replace line-item departmental budgeting for expenditure control. And by focusing on the ingredients and associated costs of instructional programs, program budgeting can

assist with data about the quality or output of programs in relation to costs. Modeling, cost-simulation, or gaming is a third relatively new administrative technique. It predicts and plans for the future by projecting what will happen to an institution operating under various assumptions. Whereas the three techniques mentioned thus far work primarily with quantitative data, management by objectives (MBO) and organization development are primarily means for working more effectively with people. MBO involves procedures that make explicit the goals and objectives of each major component of an institution and a timetable for their achievement. Organization development is the professional application of the findings of various disciplines to help an institution change. A variety of interpersonal techniques are used, such as information feedback, conflict management, sensitivity training, and confrontation meetings to bring about a planned change in an organization.

Peterson, R. E. "College Goals and the Challenge of Effectiveness." Princeton, N. J.: Educational Testing Service, 1971.

Five ways that colleges can conceive institutional effectiveness are given: *Student learning*, considered to be the first and most important criterion, is how much students learn of what the college wants them to learn. *Student values development* means that students should be better people by the time they leave the campus. *Programmatic responsiveness* refers to programming to meet educational needs as they exist and also programming to meet future needs. *Campus morale* is defined by such factors as faculty and student satisfaction—the sense that the institution is a good place to be teaching and studying—, commitment to the central values of the institution, cooperativeness, mutual respect, and interpersonal trust. *Data application* refers to the effective use of data to operate and improve the quality of the institution.

Peterson, R. E., and Loye, D. E. (Eds.). *Conversations Toward a Definition of Institutional Vitality.* Princeton, N. J.: Educational Testing Service, 1967.

This report consists of an abridgment of the proceedings of two invitational conferences attended by acknowledged experts and an appendix containing the results of a national survey. The two conferences can be characterized by their contrasts: the first was notable for its range of ideas; the second, for a deeper probing of a limited number of concepts. For example, among the concerns and concepts discussed by the first conferees were the effect of leadership on vitality, the effect of vital people and of money, the relevance of the size of an institution, of creativity (including the creative use of slush funds), of faculty negativism, of students' sense of sharing some purposes with the faculty and administration, of the sense of purposeful involvement, and of how one measures change and encourages renewal. During the second conference, the conversation considered examining colleges in terms of institutional malaise rather than vitality, or what happens when systems break down. Though it also had its continuing proponents, the word *vitality* came under repeated fire. Some felt that its emotional overtones might render it unsuitable as an operational concept for objective research. Such considerations led to the notion of "institutional functioning" as the basic underlying concept.

In 1967, an open-ended questionnaire was sent to 1,305 individuals involved in higher education across the country. The respondents were asked to name those characteristics they felt distinguished a "vital" college or university. Seven highlights of the results are given in the book: (1) Administrators (presidents and deans) more frequently mentioned staff loyalty to institutional objectives than did professors of English and student editors. (2) Student editors and deans of students, more so than presidents and professors, were concerned about who participates in setting college policies. For the student editors this was the single most frequently cited theme. (3) Student editors were relatively unconcerned about faculty research and scholarship as an attribute of a vital institution. (4) Matters of student freedom were emphasized by student editors and relatively infrequently mentioned by administrators. (5) College presidents, more so than the others, pointed to the role of the governing body in a vital institution. Openness to innovation and experimentation was the characteristic of a vital institution most frequently suggested by presidents, deans, and the group of researchers and critics. (However, this theme was used as an example on the questionnaire.) (7) Sound undergraduate instruction was the paramount concern of the English professors.

Pfnister, A. O. "Regional Accrediting Agencies at the Crossroads."
    Journal of Higher Education, 1971, *42*, 558–573.

The accrediting agencies are at the crossroads. More criticism is
being raised about them, yet viable alternatives are not forthcom-
ing. These agencies operate on three basic principles. They do not
make distinctions regarding levels of quality; they either accredit
an institution or not. They evaluate each institution as a whole,
thereby emphasizing general rather than specialized functions.
And each institution is accredited in the light of its own purposes.
Regional accrediting associations face four decisions: Can they
return to assessing the specific level of quality of an institution?
Will increased pressure for accountability have an impact on
their criteria? Can they assist more directly in the improvement
of institutions' educational programs? And can they move more
toward general accrediting functions and away from geographical
boundaries?

Popham, W. J. (Ed.). *Evaluation in Education: Current Applications.*
    Berkeley, Calif.: McCutchan, 1974.

This volume consists of nine chapters on timely theoretical issues of
evaluation, with some applications. The chapters and authors are
the following: "Evaluation Perspectives and Procedures," by
Michael Scriven; "Alternative Approaches to Educational Evaluation: A Self-Study Guide for Educators," by Daniel L. Stufflebeam;
"Designing Summative Evaluation Studies at the Local Level," by
Peter W. Airasian; "Data Analysis and Reporting Considerations in
Evaluation," by Richard M. Wolf; "The Use of Standardized Tests
in Evaluation," by Gilbert Sax; "Criterion-Referenced Measure-
ment," by Jason Millman; "Cost Analysis for Educational Program
Evaluation"; "Introduction to Matrix Sampling for the Prac-
titioner," by Kenneth A. Sirotnik; and "Formative Evaluation of
Instruction," by Eva L. Baker.

Spalding, W. B. "Policies for Higher Education in the 1970s." *Educa-
    tional Forum*, 1973, *37*, 135.

The author states that authority always rests with the recipient of a
communication or an order. Unless he grants authority to the

order by his behavior after receiving it, then it has no authority for him. Four basic reasons for failure to grant authority to a communication are given: The recipient does not understand it. The recipient is unable, through ignorance, lack of skill, or some other impediment, to do what is called for in the communication. The recipient perceives the communication as requiring him to act against his own best interest. Or the recipient perceives the communication as requiring him to act in ways that are opposed to the purposes of the organization.

Stephenson, T. E. "Organizational Development: A Critique." *Journal of Management Studies*, 1975, *12*, 249–265.

The primary concern of organizational development (OD) is with the human variable in organizations. The OD approach rests on the assumption that man is basically good and emphasizes democratic, humanistic attributes that are exemplified in man's openness and trust. This emphasis raises questions of degree and of the possibility that openness and trust can be manipulative. In addition, OD fails to distinguish between different types of relationships, such as work and friendship relationships. And since OD is largely based on intervening in a client's system, it can lead to a situation in which the developer tries to convert people to his particular point of view.

Thune, S., and House, R. "Where Long-Range Planning Pays Off." *Business Horizons*, 1970, *13*, 81–87.

Thirty-six companies in six industrial groups were matched as planners and nonplanners on the basis of a questionnaire answered by ninety-two companies. Company comparisons showed that formal planners significantly outperformed informal planners with respect to five economic measures: sales, stock prices, earnings per share, return on common equity, and return on total capital employed. In addition, they bettered the records they had achieved before they adopted formal planning.

Vaizey, J. "The Outputs of Higher Education — Their Proxies, Measurement, and Evaluation." In B. Lawrence, G. Weathersby, and V. W. Patterson (Eds.), *Outputs of Higher Education: Their*

Identification, Measurement, and Evaluation. Boulder, Colo.: Western Interstate Commission for Higher Education, 1970.

The terms *benefit-cost analysis* and *cost-effective techniques* date from Pigou's work on the *Economics of Welfare*, in which he drew attention to the indirect as well as the direct consequences of economic activity and suggested that those effects that did not appear in the sector of society where money was the measure could be estimated by analogy with money costs. Benefit-cost analysis has two weaknesses: it provides little opportunity for contrasting different sectors of the economy—it is only applicable within sectors—and the values placed on the nonmonetary benefits and losses are subject to dispute. Because the evaluation of the outputs is not independent of the evaluation of the inputs or of the procedures by which outputs are reached, many of the techniques used for measuring the results of industrial or economic activity are not necessarily applicable to education.

Winstead, P. C., and Hobson, E. N. "Institutional Goals: Where to From Here?" *Journal of Higher Education*, 1971, *42*, 669–677.

In order for an institution's goals and objectives to be valid and workable, the constituent groups must reach some agreement on them as well as on the plans for carrying them out. Participative governance involving the constituent groups—trustees, faculty members, students, community leaders, alumni, and administrators—is more responsive to the total needs of the institution than is authoritarian governance. The process includes setting goals, deriving measurable objectives which support these goals, and managing resources to enhance the probability of attaining these aims. This planning process examines basic institutional and environmental data, makes certain assumptions based on these data, formulates plans, and provides for modification of plans based on the feedback of results. This is a cybernetic process in that feedback points out when changes need to be made in addition to showing how well one is doing.

References

Adams, W. "The State of Higher Education: Myths and Realities." *AAUP Bulletin,* 1974, *60,* 119–125.

Advisory Committee on Endowment Management. *Managing Educational Endowments.* New York: Ford Foundation, 1969.

Aetna Life and Casualty Company. *A Manager's Guide To Performance Planning Appraisal and Development.* Hartford, Conn.: Aetna Life and Casualty Co., 1973.

Allison, E. K. "The Evaluation of Educational Experience." In S. R. Graubard (Ed.), *Daedalus,* 1974, *103,* 188–195.

American Alumni Council. "Alumni Relations: Definition and Role." *American Alumni Council News,* Oct.–Nov. 1956.

American Association for Higher Education. *Faculty Participation in Academic Governance.* Washington, D.C.: American Association for Higher Education, 1967.

American Association of State Colleges and Universities. *Quality and Effectiveness in Undergraduate Higher Education.* Washington, D.C.: American Association of State Colleges and Universities, 1971.

American Association of State Colleges and Universities, Resource Center for Planned Change. *Program Evaluation.* Washington, D.C.: American Association of State Colleges and Universities, 1976a.

American Association of State Colleges and Universities, Resource Center for Planned Change. *Programs for New Clientele.* Washington, D.C.: American Association of State Colleges and Universities, 1976b.

American Association of University Professors. *Depression, Recovery and Higher Education.* New York: McGraw-Hill, 1937.

American Association of University Professors. "Statement on Teaching Evaluation." *AAUP Bulletin*, 1975a, *61*, 200–202.

American Association of University Professors. "Two Steps Backward: Report on the Economic Status of the Profession, 1974–75." *AAUP Bulletin*, 1975b, *61*, 118–199.

American College Testing Program. *The Institutional Self-Study Service.* Iowa City, Iowa: American College Testing Program, 1970.

American Council on Education, National Committee on the Preparation of a Manual on College and University Business Administration. *College and University Business Administration.* Vol. 2. Washington, D.C.: American Council on Education, 1955.

Anderson, S. B., Ball, S., Murphy, R. T., and Associates. *Encyclopedia of Educational Evaluation: Concepts and Techniques for Evaluating Education and Training Programs.* San Francisco: Jossey-Bass, 1975.

Armacost, P. H., and others. "Questions for a Board of Trustees." *AGB Reports,* July/Aug. 1976, pp. 3–6.(Publication of the Association of Governing Boards of Universities and Colleges.)

Association of Graduate Schools. *The Research Doctorate in the United States.* Washington, D.C.: Association of Graduate Schools, 1976.

Astin, A. W. *The College Environment.* Washington, D.C.: American Council on Education, 1968a.

Astin, A. W. "Undergraduate Achievement and Institutional 'Excellence.' " *Science*, 1968b, *161*, 661–668.

Astin, A. W. *Preventing Students from Dropping Out.* San Francisco: Jossey-Bass, 1975.

Astin, A. W. *Academic Gamesmanship: Student-Oriented Change in Higher Education.* New York: Praeger, 1976.

Astin, A. W. *Four Critical Years: Effects of College on Beliefs, Attitudes, and Knowledge*. San Francisco: Jossey-Bass, 1977.

Astin, A. W., and Lee, C. B. T. *The Invisible Colleges*. New York: McGraw-Hill, 1972.

Auditor General. "Audit Guide for Performing Compliance Audits of Illinois State Agencies." Springfield, Ill.: Office of the Auditor General, State of Illinois, 1976.

Babbidge, H. D., Jr. "Requiem or Renaissance for the New State College Trustees?" *AGB Reports*, July/Aug. 1975, p. 40.

Bailey, S. K. "The Effective Use of Human Resources." In H. R. Bowen and S. K. Bailey, *The Effective Use of Resources*. Washington, D. C.: Association of Governing Boards of Universities and Colleges, 1974.

Balderston, F. E. *Managing Today's University*. San Francisco: Jossey-Bass, 1974.

Barton, D. W., Jr. "Preparation of Development Literature." In A. S. Knowles (Ed.), *Handbook of College and University Administration*. New York: McGraw-Hill, 1970.

Barzun, J. *The American University: How It Runs, Where It Is Going*. New York: Harper & Row, 1968.

Baskin, S., and others. *Innovation in Higher Education. Developments, Research, and Priorities*. New Dimensions in Higher Education, No. 19. Durham, N. C.: Duke University Press, 1967.

Bayer, A. E. "Faculty Composition, Institutional Structure, and Students' College Environment." *Journal of Higher Education*, 1975, *46*, 549–565.

Bean, A. "The Liberal Arts College Trustee's Next 25 Years." *AGB Reports*, May/June 1975, pp. 34–43.

Bell, D. *The Reforming of General Education*. New York: Columbia University Press, 1966.

Bennis, W. G. *The Leaning Ivory Tower*. San Francisco: Jossey-Bass, 1973.

Bennis, W. G. "Have We Gone Overboard on 'The Right to Know?' " *Saturday Review*, March 6, 1976, pp. 18–21.

Bennis, W. G., and Slater, P. E. *The Temporary Society*. New York: Harper & Row, 1968.

Berdahl, R. O. "Problems in Evaluating Statewide Boards." In R. O. Berdahl (Ed.), *New Directions for Institutional Research: Evaluating Statewide Boards*, No. 5. San Francisco: Jossey-Bass, 1975.

Berelson, B. *Graduate Education in the United States.* New York: McGraw-Hill, 1960.

Berg, B. R. "Educators' Perceptions of Obstacles to Cooperation." In Danforth Foundation, *Higher Educational Consortia: Idea of the Past or Wave of the Future?* Report of a Conference. St. Louis: Danforth Foundation, 1972.

Binning, D. W. "Admissions: A Key to Financial Stability." *Liberal Education*, 1971, *57*, 173–180.

Birenbaum, W.M. *Overlive: Power, Poverty, and the University.* New York: Dell, 1968.

Blackburn, R., and Associates. *Changing Practices in Undergraduate Education.* Berkeley, Calif. Carnegie Council on Policy Studies in Higher Education, 1976.

Blau, P. M., and Margulies, R. Z. "The Reputations of American Professional Schools: A Research Replication." *Change*, 1974–1975, *6*, 42–47.

Blocker, C. E., and others. *The Political Terrain of American Postsecondary Education.* Fort Lauderdale, Fla.: Nova University Press, 1975.

Bogard, L. "Management in Institutions of Higher Education. In A. M. Mood and others (Eds.), *Papers on Efficiency in the Management of Higher Education.* Berkeley, Calif.: Carnegie Commission on Higher Education, 1972.

Booth, W. C. "Report of the Committee on the Quality of Life in Regenstein." University of Chicago *Record*, 1976, *10*, 1–10.

Boulding, K. E. "The Management of Decline." *AGB Reports*, Sept./Oct. 1975, pp. 4–9.

Bowen, H. R. "The Products of Higher Education." In H. R. Bowen (Ed.), *New Directions for Institutional Research: Evaluating Institutions for Accountability*, No. 1. San Francisco: Jossey-Bass, 1974.

Bowen, H. R. "Systems Theory, Excellence, and Values: Will They Mix?" Address to the annual meeting of the American Association for Higher Education, Chicago, 1976.

Bowen, H. R. *Investment in Learning: The Individual and Social Value of American Higher Education.* San Francisco: Jossey-Bass, 1977.

Bowen, H. R., and Douglass, G. K. *Efficiency in Liberal Education.* New York: McGraw-Hill, 1971.

Bowen, H. R., and Minter, W. J. *Private Higher Education.* First Annual Report on Financial and Educational Trends in the Private

Sector of American Higher Education, 1975. Washington, D. C.: Association of American Colleges, 1975.

Bowen, H. R. and Minter, W. J. *Private Higher Education.* Second Annual Report on Financial and Educational Trends in the Private Sector of American Higher Education, 1976. Washington, D. C.: Association of American Colleges, 1976.

Bowen, W. G., and others. *Budgeting and Resource Allocation at Princeton University.* Princeton, N. J.: Princeton University Press, 1972.

Boyer, E. L. "Higher Education Leadership in the 1970s." In R. M. Millard and others (Eds.), *Planning and Management Practices in Higher Education: Promise or Dilemma?* Denver, Colo.: Education Commission of the States, 1972.

Bramlett, G. A. *The Academic Community: A Backup Force to State Government.* Atlanta: Southern Regional Education Board, 1974.

Bristol, J. W. "Portfolio Management by Professional Counsel." In A. S. Knowles (Ed.), *Handbook of College and University Administration.* New York: McGraw-Hill, 1970.

Broce, T. E. "Development and Foundations." In A. S. Knowles (Ed.), *Handbook of College and University Administration.* New York: McGraw-Hill, 1970.

Burke, J. C. "Coping with the Role of College or University President." *Educational Record,* 1977, *58*, 388–402.

Bursk, E., and Chapman, J. F. (Eds.). *New Decision-Making Tools for Managers.* New York: New American Library, Mentor Books, 1965.

Bushnell, D. S. *Organizing for Change: New Priorities for Community Colleges.* New York: McGraw-Hill, 1973.

Bushnell, D.S., and Zagaris, I. *Strategies for Change: A Report from Project Focus.* Washington, D. C.: American Association of Junior Colleges, 1972.

Caffrey, J., and Isaacs, H. *Estimating the Impact of a College or University on the Local Economy.* Washington, D. C.: American Council on Education, 1972.

Callan, P. M. "Evaluating Planning by Statewide Boards." In R. O. Berdahl (Ed.), *New Directions for Institutional Research: Evaluating Statewide Boards,* no. 5. San Francisco: Jossey-Bass, 1975.

Carnegie Commission on Higher Education. *Dissent and Disruption: Proposals for Consideration by the Campus.* New York: McGraw-Hill, 1971.

Carnegie Commission on Higher Education. *The More Effective Use of Resources*. New York: McGraw-Hill, 1972.

Carnegie Commission on Higher Education. *Governance of Higher Education: Six Priority Problems*. New York: McGraw-Hill, 1973a.

Carnegie Commission on Higher Education. *Opportunities for Women in Higher Education: Their Current Participation, Prospects for the Future, and Recommendations for Action*. New York: McGraw-Hill, 1973b.

Carnegie Foundation for the Advancement of Teaching, The. *Missions of the College Curriculum: A Contemporary Review with Suggestions*. San Francisco: Jossey-Bass, 1977.

Cartter, A. M. *An Assessment of Quality in Graduate Education*. Washington, D. C.: American Council on Education, 1966.

Cartter, A. M. *Ph.D.s and the Academic Labor Market*. New York: McGraw-Hill, 1976.

Cartter, A. M. "The Cartter Report on the Leading Schools of Education, Law, and Business." *Change*, 1977, *9*, 44–48.

Cary, W. L., and Bright, C. B. *The Law and Lore of Endowment Funds: Report to the Ford Foundation*. New York: Ford Foundation, 1969.

Catlin, J. B., and others. *Affirmative Action: Its Legal Mandate and Organizational Implications*. Ann Arbor, Mich.: Center for the Study of Higher Education, University of Michigan, 1974.

Centra, J. A. *The Relationship Between Student and Alumni Ratings of Teachers*. Princeton, N. J.: Educational Testing Service, 1973.

Centra, J. A. *Faculty Development Practices in U. S. Colleges and Universities*. Princeton, N. J.: Educational Testing Service, 1976.

Chait, R. P. "Nine Alternatives to Tenure Quotas." *AGB Reports*, March/April 1976, pp. 38–43.

Channing, R., Steiner, S., and Timmerman, S. "Collective Bargaining and Its Impact on Board-Presidential Relationships." In M. Brick (Ed.), *Collective Negotiations in Higher Education*. Washington, D. C.: ERIC Clearinghouse for Higher Education, 1973.

Cheit, E. F. *The New Depression in Higher Education*. New York: McGraw-Hill, 1971.

Cheit, E. F. "The Management Systems Challenge: How To Be Academic Though Systematic." Address to the annual meeting of the American Council on Education, Washington, D. C., 1973a.

Cheit, E. F. *The New Depression in Higher Education — Two Years Later.* Berkeley, Calif.: Carnegie Commission on Higher Education, 1973b.

Chesterton, G. K. *Orthodoxy.* Garden City, N. J.: Image Books, 1924.

Chickering, A. W. *Education and Identity.* San Francisco: Jossey-Bass, 1969.

Chickering, A. W. "College Advising for the 1970s." In J. Katz (Ed.), *New Directions for Higher Education: Services for Students,* no. 3. San Francisco: Jossey-Bass, 1973.

Chickering, A. W. *Commuting Versus Resident Students: Overcoming Educational Inequities of Living Off Campus.* San Francisco: Jossey-Bass, 1974.

Chickering, A. W., and others. "Institutional Differences and Student Development." *Journal of Educational Psychology,* 1969, *60,* 315–326.

Clark, M. J. "The Meaning of Quality in Graduate and Professional Education." In J. Katz and R. T. Hartnett, *Scholars in the Making: The Development of Graduate and Professional Students.* Cambridge, Mass.: Ballinger, 1976.

Cleveland, H. "The Costs of 'Openness.' " *AGB Reports,* March/April 1975, pp. 7–10.

Cohen, M. D., and March, J. G. *Leadership and Ambiguity: The American College President.* New York: McGraw-Hill, 1974.

Cole, C. C., Jr. *Encouraging Scientific Talent.* New York: College Entrance Examination Board, 1956.

The College-Rater. Allentown, Pa.: College-Rater, 1967.

Conrad, C., and Cosand, J. *The Implications of Federal Education Policy.* ERIC/Higher Education Research Report, No. 1. Washington, D. C.: American Association for Higher Education, 1976.

Corbally, J. E. "That Vital Margin of Greatness." University of Illinois *Faculty Letter,* May 10, 1976.

Cornell Center for Improvement in Undergraduate Education. *The Yellow Pages of Undergraduate Innovations.* New Rochelle, N. Y.: Change Book Department, 1974.

Coughlin, E. K. " 'The Gourman Report': a Mysterious Rating of

Universities." *The Chronicle of Higher Education,* May 8, 1978. p. 5. (See also Gourman, J.)

Council for Financial Aid to Education. *Corporate Support of Higher Education.* New York: Council for Financial Aid to Education, 1976.

Council on Postsecondary Accreditation. *The Balance Wheel for Accreditation.* Washington, D. C.: Council on Postsecondary Accreditation, 1976a.

Council on Postsecondary Accreditation. *Major Issues in Accreditation.* The President's Annual Report, 1975–1976. Washington, D. C.: Council on Postsecondary Accreditation, 1976b.

Cross, K. P. "A Realistic Look at the Future of the Student Personnel Profession." Paper prepared for the Council of Jesuit Student Personnel Administrators Workshop, Denver, 1972.

Cross, K. P. "Learner-Centered Curricula." In D. W. Vermilye (Ed.), *Learner-Centered Reform: Current Issues in Higher Education 1975.* San Francisco: Jossey-Bass, 1975.

Davis, J. S., and Batchelor, S. A. *The Effective College and University Board: A Report of a National Survey of Trustees and Presidents.* Research Triangle Park, N. C.: Research Triangle Institute, Center for Educational Research and Evaluation, 1974.

Diamond, W. J., Martin, D. F., and Miller, R. I. *Methodology for Assessing the Quality of Public Education.* Bureau of School Service, Lexington: University of Kentucky, 1969.

Dickey, F. G. "The 1970s: Time for Assessment in Accreditation." Annual Report of the Executive Director. Washington, D. C.: National Commission on Accreditation, 1970.

Dressel, P. L. "Faculty Development, Appraisal, and Reward." Unpublished document, Michigan State University, n. d.

Dressel, P. L. *The Undergraduate Curriculum in Higher Education.* New York: Center for Applied Research in Education, 1963.

Dressel, P. L. *Handbook of Academic Evaluation: Assessing Institutional Effectiveness, Student Progress, and Professional Performance for Decision Making in Higher Education.* San Francisco: Jossey-Bass, 1976.

Dressel, P. L., and DeLisle, F. H. *Undergraduate Curriculum Trends.* Washington, D. C.: American Council on Education, 1969.

Dressel, P. L., and Mayhew, L. B. *General Education: Explorations in*

Evaluation. Washington, D. C.: American Council on Education, 1954.

Dressel, P. L., and others. "Departmental Operations: The Confidence Game." *Educational Record,* 1969, *50,* 274–278.

Dressel, P. L., and others. *The Confidence Crisis: An Analysis of University Departments.* San Francisco: Jossey-Bass, 1970.

Drucker, A. J., and Remmers, H. H. "Do Alumni and Students Differ in Their Attitudes Toward Instructors?" In H. H. Remmers (Ed.), *Studies in Higher Education: Studies in College and University Staff Evaluation.* Lafayette, Inc.: Division of Educational Reference, Purdue University, 1950.

Drucker, P. F. *The Practice of Management.* New York: Harper & Row, 1954.

Drucker, P. F. "What Principles of Management Can the President of a Small College Use to Improve the Efficiency of His Institutions?" In E. J. McGrath (Ed.), *Selected Issues in College Administration.* New York: Teachers College Press, 1967.

Drucker, P. F. *Management: Tasks, Responsibilities, Practices.* New York: Harper & Row, 1974.

Dudley, J. R. *An Assessment of Remedial Skills Courses for Underprepared College Students.* Unpublished doctoral dissertation, University of Rochester, 1977.

Duryea, E. D. and Fisk, R. S. *Collective Bargaining: The State University and the State Government in New York.* Buffalo: State University of New York at Buffalo, 1975.

Dykes, A. R. *Faculty Participation in Academic Decision Making.* Washington, D. C.: American Council on Education, 1968.

Educational Testing Service. *Institutional Functioning Inventory.* Princeton, N. J.: Educational Testing Service, 1972.

Eiseley, L. "The Hope of Man." *New York Times,* November 6, 1972.

El-Khawas, E., and Furniss, W. T., *Faculty Tenure and Contract Systems: 1972 and 1974.* Washington, D.C.: American Council on Education, 1974.

Epstein, L. D. *Governing the University: The Campus and the Public Interest.* San Francisco: Jossey-Bass, 1974.

Eurich, A. C., and Tiekton, S. G. *Long-Range Planning and Budgeting at Colleges and Universities.* Paper No. 6. Washington, D. C.: Academy for Educational Development, n. d.

Falk, D. "Campus Environments, Student Stress, and Campus Planning." In B. L. Bloom (Ed.), *Psychological Stress in the Campus Community.*" New York: Behavioral Publications, 1975.

Farber, E. I., and Walling, R. *The Academic Library.* Metuchen, N. J.: Scarecrow Press, 1974.

Feldman, K. A. "Measuring College Environments: Some Uses of Path Analysis." *American Educational Research Journal,* 1971, *8,* 51–70.

Feldman, K. A., and Newcomb, T. M. *The Impact of College on Students.* Vol. 1. San Francisco: Jossey-Bass, 1969.

Fife, J. D. *Applying the Goals of Student Financial Aid.* ERIC/Higher Education Research Report, No. 10. Washington, D. C.: American Association for Higher Education, 1975.

Fisher, C. F. *The Evaluation and Development of College and University Administrators.* ERIC/Higher Education Research Currents. Arlington, Va.: ERIC Document Reproduction Service, 1977a.

Fisher, C. F. *The Evaluation and Development of College and University Administrators. Part Two: Professional Development of Administrators.* ERIC/Higher Education Research Currents. Arlington, Va.: ERIC Document Reproduction Service, 1977b.

Flanagan, J. C., and others. *Project TALENT: Five Years after High School.* Pittsburgh: American Institutes for Research and University of Pittsburgh, 1971.

Folger, J. K. "SSTRR." In R. M. Millard and others (Eds.), *Planning and Management Practices in Higher Education: Promise or Dilemma?* Denver, Colo.: Education Commission of the States, 1972.

Ford Foundation. *Research Universities and the National Interest.* New York: Ford Foundation, 1978.

Foxley, C. H. *Locating, Recruiting and Employing Women: An Equal Opportunity Approach.* Garrett Park, Md.: Garrett Park Press, 1976.

Frankel, C. "Reflections on a Worn-Out Model." In S. R. Graubard, *American Higher Education: Toward an Uncertain Future.* Vol. 1. *Daedalus,* Fall 1974, pp. 25–32.

Franz, P. J., Jr. "Capital Development Programs." In A. S. Knowles (Ed.), *Handbook of College and University Administration.* New York: McGraw-Hill, 1970.

Freedman, M. and Sanford, N. "The Faculty Member: Yesterday and Today." In M. Freedman (Ed.), *New Directions for Higher Education: Facilitating Faculty Development,* no. 1. San Francisco: Jossey-Bass, 1973.

Freeman, J. E. "Trustees, Money, and Planning." *AGB Reports,* Sept./Oct. 1976, pp. 35–40.

Gabor, D. *Innovations: Scientific, Technological, and Social.* New York: Oxford University Press, 1970.

Galloway, S. W., and Fisher, C. (Eds.). *A Guide to Professional Development Opportunities for College and University Administrators.* Washington, D.C.: Office of Leadership Development in Higher Education, American Council on Education, 1977.

Garbarino, J. W., and Assieker, B. *Faculty Bargaining: Change and Conflict.* New York: McGraw-Hill, 1975.

Gardner, J. W. *Excellence: Can We Be Equal and Excellent Too?* New York: Harper & Row, 1961.

Gardner, J. W. *Self-Renewal: The Individual and the Innovative Society.* New York: Harper & Row, 1963.

Gerth, D. R. "Institutional Approaches to Faculty Development." In M. Freedman (Ed.), *New Directions for Higher Education: Facilitating Faculty Development,* no. 1. San Francisco: Jossey-Bass, 1973.

Gilford, D. M. "Statistical Snapshots of Adult Continuing Education." 1975, *46,* 409–425.

Glenny, L. A. "State Systems and Plans for Higher Education." In L. Wilson (Ed.), *Emerging Patterns in American Education.* Washington, D. C.: American Council on Education, 1965.

Glenny, L. A. and Dalglish, T. K. *Public Universities, State Agencies, and the Law: Constitutional Autonomy in Decline.* Berkeley, Calif.: Center for Research and Development in Higher Education, 1973.

Glenny, L. A., and others. *State Budgeting for Education: Data Digest.* Berkeley, Calif.: Center for Research and Development in Higher Education, 1975.

Glenny, L. A., and others. *Presidents Confront Reality: From Edifice Complex to University Without Walls.* A report for the Carnegie Council on Policy Studies in Higher Education. San Francisco: Jossey-Bass, 1976.

Gollattscheck, J. F., and others. *College Leadership for Community Renewal: Beyond Community-Based Education.* San Francisco: Jossey-Bass, 1976.

Gourman, J. *The Gourman Report.* Phoenix, Ariz.: Continuing Education Institute, 1967. (See also Coughlin, E. K.)

Grant, W. H. "Humanizing the Residence Hall Environment." In P. A. DeCoster and P. Mable (Eds.), *Student Development and Education in College Residence Halls.* Washington: American College Personnel Association, 1974.

Greeley, A. M. *The Changing Catholic College.* Chicago: Aldine, 1968.

Greenleaf, R. F. *Trustees as Servants.* Cambridge, Mass.: Center for Applied Studies, 1974.

Griffin, G., and Burks, D. R. *Appraising Administrative Operations: A Guide for Universities and Colleges.* Berkeley, Calif.: University of California Systemwide Administration, 1976.

Gross, E., and Grambsch, P. V. *University Goals and Academic Power.* Washington, D. C.: American Council on Education, 1968.

Gross, E., and Grambsch, P. V. *Changes in University Organization, 1964–1971.* New York: McGraw-Hill, 1974.

Gross, R. F. "Facilitating Administrator Development Through Growth Contracts." Paper presented to the Conference on Evaluation and Development of Administrators, Council for the Advancement of Small Colleges/American Association for Higher Education, Arlie House, Feb. 4, 1977.

Grupe, F. H. *Interinstitutional Cooperation at the Departmental Level.* Potsdam, N. Y.: Associated Colleges of the St. Lawrence Valley, 1972.

Haggerty, M. E. *The Evaluation of Higher Institutions.* Vol. 2: *The Faculty.* Chicago: University of Chicago Press, 1937a.

Haggerty, M. E. *The Evaluation of Higher Institutions.* Vol. 3: *The Educational Program.* Chicago: University of Chicago Press, 1937b.

Haire, M. In R. I. Miller (Ed.), *The Seat of Heat.* Atlanta: Mead Educational Services, 1969.

Halsey, A. H., and others (Eds.). *Education, Economy, and Society.* New York: Free Press, 1961.

Harcleroad, F. F. "Can State Systems Adapt Models of Business Decentralization?" In R. O. Berdahl (Ed.), *New Directions for In-*

stitutional Research: Evaluating Statewide Boards, no. 5. San Francisco: Jossey-Bass, 1975.

Harcleroad, F. F. *Educational Auditing and Accountability.* Washington, D. C.: The Council on Postsecondary Accreditation, 1976.

Harcleroad, F. F., and Dickey, F. G. *Educational Auditing and Voluntary Institutional Accrediting.* ERIC/Higher Education Research Report, No. 1. Washington, D. C.: American Association for Higher Education, 1975.

Harris, M. L. "Student Financial Aid." In J. Lombardi (Ed.), *New Directions for Community Colleges: Meeting the Financial Crisis,* no. 2. San Francisco: Jossey-Bass, 1973.

Harris, S. E. *A Statistical Portrait of Higher Education.* A report of the Carnegie Commission on Higher Education Report. New York: McGraw-Hill, 1972.

Hartnett, R. T. *The New College Trustee: Some Predictions for the 1970s.* Princeton, N. J.: Educational Testing Service, 1970.

Hastings, J. L., and others. *Evaluating Geography Courses: A Model with Illustrative Applications.* Technical Paper No. 3. Washington, D. C.: Association of American Geographers, 1970.

Hays, G. D. "Evaluating A President: The Minnesota Plan." *AGB Reports,* Sept./Oct. 1976a, pp. 5–9.

Hays, G. D. "Evaluating A President: Criteria and Procedures." *AGB Reports,* Nov./Dec. 1976b, pp. 41–46.

Hefferlin, J. L. *Dynamics of Academic Reform.* San Francisco: Jossey-Bass, 1969.

Hefferman, J. M., and others. *Educational Brokering: A New Service for Adult Learners.* Syracuse, N. Y.: National Center for Educational Brokering, 1976.

Heilbron, L. H. *The College and University Trustee: A View from the Board Room.* San Francisco: Jossey-Bass, 1973.

Henderson, A. D. *The Role of the Governing Board.* Washington, D. C.: Association of Governing Boards of Universities and Colleges, 1972.

Henry, D. D. *Challenges Past, Challenges Present: An Analysis of American Higher Education Since 1930.* San Francisco: Jossey-Bass, 1975.

Herold, D. M. "Long-Range Planning and Organization Performance: A Cross-Valuation Study." *Academy of Management Journal,* 1972, *15,* pp. 91–102.

Hillway, T. "Evaluating College and University Administration." *Intellect.* 1973, *101,* pp. 426–427.

Hodgkinson, H. L. "Goal Setting and Evaluation." In R. M. Millard and others (Eds.), *Planning and Management Practices in Higher Education: Promise or Dilemma?* Denver, Colo.: Education Commission of the States, 1972.

Hodgkinson, H. L. *How Much Change for a Dollar? A Look at Title III.* ERIC/Higher Education Research Report, No. 3. Washington, D. C.: American Association for Higher Education, 1974.

Hodgkinson, H. L., and others. *A Manual for the Evaluation of Innovative Programs and Practices in Higher Education.* Berkeley: Center for Research and Development in Higher Education, 1974.

Hodgkinson, H. L., and others. *Improving and Assessing Performance: Evaluation in Higher Education.* Berkeley: Center for Research and Development in Higher Education, 1975.

Hoffer, E. *The Campus and the City: Maximizing Assets and Reducing Liabilities.* A report for the Carnegie Commission on Higher Education. New York: McGraw-Hill, l972.

Holley, E. G. "Who Runs Libraries? The Emergency of Library Governance in Higher Education." *Wilson Library Bulletin,* 1973, *48,* pp. 42–50.

Hungate, T. L., and Meeth, L. R. "The Quality and Cost of Liberal Arts College Programs." In E. J. McGrath and L. R. Meeth (Eds.), *Cooperative Long-Range Planning in Liberal Arts Colleges.* New York: Teachers College Press, 1964.

Iffert, R. E. *Retention and Withdrawal of College Students.* Bulletin No. 1. Washington, D. C.: U. S. Government Printing Office, 1957.

Jacob, P. *Changing Values in College.* New York: Harper & Row, 1957.

Jellema, W. W. *The Red and the Black: Special Preliminary Report on the Financial Status, Present and Projected, of Private Institutions of Higher Learning.* Washington, D. C.: Association of American Colleges, 1971.

Jellema, W. W. (Ed.). *Efficient College Management.* San Francisco: Jossey-Bass, 1972.

Jellema, W. W. *Study of Independent Higher Education in Indiana: In-*

terinstitutional Cooperation. Indianapolis: Associated Colleges of Indiana, 1975.

Jencks, C., and Riesman, D. *The Academic Revolution.* New York: Doubleday, 1969.

Jenny, H. H., and Wynn, G. R. *The Golden Years: A Study of Income and Expenditure Growth and Distribution of 48 Private Four-Year Liberal Arts Colleges, 1960–1968.* Wooster, Ohio: College of Wooster, 1970.

Jenny, H. H., and Wynn, G. R. *The Turning Point: A Study of Income and Expenditure Growth and Distribution of 48 Private Four-Year Liberal Arts Colleges, 1960–1970.* Wooster, Ohio: College of Wooster, 1972.

Johnson, M. "Performance Appraisal of Librarians: A Survey." *College and Research Libraries,* 1972, *33,* 359–367.

Jones, F. T. "General Procedure for Self-Evaluation." In R. J. Deferrari (Ed.), *Self-Evaluation and Accreditation in Higher Education.* Washington, D. C.: Catholic University of America Press, 1959.

Kaplin, W. A. *The Law of Higher Education: Legal Implications of Administrative Decision Making.* San Francisco: Jossey-Bass, 1978.

Karger, D. W., and Malik, Z. A. "Long-Range Planning and Organizational Performance." *Long-Range Planning,* 1975, *8.*

Katz, J., and Hartnett, R. T. *Scholars in the Making: The Development of Graduate and Professional Students.* Cambridge, Mass.: Ballinger, 1976.

Kauffman, J. F. *The Selection of College and University Presidents.* Washington, D.C.: Association of American Colleges, 1974.

Kauffman, J. F. "The New College President: Expectations and Realities." *Educational Record,* 1977, *58,* 146–168.

Keeton, M. In R. E. Peterson and D. E. Loye (Eds.), *Conversations Toward a Definition of Institutional Vitality.* Princeton, N. J.: Educational Testing Service, 1967.

Keeton, M. *Shared Authority on Campus.* Washington, D. C.: American Association for Higher Education, 1971.

Keller, J. E. "Planning and Resource Allocation." In R. M. Millard and others (Eds.), *Planning and Management Practices in Higher Education: Promise or Dilemma?* Denver, Colo.: Education Commission of the States, 1972.

Kemerer, F. R., and Baldridge, J. V. *Unions on Campus: A National*

Study of the Consequences of Faculty Bargaining. San Francisco: Jossey-Bass, 1975.

Kemerer, F. R., and Baldridge, J. V. "The Impact of Faculty Unions on Governance." *Change,* 1975–1976, 7, 50–51, 62.

Keniston, H. *Graduate Study and Research in the Arts and Sciences at the University of Pennsylvania.* Philadelphia: University of Pennsylvania Press, 1959.

Kerr, C. *The Uses of the University.* Cambridge, Mass.: Harvard University Press, 1964.

Kerr, C. "Foreword." In D. D. Henry, *Challenges Past, Challenges Present: An Analysis of American Higher Education Since 1930.* San Francisco: Jossey-Bass, 1975.

Knowles, A. S. "Faculty Personnel Policies and Regulations." In A. S. Knowles (Ed.), *Handbook of College and University Administration.* New York: McGraw-Hill, 1970.

Kotler, P. *Marketing for Nonprofit Organizations.* Englewood Cliffs, N. J.: Prentice-Hall, 1975.

Ladd, E. C., Jr., and Lipset, S. M. "U. S. Professors: The View Differs, from Inside and Outside." *The Chronicle of Higher Education,* 1976, *12,* p. 1.

Lahti, R. E. *Innovative College Management: Implementing Proven Organizational Practice.* San Francisco: Jossey-Bass, 1973.

Lanier, L. H., and Andersen, C. J. *A Study of the Financial Condition of Colleges and Universities: 1972–1975.* Washington, D. C.: American Council on Education, 1975.

Lasher, W. F. "Institutional Research: Coming of Age in the 1970s." *Planning for Higher Education* 1976, *5.* (Publication of the Society for College and University Planning.)

Leslie, D. W. *Conflict and Collective Bargaining.* ERIC/Higher Education Research Report, No. 9. Washington, D. C.: American Association for Higher Education, 1975.

Levi, E. H. "The University and the Modern Condition." In E. H. Levi, *Points of View.* Chicago: University of Chicago, 1970.

Levine, A. "Reflections of an Itinerant Interviewer: A Sketch of Undergraduate Curriculum Trends." A monograph prepared for the Carnegie Council on Policy Studies in Higher Education. Berkeley, Calif., 1976. (Mimeograph.)

Levine, A., and Weingart, J. R. *Reform of Undergraduate Education.* San Francisco: Jossey-Bass, 1973.

Lewin, K. "Frontiers in Group Dynamics." *Human Relations,* 1947, *1,* 5–41.

Lewis, M. O. (Ed.). *The Foundation Directory.* (5th ed.) New York: The Foundation Center, 1975.

Litchfield, E. H. "Notes on a General Theory of Administration." *Administrative Science Quarterly.* 1956, *1,* 28.

London, A. "Experimental Colleges' University Without Walls: Reform or Rip Off?" *Saturday Review,* Sept. 16, 1972.

London, H. E. "The Case for Nontraditional Education." *Change,* 1976, *8,* 25–29.

Long, H. J. "What Are the Private Colleges Doing to Meet the Crisis Ahead?" *School and Society,* 1951, *73,* 410–411.

Lupton, A. H., Augenblick, J., and Heyison, J. "The Financial State of Higher Education." *Change,* 1976, *8,* 20–38.

Lykins, R. G. "Techniques for Improving Cash Management." *NACUBO Studies in Management,* 1973, *2,* 1–4.

Lyle, G. R. *The Administration of the College Library.* New York: A. W. Wilson, 1974.

Lynch, B. P. "The Academic Library and Its Environment." *College and Research Libraries,* 1974, *35,* 126–132.

McAnnally, A. M., and Downs, R. B. "The Changing Role of Directors of University Libraries." *College and University Libraries,* 1973, *34,* 103–125.

McClelland, D. C. "Testing for Competence Rather than for 'Intelligence,'" *American Psychologist,* 1973, *28,* 1–14.

McConnell, T. R. "Needed Research in College and University Organization." In T. F. Lunsford (Ed.), *The Study of Academic Administration.* Boulder, Colo.: Western Interstate Commission for Higher Education, 1963.

McGee, R. *Academic Janus: The Private College and Its Faculty.* San Francisco: Jossey-Bass, 1971.

McGrath, E. In R. E. Peterson and D. E. Loye (Eds.), *Conversations Toward a Definition of Institutional Vitality.* Princeton, N. J. Educational Testing Service, 1967.

McGregor, D. "On Leadership." In W. G. Bennis and E. A. Schein (Eds.), *Leadership and Motivation.* Cambridge, Mass.: M. I. T. Press, 1966.

McHenry, D. E., and Associates. *Academic Departments: Problems, Variations, and Alternatives.* San Francisco: Jossey-Bass, 1977.

McNeeley, J. J. *College Student Mortality*, Bulletin 1937–11. Washington, D. C.: U. S. Office of Education, 1938.

Mali, P. *Developing and Using a Personnel Evaluation System*. Groton, Conn.: Paul Mali and Associates, n. d.

Manning, B. A. *The "Trouble Shooting" Checklist for Higher Educational Settings*. Austin, Tx.: Research and Development Center for Teacher Education, 1976.

Margulies, R. Z., and Blau, P. M. "America's Leading Professional Schools: The Pecking Order of the Elite." *Change*, 1973, *5*, 21–27.

Marks, A. C. "Organization and Administration of Nonacademic Personnel." In A. S. Knowles (Ed.), *Handbook of College and University Administration*. New York: McGraw-Hill, 1970.

Martin, W. B. In R. E. Peterson and D. E. Loye (Eds.), *Conversations Toward a Definition of Institutional Vitality*. Princeton, N. J.: Educational Testing Service, 1967.

Martorana, S. V. "Commentary." In *The Two-Year College Trustee: National Issues and Perspectives*. A special report. Washington, D. C.: Association of Governing Boards of Universities and Colleges, 1972.

Martorana, S. V., and Kuhns, E. *Managing Academic Change: Interactive Forces and Leadership in Higher Education*. San Francisco: Jossey-Bass, 1975.

Massy, W. F. "Resource Management and Financial Equilibrium." *NACUBO Professional File*, 1975, *7*, 1–7.

Mautz, R. K., and Sharaf, H. A. *The Philosophy of Auditing*. Chicago: American Accounting Association, 1961.

Maxey, J. Unpublished report prepared for the American College Testing Program. Iowa City, Iowa, 1975.

Mayhew, L. B. "Curriculum Construction and Planning." In A. S. Knowles (Ed.), *Handbook of College and University Administration*. New York: McGraw-Hill, 1970.

Mayhew, L. B. *How Colleges Change: Approaches to Academic Reform*. Palo Alto, Calif.: School of Education, Stanford University, 1976.

Mayhew, L. B., and Ford, P. J. *Changing the Curriculum*. San Francisco: Jossey-Bass, 1971.

Means, H. B., and Semas, P. W. "Do Unionized Faculty Members

Get Bigger Pay Increases?" *Chronicle of Higher Education,* Dec. 6, 1976.

Meeth, L. R. *Quality Education for Less Money: A Sourcebook for Improving Cost Effectiveness.* San Francisco: Jossey-Bass, 1974.

Middle States Association of Colleges and Schools, Commission on Higher Education. *Policies and Procedures Handbook.* Philadelphia: Middle States Association of Colleges and Schools, 1973.

Middle States Association of Colleges and Schools, Commission on Higher Education. *Handbook on Institutional Self-Study.* Philadelphia: Middle States Association of Colleges and Schools, 1974.

Middle States Association of Colleges and Schools, Commission on Higher Education. *Handbook for Institutional Self-Study.* Philadelphia: Middle States Association of Colleges and Schools, 1977.

Miles, M. B. "Planned Change and Organizational Health: Figure and Ground." A paper for the Seminar on Change Processes in Public Schools, University of Oregon, Oct. 14–16, 1964.

Millard, R. M. "Introduction." In R. M. Millard and others (Eds.), *Planning and Management Practices in Higher Education: Promise or Dilemma?* Denver, Colo.: Education Commission of the States, 1972.

Millard, R. M. *State Boards of Higher Education.* ERIC/Higher Education Research Report. No. 4. Washington, D. C.: American Association for Higher Education, 1976.

Miller, R. I. *Teaching About Communism.* New York: McGraw-Hill, 1966.

Miller, R. I. *Evaluating Faculty Performance.* San Francisco: Jossey-Bass, 1972.

Miller, R. I. *Developing Programs for Faculty Evaluation: A Sourcebook for Higher Education.* San Francisco: Jossey-Bass, 1974.

Miller, T. K., and Prince, J. S. *The Future of Student Affairs: A Guide to Student Development for Tomorrow's Higher Education.* San Francisco: Jossey-Bass, 1976.

Millett, J. D., *The Academic Community.* New York: McGraw-Hill, 1962.

Mills, D. K. "Community College Trustees: A Survey." In *Two-Year College Trustee: National Issues and Perspectives.* A special report.

Washington, D. C.: Association of Governing Boards of Universities and Colleges, 1972.

Moore, R. S. *Consortiums in American Higher Education: 1965–66. Report of an Exploratory Study.* Washington, D. C.: U. S. Government Printing Office, 1968.

Morgens, H. J. "Business and the Universities: A Call for Mutual Understanding." St. Louis: Washington University, 1973.

Morse, P. M. *Library Effectiveness.* Cambridge, Mass.: M. I. T. Press, 1968.

Muller, S. "Higher Education or Higher Skilling? In S. R. Graubard, *American Higher Education: Toward an Uncertain Future.* Vol. 1. *Daedalus,* Fall 1974.

Munitz, B. "Measuring a President's Performance." *AGB Reports,* Jan./Feb. 1976, pp. 36–39.

Nash, G., and others. *The University and the City.* A report of the Carnegie Commission on Higher Education. New York: McGraw-Hill, 1973.

Naples, C. J. "Collective Bargaining: Opportunities for 'Management.' " In J. H. Schuster (Ed.), *New Directions for Higher Education: Encountering the Unionized University,* no. 5. San Francisco: Jossey-Bass, 1974.

Nason, J. W. "The Trustee's Ten Responsibilities." *AGB Reports,* Jan./Feb. 1976, pp. 45–48.

National Association of College and University Business Officers. *The Sixty College Study.* Washington, D. C.: National Association of College and University Business Officers, 1956.

National Association of College and University Business Officers. *Sixty College Study . . . A Second Look.* Washington, D. C.: National Association of College and University Business Officers, 1960.

National Association of College and University Business Officers. *College and University Business Administration.* (3rd ed.) Washington, D. C.: National Association of College and University Business Officers, 1974.

National Association of College and University Business Officers. *A College Planning Cycle: People, Resources, Process.* Washington, D. C.: National Association of College and University Business Officers, 1975a.

National Association of College and University Business Officers. *Results of the 1975 NACUBO Comparative Performance Study and Investment Questionnaire.* Washington, D. C.: National Association of College and University Business Officers, 1975b.

National Center for Higher Education Management Systems, Western Interstate Commission for Higher Education. *Outcome Measures and Procedures Manual: Field Review Edition.* Technical Report No. 70. Boulder, Colo.: Western Interstate Commission for Higher Education, 1975.

National Commission on the Financing of Postsecondary Education. *Financing Postsecondary Education in the United States.* Washington, D. C.: U. S. Government Printing Office, 1973.

Nelson, C. "The Temptation to Resign." *AGB Reports,* 1966.

Nelson, R. E. "Development of Corporate Financial Support." In A. S. Knowles (Ed.), *Handbook of College and University Administration.* New York: McGraw-Hill, 1970.

New York Board of Regents, Project on Self-Assessment for Colleges and Universities. *Guidelines for Self-Assessment.* New York: New York Board of Regents, 1977.

New England Association of Schools and Colleges, Inc., Commission on Institutions of Higher Education. *Evaluation Procedures.* Burlington, Mass.: New England Association of Schools and Colleges, 1973.

New York State Education Department, Higher Education Management Services. *Interinstitutional Cooperative Arrangements in Higher Education in New York State.* Albany, N. Y.: State Education Department, 1970.

Newcomb, T. M., and Wilson, E. K. *College Peer Groups: Problems and Prospects for Research.* Chicago: Aldine, 1966.

Newman, F. (Ch.). *Report on Higher Education.* Washington, D. C.: U. S. Government Printing Office, 1971.

Northwest Association of Schools and Colleges, Commission on Colleges. *Accreditation Procedural Guide.* Seattle: Northwest Association of Schools and Colleges, 1975.

O'Connell, W., Jr., and Meeth, L. R. *Evaluating Teaching Improvement Programs.* New Rochelle, N. Y.: National Teaching Program, 1978.

O'Neil, R. M. "Pros and Cons of Learner-Centered Reform." In D. W. Vermilye (Ed.), *Learner-Centered Reform: Current Issues in Higher Education 1975*. San Francisco: Jossey-Bass, 1975.

O'Neill, J. *Resource Use in Higher Education: Trends in Output and Inputs, 1930 to 1967*. Berkeley, Calif.: Carnegie Commission on Higher Education, 1971.

Orlans, H., and others. *Private Accreditation and Public Eligibility*. Vol. 1. Washington, D. C.: Brookings Institution, 1974.

Ostar, A. W. "Federal Effects on State and Institutional Policies." In *Changing Patterns of Governance in Higher Education*. Tucson: Higher Education Program, University of Arizona, 1976.

Pace, C. R. *Preliminary Technical Manual: College and University Environment Scales*. Princeton, N. J.: Educational Testing Service, 1963.

Pace, C. R. *College and University Environment Scales: Technical Manual*. (2nd ed.) Princeton, N. J.: Educational Testing Service, 1969.

Pace, C. R. *Thoughts on Evaluation in Higher Education*. Essays on Education, No. 1. Iowa City, Iowa: American College Testing Program, 1972.

Pace, C. R., and Stern, G. "An Approach to the Measurement of Psychological Characteristics of College Environment." *Journal of Educational Psychology*, 1958, *49*, 269–277.

Palola, E., Lehmann, T., and Blischke, W. R. "The Reluctant Planner: Faculty in Institutional Planning." *Journal of Higher Education*, 1971, *43*, 587–602.

Paltridge, J. G., and others. *Boards of Trustees: Their Decision Patterns*. Berkeley, Calif.: Center for Research and Development in Higher Education, 1973.

Patterson, F. *Colleges in Consort: Institutional Cooperation Through Consortia*. San Francisco: Jossey-Bass, 1974.

Patterson, L. D. *Evolving Patterns of Cooperation*. ERIC/Higher Education Research Currents. Arlington, Va.: ERIC Document Reproduction Service, 1975.

Perkins, J. A., Johnson, A. D., and Kerley, R. F. *The Impact of Federal Regulations on Research Management in Colleges and Universities*. Berkeley, Calif.: Research Management Improvement Project, 1976.

Pervin, L. A. "Satisfaction and Perceived Self-Environment Similarity: A Semantic Differential Study of Student-College Interaction." *Journal of Personality*, 1967a, *35*, 623–634.

Pervin, L. A. "A Twenty-College Study of Student X College Interaction Using TAPE (Transactional Analysis of Personality and Environment): Rationale, Reliability, and Validity." *Journal of Educational Psychology*, 1967b, *58*, 290–302.

Pervin, L. A. "Performance and Satisfaction as a Function of Individual-Environment Fit." *Psychological Bulletin*, 1968, *69*, 56–68.

Perry, R. R. *Criteria of Effective Teaching in an Institution of Higher Education*. Toledo, Ohio: Office of Institutional Research, Toledo University, 1969.

Peterson, R. E. "On the Meaning of Institutional Vitality: A Statistical Summary of a Survey." Research Memorandum. Princeton, N. J.: Educational Testing Service, 1967.

Peterson, R. E. *Goals for California Higher Education*. Berkeley, Calif.: Educational Testing Service, 1973a.

Peterson, R. E. *Goals for California Higher Education: A Survey of 116 Academic Communities*. Sacramento, Calif.: Joint Committee on the Master Plan for Higher Education, California State Legislature, 1973b.

Peterson, R. E., and Loye, D. E. (Eds.). *Conversations Toward a Definition of Institutional Vitality*. Princeton, N. J.: Educational Testing Service, 1967.

Peterson, R. E., and Uhl, N. P. *Formulating College and University Goals: A Guide for Using the IGI*. Princeton, N. J.: Educational Testing Service, 1977.

Peterson, R. E., and others. *Institutional Functioning Inventory: Preliminary Technical Manual*. Princeton, N. J.: Educational Testing Service, 1970.

Petrowski, W. R., Brown, E. L., and Duffy, J. A. " 'National' Universities and the ACE Ratings." *Journal of Higher Education*, 1973, *44*, 495–513.

Pitcher, R. W., and Blaushild, B. *Why College Students Fail*. New York: Funk & Wagnalls, 1970.

Pottinger, P. E. "Some Comments on the Effective Use of Consultant and External Advisors." Paper presented to a project directors' meeting of the Fund for the Improvement of Postsecondary Education. Boston: Institute for Competence Assessment, Division of McBer and Co., 1975.

Princeton University. *Budgeting and Resource Allocation at Princeton University.* Princeton, N. J.: Princeton University, 1972.

Radock, M. "Fund-Raising Tips for Trustees." *AGB Reports,* Jan./ Feb. 1976, pp. 18–27.

Rauh, M. A. *The Trusteeship of Colleges and Universities.* New York: McGraw-Hill, 1969.

Report of the Harvard Committee. *General Education in a Free Society.* Cambridge, Mass.: Harvard University Press, 1962. (Originally published 1945.)

"Report of the Visiting Committee to Evaluate the Department of Anatomy." University of Chicago *Record,* 1975, *3,* 109.

Richman, B. M., and Farmer, R. N. *Leadership, Goals, and Power in High Education: A Contingency and Open-Systems Approach to Effective Management.* San Francisco: Jossey-Bass, 1974.

Riesman, D. *Constraint and Variety in American Education.* New York: Doubleday, 1958.

Riesman, D. "Can We Maintain Quality Graduate Education in a Period of Retrenchment?" Chicago: University of Illinois at Chicago Circle, 1975.

Roose, K. D., and Andersen, C. J. *A Rating of Graduate Programs.* Washington, D. C.: American Council on Education, 1970.

Roueche, J. E., and Kirk, R. W. *Catching Up: Remedial Education.* San Francisco: Jossey-Bass, 1973.

Rourke, F. E., and Brooks, G. E. "The 'Managerial Revolution' in Higher Education." *Administrative Science Quarterly,* 1964, *9,* 154–181.

Roy, R. "University-Industry Interaction Patterns." *Science,* 1972, *178,* 955–960.

Sanford, N. *Where Colleges Fail: A Study of the Student as a Person.* San Francisco: Jossey-Bass, 1967.

Sanford, M. *Making It in Graduate School.* Berkeley, Calif.: Montaigne, 1976.

Schuster, J. A. *Encountering the Unionized University.* San Francisco: Jossey-Bass, 1974.

Scott, E. L. *Higher Education Salary Evaluation Kit.* Washington,

D. C.: American Association of University Professors, n. d.

Shuck, E. C. "The Best Laid Plans. . . ." Paper presented to the 16th annual meeting of the American Association of State Colleges and Universities, New Orleans, Nov. 1976.

Shelton, K. M. "The Growth of Student Trusteeship." *AGB Reports,* March/April 1976, pp. 24–26.

Shulman, C. H. "Keeping Up with Title IX." ERIC/Higher Education Research Currents. *College and University Bulletin,* 1977, *29,* 3–6.

Solomon, L. C., Bisconti, A. S., and Ochsner, N. L. *College as a Training Ground for Jobs.* New York: Praeger, 1977.

Solomon, L. C., and Taubman, P. J. *Does College Matter: Some Evidence on the Impacts of Higher Education.* New York: Academic Press, 1973.

Spaeth, J. L., and Greeley, A. M. *Recent Alumni and Higher Education.* A general report prepared for the Carnegie Commission on Higher Education. New York: McGraw-Hill, 1970.

Spriegel, W. R., and Myers, C. E. (Eds.). *The Writings of the Gilbreths.* Homewood, Ill.: Irwin, 1953.

State of Illinois, Office of the Auditor General. *Audit Guide: For Performing Compliance Audits of Illinois State Agencies.* Springfield, Ill.: Office of the Auditor General, 1976.

State University of New York. *The Economic Impact Study and Its Use.* Albany: State University of New York, 1978.

Stern, G. "Environments for Learning." In N. Sanford (Ed.), *The American College: A Psychological and Social Interpretation of the Higher Learning.* New York: Wiley, 1962a.

Stern, G. "The Measurement of Psychological Characteristics of Students and Learning Environments." In S. Messick and J. Ross (Eds.), *Measurement in Personality and Cognition.* New York: Wiley, 1962b.

Stern, G. "Time Present and Time Past." Paper prepared for the annual meeting of the American Educational Research Association Convention, New York City, Feb. 6, 1971.

Sturner, W. F. *Action Planning on the Campus.* Washington, D. C.: American Association of State Colleges and Universities, 1974.

Surwill, B. J., and Heywood, S. J. *Evaluation of College and University Top Brass: The State of the Art.* Washington, D. C.: American Association of State Colleges and Universities, 1976.

Taylor, F. W. *The Principles of Scientific Management.* New York: Harper & Row, 1911.

Taylor, H. *How To Change Colleges: Notes on Radical Reform.* New York: Holt, Rinehart and Winston, 1971.

Tennessee Higher Education Commission. *The Performance Funding Project: A Status Report.* Nashville: Tennessee Higher Education Commission, 1977.

Thresher, B. A. "Admissions in Perspective." In A. S. Knowles (Ed.), *Handbook of College and University Administration.* New York: McGraw-Hill, 1970.

Thune, S., and House, R. "Where Long-Range Planning Pays Off." *Business Horizons,* 1970, *13*, 81–87.

Tinto, V., and Sherman, R. H. *The Effectiveness of Secondary and Higher Education Intervention Programs: A Critical Review of the Research.* New York: Teachers College Press, 1974.

Toffler, A. *Future Shock.* New York: Bantam Books, 1970.

Trow, M. "Higher Education and Moral Development." In *Proceedings of the 1974 ETS Invitational Conference.* Princeton, N. J.: Educational Testing Service, 1974.

Trow, M. (Ed.). *Teachers and Students.* A report of the Carnegie Commission on Higher Education. New York: McGraw-Hill, 1975.

Trow, M. "Surveys Show Drop in Social-Science, Humanities Majors." *Chronicle of Higher Education,* Dec. 19, 1977.

Tyler, R. W. *Basic Principles of Curriculum and Instruction.* Chicago: University of Chicago Press, 1949.

University of California at Berkeley, "Staff Personnel Policy, Berkeley Campus Procedure." Berkeley: University of California, n. d.

University of Illinois at Urbana-Champaign. *Nonacademic Employee Appraisal Handbook.* Urbana: University of Illinois, n. d.

University of Illinois at Urbana-Champaign, Office of Planning. "Facts Supporting Restoration of Reduction in the University of Illinois FY 77 Appropriation Bill S-1628." Urbana: University of Illinois, 1976.

University of Pittsburgh, Office of Planning and Budget. *Planning and Resource Management System Procedures Manual.* Pittsburgh: University of Pittsburgh, 1976.

University System of Georgia. *The System Summary,* 1976, *12,* 14–15.

Van Alstyne, C. "Comments on *The Financial State of Higher Education: A Special Report,* by Andrew Lupton, John Augenblick, and Joseph Heyison, *Change,* September 1976." Unpublished memorandum, 1976.

Van Alstyne, C., and Coldren, S. L. *Costs to Colleges and Universities of Implementing Federally Mandated Social Programs.* Washington, D. C.: American Council on Education, 1976.

Waples, D. *The Evaluation of Higher Institutions.* Vol. 4: *The Library.* Chicago: University of Chicago Press, 1937.

Wattenbarger, J. L., and others. "State-Local Financing for the Seventies." In J. Lombardi (Ed.), *New Directions for Community Colleges: Meeting the Financial Crisis,* no. 2. San Francisco: Jossey-Bass, 1973a.

Wattenbarger, J. L., and others. "Tuition and the Open Door." In J. Lombardi (Ed.), *Meeting the Financial Crisis: New Directions for Community Colleges,* no. 2. San Francisco: Jossey-Bass, l973b.

Webster, D. E. "The Management Review and Analysis Program: An Assisted Self-Study to Secure Constructive Change in the Management of Research Libraries." *College and Research Libraries,* 1974, *35,* 114–125.

Werdell, P. R. "Teaching and Learning: The Basic Process." In P. Runkel and others (Eds.), *The Changing College Classroom.* San Francisco: Jossey-Bass, 1969.

Wethersby, G. B. "Tools and Techniques for Planning and Resource Allocation." In R. M. Millard and others (Eds.), *Planning and Management Practices in Higher Education: Promise or Dilemma?* Denver, Colo.: Education Commission of the States, 1972.

Wood, F. C. "Space Requirements for Physical Facilities." In A. S. Knowles (Ed.), *Handbook of College and University Administration.* New York: McGraw-Hill, 1970.

Yankwich, P. E. *Administrator Evaluation Project.* Urbana: University of Illinois, 1975.

Youston, D. J., and others. *Decision Making and University Information Systems: Analysis and Design.* New York: Ford Foundation, 1969.

Yuker, H. E. *Faculty Workload: Facts, Myths, and Commentary.* ERIC/ Higher Education Research Report, No. 6. Washington, D. C.: American Association for Higher Education, 1974.

Yuker, H. E. "How Hard Do Faculty Really Work?" *AGB Reports,* July/Aug. 1975, pp. 26–33.

Zook, G. F., and Haggerty, M. E. *The Evaluation of Higher Institutions.* Vol. 1: *Principles of Accrediting Higher Institutions.* Chicago: University of Chicago Press, 1936.

Zwingle, J. L. "Build a Better Board." *AGB Reports,* May/June 1976, pp. 32–36.

Zwingle, J. L., and Mayville, W. V. *College Trustees: A Question of Legitimacy.* ERIC/Higher Education Research Report, No. 10. Washington, D. C.: American Association for Higher Education, 1974.

Index